W9-AVR-097

cookin' up good vibrations

Deliciously healthy
gluten-free & dairy-free dishes
in harmony with the seasons

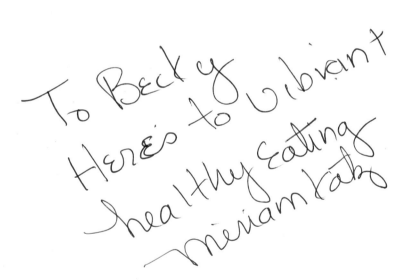

To Becky
Here's to vibrant
healthy eating
Miriam Katz

INSPIRED WISDOM PRESS

Copyright © 2010 by Inspired Wisdom Press.

All rights reserved. No part of this book may be reproduced or transmitted in any form or by any means, electronic or mechanical, including photocopying, recording, or by any information storage and retrieval system, without permission in writing from the publisher.

Published by Inspired Wisdom Press, Whitefish, Montana.

Printed in China.

ISBN   0-9846138-0-3
          978-0-9846138-0-9

First Edition

Inspired Wisdom Press
P. O. Box 4490
Whitefish, MT 59937
www.inspiredwisdom.org

contents

acknowledgments

The Cookbook Project Crew

Project Manager
Robin Kelson

Managing Editors
Robin Kelson
Kathleen Grace Kint

Research & Development
Lee Anne Byrne
Trudy Dunfee
Miriam Katz
Robin Kelson
Vickie Kelson
Kathleen Grace Kint
Janet Morrow
Adrienne Swiatek

Special Resources

Editing
Heidi Duncan
Julie Greiner
Joan M. Kelley
Alli Shapiro

Promotion & Distribution
Jessica Cripe
Christine Phillips

Book Production & Promotion Mentor
Barry Scheiber

Design & Printing

Book & Cover Design
Jennifer Nelson Golan Graphic Design

Book Production & Manufacturing
Global Interprint

Production Design
Jill Blessing, blue iguana productions
Jennifer Nelson Golan Graphic Design

Illustrations
Shane Svee

Photo Credits
The Green Tea House:
Courtesy of Whitefish Convention
and Visitors Bureau

JMSI Board of Directors 2009-2010

Susan Clarke, *Chair*
Miriam Katz
Sharlea Leatherwood
Terri Oshiro
Ann Schauber, *Vice-Chair*

JMSI Officers 2009-2010

Executive Director
Robin Kelson

Chancellor
Carolyn Rutherford Muldoon

Deans
Lee Anne Byrne
Vickie Kelson

Local Farms and Ingredient Resources

We'd like to thank all the local farmers
and natural foods stores in our area who
have been providing our valley with
delicious organic produce and healthy
ingredients for many years. We sure
hope we didn't forget anybody!

Butterfly Herbs
Country Fresh Farm
Honthass Herbs
Loon Lake Gardens
Meadowsweet Herbs
Mountain Valley Foods
Ottey's Gardens
Purple Frog Farms
Raven Ridge Farm
Sundrop Natural Foods
Swan Valley Herbs
Taste of Sunshine Sprouts
Ten Lakes Farm
Terrapin Farms
Third Street Market
Withey's Natural Foods

Greetings and Welcome to "Cookin' Up Good Vibrations"!

We are delighted and thrilled to be offering this book of recipes and information to you — it has been many years in the making. Our sincere wish is that you find these recipes helpful and delicious, and that the book itself will be of assistance in your own journey of greater self-knowing...what we call accessing the wisdom of your own True Self.

We believe that the more we balance the whole self at all levels — emotionally, mentally, physically and energetically, the better we access our own inner knowing, and the more comfortable we are hanging out in the space of infinite possibilities. This is the space where we know our spiritual purpose in the world and we know how to respond in each moment for the highest good of all concerned. It is the space where we access joy. It is a space of high vibration.

For the past 15 years, all of us at the Jwalan Muktikā School for Illumination (JMSI) — students, faculty and alumni, have been exploring the profound role that food plays in balancing the whole self. With the help of the "Teachers," a collective consciousness that the school's founder, Carolyn Rutherford Muldoon channels, we have been bringing forth and connecting new and ancient information across multiple disciplines and cultures. Our intention has been to define key ingredients that support balancing the 'modern day' body, and eliminate ingredients that our bodies no longer tolerate as well. Among ancient traditions of body balancing through food, we have particularly focused on the East Indian Ayurvedic, Chinese Five Elements and Essene traditions. We've spent years developing nutritious recipes with this "new" combination of ingredients, all with the intention that the dishes be easy to create, delightful to look at, and delicious to eat. It has been a fabulous journey!

In putting the recipes together, Miriam Katz has endeavored to give you an array of dishes that are both fun to prepare and satisfying to your body in each season. Hopefully, the recipes also provide a springboard for you to begin creating your own dishes, that are unique to you, your own body's inspiration, and your own ever-unfolding sense of Self. In Miriam's own words:

All my life, I have appreciated the gift of food and its power to impact health. I have studied nutritional philosophies from all over the world and incorporated the learnings in my practice for over thirty years as a nutritionist. Still, what I have discovered is that the most reliable resource for determining the "right" nutrition plan for any person lies within that individual. When I work with clients and students, my job is to assist them in accessing that source of information for themselves.

We invite you to pay attention to all your senses as you prepare and eat these meals: the colors, the aromas, the tastes and the sounds. Which foods do you like best together and why? How do you feel preparing certain foods and eating them? Why might this be so? Just observe, engage, explore and enjoy. There is information for you in all of it. Bon appetit!

Robin Kelson
Executive Director
Jwalan Muktikā School for Illumination

Miriam Katz, M.A.
Faculty & Staff Nutritionist
Jwalan Muktikā School for Illumination

special thanks

The recipes and information in this book is the result of experimentation, research and good eating by the faculty, students, friends and family of the Jwalan Muktikā School for Illumination. Among them all, we particularly want to thank —

Adrienne Swiatek
Carolyn Rutherford Muldoon
Janet Morrow
Kathleen Grace Kint
Lee Anne Byrne
Trudy Dunfee
Vickie & Robin Kelson

In addition, Miriam offers special thanks and acknowledgment to the following farmers, Judy Owsowitz, Martin & Atina Diffley, and Julian Cunningham —

Thank you for helping me make a special connection to the earth, the environment and food.

dedication

To all of JMSI's students, past, present and future —

Your willingness to participate and open to the wisdom of infinite possibilities within yourself is what makes this work possible and brings it out into the world for others.

- jmsi

To Annie Fox, who started me on my path so many years ago —

Thank you for showing me the way. I would not be where I am today without your assistance.

- mk

A Word About…

What follows is a BRIEF comment on various foods and ingredients. For more details on these and other food-related topics, please visit our Nutrition Blog at cookinupgoodvibrations.org.

Allergens

Looking through this cookbook you'll see that in addition to being gluten-free and dairy-free, these recipes are, for the most part, free of a lot of other ingredients. Namely:

soy, corn, garlic, onions, nightshades (ie., peppers, eggplant, potatoes, tomatoes), caffeine (chocolate or coffee), fermented foods, mushrooms and other fungi, and most nuts, with the exception of almonds and pine nuts.

Why? Well, for one reason or another these foods, like gluten and dairy, also have become general allergens in our systems. This means they tend to stress our body in some way, triggering our chronically stimulated immune systems into more activity, which sends our bodies further out of balance. For some people the reactions can feel like a full-blown allergic response, as significant as eating gluten is for someone with celiac disease. For others, the reaction may feel more like a food sensitivity – bloating and digestive gas for example, or temporary joint pain. It can even look like irritability and agitation. The fact is that today, more and more people are developing ever-greater sensitivity to foods we used to rely on for nutrition and nurturance.

While we don't profess to know all the reasons these foods are increasingly taxing our bodies today, we do have an idea about some of the likely reasons. LIke gluten and dairy, a number of these foods -- soy, corn, garlic, onions and nightshades, likely have become general allergens due to their near ubiquitous inclusion in processed foods. (It's like developing hay fever after years of living in a location with a high pollen concentration.) The high degree to which many of these foods have been genetically modified also may play a role. The response also may be due to how these foods tax particular systems in the body. For example, highly refined sugars tax the metabolic, endocrine and cardiovascular systems; caffeine taxes the adrenal system.

The increased reactivity to mushrooms and other fungi, fermented foods, and many nuts appears to coincide with the advent of antibiotics, synthetic pesticides, and synthetic food molecules in the modern diet. For mushrooms and other fungi, like yeast, likely it is a combination of increased consumption of these foods today, together with increased exposure to antibiotics, (originally derived from fungi), that over-stimuates the immune system.

Our intention is to support balancing the whole self at all levels, so we choose to avoid these allergens and do not include them generally in our cooking. If we do include them, it is infrequently, in small quantities, and always with organic, heirloom, and non-GMO versions. This way we support the immune system in re-balancing, which supports vitalizing the whole body. It also may allow the potent balancing properties inherent in certain of these allergens, like garlic for example, to become available to the body again as occasional, special-use medicinals.

Beans

We love beans. Humans have been cultivating beans around the world literally for thousands of years. Members of the legume family, beans are a rich source of dietary fiber, vitamins and minerals. While a rich source of protein, most beans are deficient in one or more essential amino acids. Eating cooked beans together with a grain will provide the missing amino acids, fulfilling our dietary intake needs. Because germination typically stimulates the production of amino acids, sprouted beans can be a complete source of essential amino acids even when the dried bean is not.

The following suggestions will help your body digest beans more easily:

- Keep meals simple when eating beans. For example, create a meal of beans, a grain or bread, and a simple green salad or vegetable.

- Eat beans in small amounts, especially when first beginning to eat them. You can increase the quantity you eat as your body adapts to them.

- Cook beans for at least 2 hours until they are very soft. See page 19 for cooking directions.

- Add salt only near the end of cooking.

- Soaking the dried beans in water for at least 8 hours before cooking improves their digestibility and supports faster cooking. Rinse the soaked beans, and use fresh water for cooking.

- Sprouting beans (or any grain, nut or legume) until they germinate (a three to five day process, depending on the bean) also enhances their digestibility and nutrient potential. To sprout: soak beans overnight in water, rinse and drain, and place in a jar (one-third full). Cover with screen or cloth lid and place, inverted, in a cool, dark, dry location. Rinse beans at least twice a day. Beans are germinated when a white sprout appears. Germinated beans cook faster, so begin testing for doneness after one-half hour.

Broths

Vegetable Broths

You will see vegetable broth used throughout this cookbook. We rely on it to provide flavor and nutrients as a liquid ingredient of soups, stews, and a host of main dishes. That being said, we are fussy about our broth - we want it to be made from organic ingredients, free of additives and, wherever possible, free of or low in garlic, onions and nightshades.

Making your own broth is the best way to ensure the source of the ingredients in your broth. We offer a vegetable broth recipe on page 227. In this day and age, however, few of us choose to spend our time making enough broth that we have it on hand and thawed when we want to make a soup or dinner. So, having a reliable source of good prepared vegetable broth is key. Various high quality boxed broths use organic ingredients and are readily available in local natural food stores and larger supermarkets. Check the ingredient list and choose your favorite. Personally, we prefer high-quality, organic vegetable broth cubes. For one thing, there's no box to throw out. Also, the Rapunzel Pure Organics brand pretty much fits the bill: organic vegetables, lots of herbs, no nightshades or onions, and unrefined Celtic sea salt.

Chicken or Turkey Broth

Make sure it is organic. Various high-quality organic chicken broths are available in box form, and can be found in natural foods stores and larger supermarkets. If you cannot find prepared, organic chicken broth, make your own.

Dairy

Dairy means animal milks and their products, like butter, cheese and yogurt. While as a species our digestive systems have evolved to tolerate some dairy (we are the only species that ingests animal milk of any kind into adulthood, let alone the milk of another species), our systems don't tolerate well the large quantities we ingest today. Lactose, casein and whey are common sources of milk sensitivities, among others, and symptoms can range from indigestion to chronic sinusitis. We recommend switching to organic nut and seed milks. Our favorites are hemp and almond milks.

Fish & Seafood

We recommend eating wild-caught rather than cultivated fish. Cultivated fish, known as farm-raised or ocean-raised fish, are grown in pens and can be grown in spaces so crowded that the fish are subject to diseases, infestations, infections and stress, for which they are given antibiotics and other chemical treatments. These chemicals then deposit in their flesh and also make their way into the local environment. Some farm-raised fish also have been reported to have high levels of toxins in their bodies. Finally, the flesh of certain fish, such as farm-raised salmon, is artificially colored. For wild-caught ocean fish, we recommend fish from the Pacific Ocean.

Our comments on fish apply to seafood as well.

Adding a bit of dulse (seaweed) to the fish while cooking assists the body in digesting fish protein. Dulse typically comes in a shaker bottle, like salt or pepper, and is available in natural foods stores, larger supermarkets and Asian specialty foods stores.

Food Combining

The enzymes and digestive environment required for breaking down and extracting nutrients from certain foods (for example, a concentrated protein like fish, poultry, beans or nuts) differs significantly from that required for breaking down other foods, such as concentrated carbohydrates like breads, pastas and grains. Combining these different foods tends to slow the digestive process down and can even inhibit it, limiting your body's ability to extract nutrients, and taxing the digestive system. Below, we've put together our general "rule of thumb" with respect to food combining. We think you'll find it makes sense, and your body will appreciate the support.

On the subject of fruit:

With the exception of citrus, raw fruit generally is best eaten alone, either before you eat anything else, or at least a half hour after having eaten your main meal. This is because raw fruit is so rapidly broken down in the body that if it is delayed in moving through the digestive system by slower processing foods, it can start to ferment in the body, which limits the nutrient extraction from both the fruit and the other food in your digestive system. The fermentation also can cause gas, bloating and other unpleasant side effects.

One more thing — melons:

Eat melons by themselves, not even in combination with other fruit. Melons are one of the fastest raw fruits to be processed by the body, and also one of the quickest to decompose, once their thick rinds have been cut open and the flesh exposed to air. If melon has to compete with anything else in the stomach for digestion, it will just start breaking down (basically, fermenting) right where it is...in your tummy.

Rule of thumb:

DO combine

- Poultry, fish or eggs with vegetables
- Vegetables with grains, pasta or bread
- Poultry, fish or eggs with nuts, seeds or citrus

AVOID combining

- Poultry, fish, or eggs with grains, Pasta and bread
- Poultry, fish or eggs with non-citrus fruit
- Poultry, fish or eggs with sweetener
- Grains, pasta or bread with raw fruit (cooked fruit is okay)
- Fruit with vegetables

Gluten-Free Grains

Gluten is a composite of two proteins found in certain grass-related grains, notably wheat, spelt, Kamut®, barley and rye. It is nearly ubiquitous in processed foods today, which is likely why celiac disease and gluten-sensitivity diagnoses are on the rise. Symptoms range from bloating, mental fogginess, irritability, or drowsiness to full-blown auto-immune reactions like arthitis or asthma, as well as classic intestinal symptoms.

The following grains and vegetables do not contain gluten, and work well as gluten-free whole grains or flours for baking. We particularly like the foods on this list as they are nutrient-dense, complex carbohydrates that our bodies still recognize as friendly. See the associated recipe for more details on each grain.

- Amaranth, page 208
- Arrowroot, page 109
- Buckwheat, page 151
- Chickpea (garbanzo), page 99
- Fava, page 210
- Millet, page 149
- Oats (Be sure to buy only certified gluten-free oats, as most oats processed in the United States are contaminated with wheat or other gluten-containing grains. Bob's Red Mill™ is one reliable source.)
- Quinoa, page 257
- Rice – particularly hulled rices like the brown and red rices, page 258
- Sorghum, page 314
- Tapioca, page 268
- Teff, page 119
- Wild rice, page 259

Oils

This is potentially an enormous subject, and here is our bottom line.

Processing: We recommend using only specific, organic, unrefined, minimally processed plant oils. This way, the oil retains its nutritional value and the fatty acid chains that make up the oil are less likely to be modified by the refining process into forms that the body does not recognize and/or cannot process. In our world, this means cold-press processing only. For oils such as olive oil that can undergo multiple pressings, we recommend only extra-virgin, which refers to the first pressing. (Many commercial oil companies utilize heat, pressure and/or chemicals to enhance oil extraction, all of which compromise the oil's integrity. In addition, the word "refined" allows the inclusion of chemicals to clarify the oil and even mask rancid odor.)

Storage: Keeping oil in colored glass bottles in a cool dark place minimizes oxidation and degradation of the oil. Certain oils (see below) must be refrigerated. Others, such as the oils suggested below for cooking, can be left at room temperature if you use them frequently. Because the recommended oils are unrefined, they may appear cloudy, particularly when refrigerated. This is normal.

Our Preferred Oils: The following oils are the only oils we use. We like them because of their high nutritional value, and because the body recognizes them as beneficial. Note that each oil has its own "smoke point", the temperature at which the heated oil begins literally to smoke and break down. Accordingly, not all oils are suitable for cooking, and some are recommended only for cold applications, such as salad dressings.

Oils for cooking, baking, all-around uses:

- Extra-virgin olive oil
- Coconut oil
- Grape seed oil

Cold-use only oils:

- Sunflower
- Safflower

Specialty Oils

Specialty oils are strongly flavored, use them sparingly.

- Sesame seed - hot or cold uses
- Flax seed - cold use only
- Hemp seed - cold use only
  (Both flax and hemp seed oils have high nutritional value as sources for Essential Fatty Acids (EFA), and provide a vegan alternative for the EFA often sought by those taking fish oil supplements.)

Poultry & Eggs

Whenever possible, we recommend buying poultry and eggs from small local farms where you can see for yourself how the chickens are raised, what they are fed, and how eggs are produced. What you want to see are chickens that roam around outside in a pesticide-free natural space; that are fed organic grains that they can supplement with the plants and bugs they get to eat outside; that are not given with hormones, antibiotics or other chemicals; and that are not stimulated artificially to enhance egg production.

Where local resources are not available, we recommend eating poultry and eggs that are certified organic. Commercially raised birds, even those considered "free-range", can be grown in spaces so crowded that they are subject to diseases, infestations, infections and stress, for which they are given antibiotics and other chemical treatments. In addition, these birds may be fed a host of other chemicals to "assist" in the management of mass egg and poultry production, including chemicals that speed up bird growth and/or egg production, and/or that sedate the birds. Traces of all these chemicals can be found in their flesh and eggs, and also make their way into the local environment.

One more thing — replacing eggs in baking recipes:

- Replacing more than two eggs in a given recipe changes the integrity of the recipe.
- Because egg substitutions typically increase the moisture content of the dish, you may need to increase baking time.

Here's what we like to use. For each egg, substitute any one of the following:

- 2 Tablespoons unsweetened applesauce plus 1 teaspoon baking powder.
- 1 Tablespoon flax meal plus 3 Tablespoons hot water. Let stand, stirring occasionally, about 10 minutes or until thick. Use without straining.
- Dissolve 1 Tablespoon plain agar powder into 1 Tablespoon water. Beat, chill for 10 minutes, and beat again.

Processed Foods

As a general rule, we choose not to include processed foods in our cooking. That being said, there are a few we rely on as time savers and have included in the cookbook (see below). In our opinion, these particular processed foods are sufficiently wholesome and are used with such limited frequency and quantity that they are not likely to impact the body adversely.

- Bragg Liquid Aminos™, see page 32
- Dijon mustard, organic, made from brown mustard seeds and verjuice (a sour liquid made from unripe grapes) or vinegar
- Vegenaise™ dressing, see page 25
- Vegetable broth cubes, see "A Word About…Broth," see page 8

Salt

We recommend using high quality unrefined sea or crystal salts, which are rich in a variety of minerals and trace elements, rather than conventional table salt. Refined salts, including table salt, typically have the minerals and trace elements removed, except sodium chloride. In addition, refined salts often are filled with salicilates, dextrose, and other additives intended to make the salt uniformly white and easily pourable. As a result, they are a processed food and can create imbalances in the body.

Here's how the balanced system works:

Plants convert solar energy into carbohydrates through a photosynthetic process. Humans utilize this "hydrated carbon" energy when they eat the plant, specifically, by converting it into a molecule called ATP. What the body does not utilize in the moment it stores for the future in a form called glycogen. That really is the end of the story, in a balanced system where we simply eat what we need, in its most natural, unprocessed form. However, as a species, we've gone quite beyond that time, so here are more details:

The most common carbohydrates (aka simple sugars) are glucose, fructose, sucrose and maltose. Sucrose is just fructose and glucose bonded together; maltose is two molecules of glucose bonded together. Many plants store these sugars in long chains, called complex carbohydrates. There are two primary kinds of complex carbohydrates: (1) amylum (aka 'starch'), which is a chain of glucose units only, and is commonly found in potatoes, corn, wheat and cassava. The other form, (2) inulin (aka 'fructan'), is a chain of fructose units with a glucose molecule on either end, and is commonly found in agave, artichokes, Jerusalem artichokes, leeks, green beans and jicama, among other vegetables.

Glucose enters the bloodstream fastest of all the simple sugars, giving it the highest glycemic index (five times that of fructose, twice that of sucrose.) Excessive glucose intake can yield blood sugar spikes, which stress the body generally, and particularly impact folks subject to hyper- or hypo-glycemia and/or diabetes. On the other hand, excessive fructose intake mucks up the ATP conversion process (it can't keep up) which can result in triglycerides (fats) being dumped into the bloodstream. This stresses the heart and the whole cardiovascular system.

All this becomes part of the conversation because for the last half-century or so our daily sugar intake has increased somewhere around 30%, mostly from the inclusion of sugar in processed foods and beverages, e.g., sodas. Interestingly, a primary form of this added sugar is high-fructose corn syrup, itself a highly processed sweetener. (As you read above, corn does not make fructose naturally. Moreover, the corn used to make high-fructose corn syrup is almost assuredly a GMO corn.)

Unrefined sea or crystal salt is available in the condiment section of natural foods stores and larger supermarkets. Our favorite sea salts are the "Celtic" sea salts, from the northwestern coast of France, and the Hawaiian salts. Our favorite crystal salts are the "Himalayan" salts.

Sugars & Sweeteners

This too is a "big" subject, with lots of opinions and conflicting data. This laser focus on sugar stems from the fact that our daily sugar intake has increased significantly over the last 50 years. Basically, we've been taking in too much of it and this impacts a number of our body's systems. You can read "The Sugar Details" in the side bar for the subtleties of this impact. Here's our bottom line:

We recommend using natural sweeteners in moderate amounts, and staying away from highly processed sweeteners altogether. Our favorite sweeteners are raw honey, pure maple syrup, raw agave nectar, date sugar, dried fruit, fruit juice, or fruit, in no particular order. It's a matter of taste. As always, we use only organic, minimally processed forms of these sweeteners, so we can get as many nutrients as possible from them and because they are more easily metabolized by the body. Of these sweeteners, agave nectar has the lowest glycemic index (slowest to enter bloodstream). For more details on the particular sweetener, see the associated recipe.

- Agave nectar, page 161
- Date sugar, page 328
- Honey, page 156
- Maple syrup, page 197

Vegetables & Everything Else

Please buy or grow organic, non-GMO vegetables, grains, beans and fruit. Food grown on local, personally tended farms is best. Certified or not, organic means grown without chemical or sewage sludge fertilizers, bioengineering, ionizing radiation, or man-made chemical insecticides, herbicides or pesticides.

Know Your Foods

Throughout the cookbook you'll find:

- information on particular ingredients about which you might be curious

- cooking tips intended to make your experience in the kitchen one of grace and ease, whatever your cooking skill level

- body balancing tips for supporting your body in being nourished

spring SEASON

shifting your food choices with spring | gluten-free & dairy-free recipes

CONTENTS

Harmony with Spring

In the spring the body begins a process of reawakening after the resting season of winter. As part of this process, it naturally wants to cleanse — to 'clean house', so to speak. The liver and gall bladder are the primary organs that make this process possible. Transitioning from the heavy, warming foods of winter to the lighter foods of spring will assist the liver and gall bladder in this process.

If the liver and gall bladder are not allowed to cleanse properly, a build up of toxins in the body may result.

Blockages or imbalances in the liver or gall bladder may present as one or more of the following symptoms:

- Feeling groggy and having trouble waking up in the morning
- Feeling symptoms of allergic sensitivities
- Having soreness on the top of the head
- Having burning, itching or watery eyes
- Having congestion, cold, or flu-like symptoms
- Having muscle fatigue or weakness
- Feeling stiffness in the neck or back
- Having headaches
- Feeling crabby or irritable
- Having bursts of anger
- Feeling lethargic and nothing tastes good

The following suggestions are a natural way to assist the body in cleansing:

- Drink a light, system-cleansing drink.

  As a general rule, a natural way to cleanse is to drink the following mixture once a day for 2–3 weeks:

    3 Tablespoons lemon or lime juice
    2 Tablespoons pure maple syrup
    ¼ teaspoon cayenne pepper (use more if desired)
    8 ounces water

  Place all ingredients in an 8 ounce glass and mix well. Drink slowly.

- Cut down or eliminate baking.

- Cook more gently. Use lower heat and cook vegetables only until they are tender/crisp.

- Steaming, light and gentle stewing, and low oil sautéing are the best techniques to use in cooking during this season.

- Cut vegetables in small pieces when making soup to create less cooking.

- Use less salt than usual. Plan for meals and days when salt is not used at all. This will open up the body to release winter storage. When using salt, we recommend using an unrefined sea or rock salt rather than regular table salt. Unrefined salts are rich in minerals and trace elements. See "A Word About...Salt" page 11.

- Increase the flavor of meals with green herbs as a substitute for salt (i.e., cilantro, dill, basil, parsley, thyme, oregano, and marjoram). Green onions, chives, and ginger also provide interesting flavors.

- Eat a little less protein. At least once daily, use a sprinkling of freshly roasted seeds, almonds or pine nuts over whole grains to replace heavier protein foods such as beans, eggs, fish, seafood or poultry.

- Use less oil in cooking and eliminate fried foods. We recommend using unrefined, organic oils. Coconut, grape seed, olive, safflower, hemp, flax, sesame, and sunflower oils are most beneficial to the body. Use only olive, coconut or grape seed oils for cooking. See "A Word About Oils" page 10.

- Eat more greens. Fresh spring leafy greens such as dandelion, watercress, sorrel, and arugula are delicious, healing and detoxifying. Asparagus, artichokes, and all leafy greens are excellent liver cleansers.

- Use orange, lemon, or lime juice in cooking, as seasoning or in salad dressings. They are excellent for digestion and the liver.

- Drink freshly made fruit and/or vegetable juices as often as desired (i.e., carrot, celery, beet, spinach, kale, parsley, apple, orange in any combination). A little ginger or lemon juice also` can be added.

- Use grated fresh horseradish in salads, dressings, sauces or sprinkle over cooked food.

- Supplement the diet with chlorophyll, spirulina or blue green algae.

- Drink two quarts of water each day.

- Don't eat after 8 p.m.

- Spend more time outdoors by taking walks and exercising in nature.

SPRING FOODS LIST

This list describes foods available in the spring and which support your body's natural spring cleansing process. Their availability may vary according to your location. Some may come earlier in one location and later in another. Generally, we recommend eating foods grown locally whenever possible, so that your body's rhythm matches that of your environment. While some of the foods on this list are not local to all locations, they still have valuable balancing properties at this time of the year and we recommend them during this season even if they come to you from other locations.

BEANS

Aduki beans
Cannelini beans
Chickpeas
Fava beans
Lima beans
Pinto beans
Red beans
Red lentils
White beans

Soaked or sprouted beans are lighter and assist with the cleansing process. See "A Word About...Beans," page 7.

FRUITS

Apples
Avocado
Bananas
Grapefruit
Grapes
Lemons
Limes
Mango
Oranges
Strawberries
(Only during their natural season: late May–mid July)
Tangelos
Tangerines

EDIBLE FLOWERS

Chive blossoms
Gem marigolds
Johnny-jump-ups
Pansies
Tulips
Violets

Flowers add vibrant color to salads and as garnishes. It is best to use only organic flowers, collected in the wild, away from roadsides, or purchased from an organic farm. Flowers purchased from green houses typically are heavily sprayed with chemicals and are not grown for human consumption. See "A Note on Edible Flowers," page 67.

GRAINS

Millet
Oats *(certified gluten-free)*
Quinoa
Rice
(Basmati: brown and white, Brown: long grain, Jasmine: brown and white, Sushi, Wild)

HERBS TO EAT MOST OFTEN

Chives
Cilantro
Comfrey
Dill
Mint
Parsley

All other fresh herbs are appropriate to eat as well, but not as often as these listed.

VEGETABLES

Arugula
Artichokes
Asparagus
Beet greens
Bok choy
Burdock root
Carrots *(new spring carrots)*
Carrot tops
Celery
Chickweed
Chicory
Collard greens
Dandelion greens
Endive
Green onion
Horseradish
Jicama
Kale *(all types)*
Lambsquarters
Landcress
Leeks
Lettuce greens
(all types except iceberg, which the body does not tolerate in any season)
Mustard greens
Nettles
Radicchio
Radishes
Snow peas
Sorrel greens
Spinach
Sprouts
(clover, radish, sunflower)
Swiss chard
Watercress

We offer the following recipes as suggestions for enhancing your spring meals.

ENJOY!

spring APPETIZERS

CONTENTS

Guacamole

This can be served as an accompaniment to Mexican-style dishes or other bean dishes. It tastes great served on rice crackers, dipped with raw vegetables, or on a simple sandwich. Extra lemon juice can be added for more lemon flavor, if desired.

SERVES 4 – 6

2 avocados, mashed
6 Tablespoons lemon juice
1 teaspoon ground cumin
1 Tablespoon fresh cilantro, chopped
4 Tablespoons green onion, finely chopped, including green tops
Pinch of cayenne pepper (or more) for a spicier taste, if desired

1. Place the avocado in a medium-size bowl with the lemon juice, ground cumin, and cayenne pepper.

2. Mash with a fork until it is slightly chunky.

3. Add the remaining cilantro and green onions and mix well.

ABOUT: CUMIN

A member of the parsley family native to the Mediterranean and East India, cumin seed has been harvested as a spice since ancient times. The seeds can be used whole or ground into a powder. Cumin's strong, aromatic and slightly bitter flavor has made it a favorite spice in cultural dishes around the world, adding an earthy and warming feeling to stews, soups, curries and dips.

In the East Indian Ayurvedic tradition of body balancing through food, cumin is valued as a digestive system re-balancer and overall body tonic. Cumin also has significant antiseptic and antiviral properties.

Spring Bean Dip

This unusual dip is both satisfying and cleansing. It can be served with rice crackers or rice cakes and can also be eaten during summer.

MAKES 2 ½ CUPS

¼ cup leeks, finely chopped
1 green onion, finely chopped, including green tops
2 Tablespoons cold-pressed extra-virgin olive oil
½ cup artichoke hearts frozen or canned (in water), drained, quartered
½ cup hearts of palm (canned), chopped in ½ inch pieces
½ teaspoon salt
¼ teaspoon white pepper
¼ teaspoon paprika
1 (15 ounce) can aduki beans, cooked, drained (see instructions below on cooking dried beans)
2 Tablespoons lime juice
¼ teaspoon cayenne pepper

1. In frying pan, sauté leeks and green onion in olive oil until they are soft. Add artichoke hearts, hearts of palm, salt, pepper, and paprika. Sauté 1–2 minutes until well mixed.

2. Add aduki beans and sauté 1–2 minutes more.

3. Place in bowl, add lime juice and cayenne pepper. Blend with a hand blender or food processor until smooth. Taste for seasoning. Add more juice, salt or pepper to suit your taste.

VARIATION:

•   Substitute lemon juice for lime juice.

COOK'S TIP: COOKING DRIED BEANS

If you wish to use cooked dried beans in place of canned beans, here are two methods you can use. These methods work for cooking any dried beans.

Overnight version: Place 1 cup dried beans in a bowl, cover with water about 3 inches above the beans. Soak beans overnight or for about 8 hours. Discard water, rinse beans, and place beans in a saucepan. Add fresh water about 3 inches above beans. Bring to a boil, turn heat to low, cover pot and cook for about 1–1½ hours until beans are tender.

3-hour version: Place 1 cup dried beans in a saucepan. Cover with water about 3 inches above the beans. Cover pan, bring to a boil, and turn off the heat and let set for 1 hour. Discard water. Add fresh water to the pan about 3 inches above the beans. Bring to a boil, cover pot, turn heat to low and cook for 1– 1½ hours until beans are tender.

Vegetarian Nori Rolls with Citrus Horseradish Dipping Sauce

Dinner guests are always delighted when these are served. They also make an excellent spring lunch. The rolls are a bit time consuming, but not difficult to make. They are well worth the effort because they are delicious, especially when dipped in the sauce!

MAKES APPROXIMATELY 30 PIECES

2 cups sushi rice (Sushi rice is a sticky, short-grain rice, ideal for rolling.)
4 cups water
5 sheets toasted Nori sheets
1 sushi mat
1 avocado, sliced in ½-inch strips
1 carrot, cut into small pieces, 1-inch long and ¼-inch wide
2 stalks celery, cut into small pieces, 1-inch long and ¼-inch wide
2 green onions, cut in small pieces, 1-inch long and ¼-inch wide, including green tops
½ cup fresh cilantro, chopped

1. Wash rice. Bring water to boil in saucepan. Add rice, bring to a boil again, cover pot and turn heat to low. Cook for 20 minutes. Turn off heat and let set covered for another 15 minutes before using.

2. Place one sheet of Nori, shiny side down, on sushi mat. Spread ¼ cup rice over the Nori, leaving a 2-inch border on the two longer sides.

3. Place a row each of avocado, carrots, celery, green onion, and cilantro lengthwise down the center of the rice, as shown in the illustration on the next page.

4. Using the mat to help, roll the Nori into cigar shape, shown in Step 2. Press gently as you roll, so the Nori roll is firm.

5. Unroll the mat. Continue this procedure until all the sheets of Nori are used. If there are any leftover vegetables, toss them in a salad.

6. To serve, slice the rolls into 1½-inch rounds using a very sharp knife. Serve with Citrus Horseradish Dipping Sauce (see recipe next page.)

Citrus Horseradish Dipping Sauce

½ cup grated fresh horseradish
¼ cup fresh orange juice
2 teaspoons agave nectar or honey
3 Tablespoons cold-pressed extra-virgin olive oil

1. Blend all ingredients together. Use as a dipping sauce.

VARIATIONS:

• Add pieces of cooked or raw sushi-grade tuna fish.

• Add pieces of cooked halibut, cod, or salmon.

• Substitute lemon or lime juice in the sauce for the orange juice.

COOK'S TIP: HORSERADISH

If you don't have access to fresh horseradish you can substitute 1/4 cup prepared horseradish. We tend to avoid this as prepared horseradish typically is made with vinegar. Our favorite prepared brand is Bubbies™.

COOK'S TIP: ROLLING SUSHI

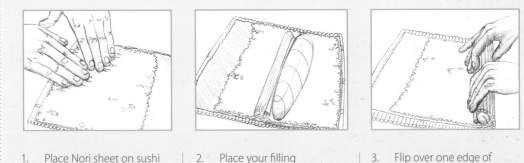

1. Place Nori sheet on sushi mat. Spread rice onto sheet, making sure there are no empty spaces. Leave about a half-inch margin of Nori edge showing all around.

2. Place your filling lengthwise down the center of the rice layer.

3. Flip over one edge of sushi mat by about a third. Now roll that folded side of the mat, pressing gently. The Nori roll will roll up as a cylinder under the mat.

COOK'S TIP: NORI AND SUSHI MATS

Nori is a seaweed, dried as a sheet, and used to create the "skin" that holds the rice and vegetables. It is readily available in natural foods stores, Asian specialty food stores, and larger supermarkets.

Sushi mats are available in natural foods stores and Asian specialty food stores.

spring SOUPS

CONTENTS

Creamy Asparagus Soup

This light soup has a deliciously rich flavor. The addition of lots of herbs to the water, along with the spices and leeks, creates a light, spring broth that tastes great and supports your body in its natural rhythm of spring cleansing.

SERVES 6

½ cup leeks, chopped
2 Tablespoons cold-pressed extra-virgin olive oil
5 cups water, divided
¼ cup each: fresh cilantro, dill, parsley, finely chopped
1 Tablespoon fresh ginger, grated
1 bay leaf
1 teaspoon salt
¼ teaspoon white pepper
1½ bunches asparagus
½ teaspoon dried coriander
3 Tablespoons lime or lemon juice
2 Tablespoons Vegenaise™ dressing (optional)
½ cup toasted almonds, chopped (optional)

ABOUT: VEGENAISE™

Veganaise® is a prepared, egg-free vegan spread that tastes remarkably like mayonnaise. Follow Your Heart®, the company that makes the product, offers four varieties, which vary primarily in the type of oil used. We prefer the version with the purple lid, which is made with grape seed oil. The other primary ingredients in Veganaise®, all non-GMO, are filtered water, apple cider vinegar, brown rice syrup, soy protein, sea salt, lemon juice, and dry mustard powder.

1. Sauté leeks in olive oil in a 2–4 quart soup pot for 5 minutes or until slightly browned.

2. Add 3 cups water, cilantro, dill, parsley, ginger, bay leaf, salt and pepper. Bring to a boil, turn to medium low and cook for about 20 minutes.

3. Break woody ends off asparagus and cut in 2-inch pieces.

4. Add asparagus, coriander and 2 cups water to cooking vegetable broth. Simmer 5–10 minutes, until asparagus can be pierced with a fork.

5. Turn off heat, remove bay leaf, and blend soup with hand blender or food processor.

6. Stir in lime or lemon juice. Taste for seasoning. Stir in the Vegenaise™ (optional, for a creamier taste).

7. Serve sprinkled with toasted almonds, if using (see "Toasting Seeds and Nuts" page 36.)

Curried Red Lentil Soup

This is a light refreshing soup. Served with a salad, it makes a delightful lunch or light dinner meal.

SERVES 6

2 Tablespoons cold-pressed extra-virgin olive oil
½ cup leeks, chopped
1 Tablespoon fresh ginger, grated
1 - 2 teaspoons curry powder
5 cups water
2 vegetable broth cubes
1 cup dried red lentils
2 large strips of lemon rind (about 1-inch wide by 2-inches long, each)
1 Tablespoon lemon juice, or to taste
6 thin slices of lemon for garnish (optional)

1. In a 3–4 quart soup pot, heat oil over medium heat. Add leeks and ginger and sauté in olive oil until soft, about 3–4 minutes. Add curry powder and sauté for 1 minute.

2. Add water and vegetable pieces. Bring to a boil. Turn heat to medium and cook 3 minutes.

3. Pick over red lentils and discard any stones. Rinse and add to pot. Bring to a boil, skimming off foam if necessary.

4. Reduce heat and add lemon rind and simmer 25 minutes or until beans are tender. Discard lemon rind.

5. Add lemon juice to the soup and stir.

6. Pour into soup bowls and garnish each with a slice of lemon.

VARIATION:

•   Add 1 cup each, chopped carrots and celery, and sauté with the leeks before adding the vegetable cubes.

Golden Dragon Soup

This soup has a golden hue and a bright flavor. It is light, satisfying, and cleansing at the same time.

SERVES 6

½ cup leeks, chopped
1½ cup carrots, chopped in ¼-inch pieces
1 cup fennel, chopped in ½-inch pieces
1 Tablespoon cold-pressed extra-virgin olive oil
3 teaspoons curry powder
5 cups water
1 cube vegetable broth
2 lime leaves (optional)
⅛ - ¼ teaspoon cayenne pepper, or to taste
2 cups asparagus, cut in ½-inch pieces (woody ends removed)
1 can light coconut milk
¼ cup lime juice

1. Sauté leeks, carrots, and fennel in olive oil until glazed, about 5 minutes.

2. Add curry powder and sauté for 20 seconds or until there is an aroma. Add water, vegetable broth cube, lime leaves, and cayenne pepper. Cover and bring to a boil. Simmer about 10 minutes.

3. Add asparagus. Cover and cook another 5–7 minutes or until asparagus is bright green and can be pierced with a fork.

4. Add coconut milk and purée with a hand blender until soup has a smooth consistency. Add lime juice. Let simmer about 2–3 minutes. Taste for seasoning.

ABOUT: FENNEL

Native to the Mediterranean and Western Asia, fennel is valued as a crisp vegetable, herb and spice. The plant grows as a greenish-white "bulb" extending into tubular stalks that end in feathery leaves or fronds. The edible white "bulb", rich in vitamin C, is actually not a bulb, but tightly stacked leaves that unpack like the base of a celery stalk. Its texture is light and crisp, with a slight flavor reminiscent of licorice. Slice up the bulb for salads or vegetable sautés, chop the stalks for soups and sauces, and use the fronds as a garnish or chopped fine in salad dressings, soups, sauces and stews. The seeds, ground or whole or crushed, are used to flavor sauces, stews and breads in cultural dishes everywhere. Fennel seed is one of the five essential spices in Chinese five-spice powder, and a staple in Indian curries.

Fennel has been used as a digestive aid for centuries: to stimulate appetite, relieve indigestion, calm colic in children, and freshen the breath. It is a wonderful body-balancing food for spring.

Cleansing Spring Soup

This soup is light, refreshing and satisfying. It tastes great on a cool spring day.

4 cups water
1 vegetable broth cube
½ Tablespoon fresh ginger, grated
¼ teaspoon cayenne pepper (add more for a hotter taste)
½ cup fresh asparagus, cut in ¼-inch pieces (woody ends removed)
½ cup snow peas, cut in thirds
1 cup spinach, coarsely chopped
3 green onions, coarsely chopped, including green tops
2 Tablespoons fresh cilantro, finely chopped

1. Add water, vegetable broth cube, ginger, and cayenne pepper to a 2½-quart pot. Bring to a boil.

2. Add asparagus and snow peas.

3. Bring to a boil again and turn heat down to medium. Allow vegetables to cook until asparagus turns bright green and can be pierced with a fork, 5–8 minutes.

4. Add spinach and green onions. Cook until spinach wilts.

5. Mix in the cilantro and serve in soup bowls.

VARIATIONS:

- Substitute bok choy or Napa cabbage for spinach.
- Substitute dill or parsley for cilantro.

spring SALADS

CONTENTS

Mixed Spring Greens with Honey Lemon Dressing

This is a delicate spring salad. The wild flowers give the salad a colorful, elegant look, and the astringent, tart flavor of the dandelion greens brightens all the flavors. Violets and Johnny-jump-ups can be found growing wild at this time of year. Be sure to pick flowers in areas that have not been sprayed with pesticides See "A Note On Edible Flowers," page 67.

SERVES 4

4 cups organic mixed greens
1 cup dandelion leaves, chopped
1 small carrot, grated
⅓ cup violets or Johnny-jump-ups, stems removed

1. Combine mixed greens, dandelion leaves, and grated carrot in a large salad bowl.
2. Toss with Honey Lemon Dressing (see recipe below.)
3. Garnish with wild flowers.

VARIATION:

• Substitute chives and chive flowers for the violets/Johnny-jump-ups.

Honey Lemon Dressing

MAKES ¾ CUP

½ cup fresh lemon juice
¼ cup cold-pressed extra-virgin olive oil
3 Tablespoons agave nectar or honey

1. Place all ingredients in small sauce pan.
2. Mix well and heat until *almost* boiling.
3. Remove from heat and toss with salad.

VARIATION:

• Substitute lime or orange juice for lemon juice.

COOK'S TIP:
DRESSING AS MARINADE

This dressing can be used as a marinade for halibut, cod or salmon. Mix 1 Tablespoon dill into the dressing and pour over fish.

Mixed Green Salad with Creamy Dill Dressing

The slightly tart flavor of watercress and the arugula's nutty flavor blend well to create a crisp, bright salad with an unusual taste The Creamy Dill Dressing described here can be used on almost any salad. Adding cooked fish such as halibut, cod, tuna, or salmon to the salad makes a light spring meal.

SERVES 4 – 6

1 cup bib lettuce, torn in pieces
1 cup red leaf lettuce, torn in small pieces
1 cup watercress, torn in small pieces
1 cup arugula, torn in small pieces
¼ cup fresh basil, chopped (optional)

1. Place all ingredients in large salad bowl.
2. Add Creamy Dill Dressing and toss (see recipe below.)

Creamy Dill Dressing

This dressing also can be used as a sauce for fish, as a spread on sandwiches, or as a dip for vegetables or chips.

MAKES 1 CUP

¾ cup Vegenaise™ dressing
¼ cup lemon juice
Zest of 1 lemon (optional)
3 green onions, finely chopped, including green tops
3 Tablespoons fresh dill, chopped or 1 Tablespoon dried

1. Mix all ingredients in a medium-size bowl.
2. Pour into salad and toss.

> BODY BALANCING TIP:
> INCORPORATING SALADS
>
> We recommend incorporating salads gradually into your diet at the beginning of spring. Add more salads as the season progresses. Your body does best if given time to adjust to the inclusion of raw foods after a winter of cooked foods. Too much raw food too quickly can place an unnecessary strain on your digestive system.

Crunchy Napa Cabbage Slaw with Creamy Oriental Dressing

This slaw is a delicious and fun variation on coleslaw. It tastes best after chilling for at least 30 minutes.

SERVES 6 – 8

⅓ cup slivered almonds, toasted (see "Toasting Seeds and Nuts," page 36)
4 cups Napa cabbage, coarsely shredded
½ cup snow peas, strings removed, rinsed and thinly sliced
¾ cup radishes, thinly sliced
¾ cup green onions, sliced, including green tops
½ cup fresh cilantro, chopped

1. Combine all ingredients in a large bowl.

2. Toss with Creamy Oriental Dressing (see recipe below.)

VARIATION:

•   Substitute toasted sunflower seeds for almonds.

Creamy Oriental Dressing

1 cup Vegenaise™ dressing
1¼ Tablespoons agave nectar or honey
1 Tablespoon Bragg Liquid Aminos™
1 Tablespoon fresh ginger, grated
⅛ teaspoon cayenne pepper

1. Mix all ingredients in a small bowl.

2. Adjust seasoning to taste.

ABOUT: BRAGG LIQUID AMINOS™

Bragg Liquid Aminos™ is a liquid seasoning that mimics soy or tamari sauce in flavor. It is made from NON-GMO soybeans and purified water. Soy beans are a complete protein, meaning they contain all the essential amino acids we cannot make ourselves. The soybean protein is processed to its constituent amino acids, a process that releases a small amount of natural-occurring sodium, giving this liquid seasoning its characteristic salty taste. It is not fermented or heated, and it is gluten-free. While we generally abstain from using soy beans in our cooking, we do use this product for seasoning.

Dandelion and Watercress Salad with Ginger Dressing

The sweet flavor of the ginger dressing balances the tartness of the dandelion greens nicely. This is a nutrient-rich and mouth-watering salad.

SERVES 6

3 cups dandelion greens, torn
1 bunch watercress, torn
2 green onions, chopped, including green tops
2 radishes, cut in small pieces
½ cup fresh cilantro, chopped

1. Combine all salad ingredients in a salad bowl.

2. Toss with Ginger Dressing (see recipe below)

VARIATION:

*   Substitute spinach for watercress or dandelion greens.

Ginger Dressing

4 Tablespoons fresh lime juice
1 Tablespoon Bragg Liquid Aminos™
1 teaspoon toasted sesame oil
1 Tablespoon cold-pressed extra-virgin olive oil
1 teaspoon crushed red pepper flakes or ¼ teaspoon
    cayenne pepper (more if you want it hotter)
4 teaspoons agave nectar or honey
1 Tablespoon fresh ginger, grated

1. Whisk all dressing ingredients in a small bowl. Drizzle over salad and toss gently.

ABOUT: WATERCRESS

This fast-growing, aquatic or semi-aquatic perennial plant, native to Europe and Central Asia, is one of the oldest known green leaf vegetables eaten by humans. A member of the mustard family, it is known for its peppery taste. Enjoy it raw in salads and as a crunchy sandwich green, wilted as a vegetable sauté, or cooked in soups. Rich in minerals and vitamins, particularly vitamin C, it historically was used to treat scurvy. Valued for its high iodine content which, supports proper thyroid function, and as a digestive aid, watercress is particularly wonderful to eat in the spring when the body naturally detoxifies.

spring VEGETABLES

CONTENTS

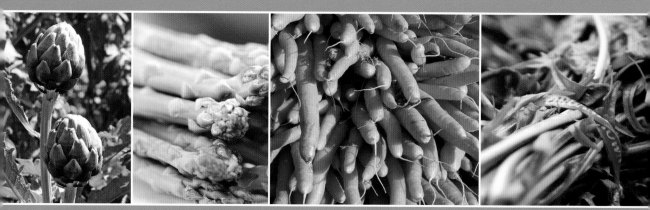

Oriental Stir Fry

This is a quick and easy way to prepare vegetables. They are tasty served with pan-seared halibut, cod or tuna.

SERVES 6

½ cup leeks, chopped
1 Tablespoon fresh ginger, finely chopped or grated
2 Tablespoons cold-pressed extra-virgin olive oil
2 cups carrots, cut in thin strips, 1-2 inches long
2 stalks celery, cut in ¼-inch pieces
1 teaspoon salt
½ teaspoon white pepper
1 bunch red chard, chopped in ½-inch pieces (include red stems)
1 cup snow peas, cut in thirds

1. In large frying pan or wok, sauté leeks and ginger at medium heat in olive oil until leeks are soft, about 3 minutes.

2. Add carrots and celery.

3. Sprinkle salt and pepper over vegetables.

4. Sauté for 2–3 minutes, cover and let cook until almost tender, about 5 minutes.

5. Add the chard and snow peas.

6. Cover and cook until chard is wilted and snow peas are slightly tender, about 3–4 minutes. Snow peas will be slightly crisp. Add in a little water if there is difficulty getting chard to wilt.

7. Serve immediately.

VARIATIONS:

• Substitute 2 cups of asparagus, cut in ½-inch pieces, for the chard.

• Substitute spinach, kale, Napa cabbage, Savoy cabbage or bok choy (or any combination of these) for the chard.

• Use 4 green onions, chopped, including green tops, in place of the leeks.

• Just before the vegetables are cooked, add the juice of ½ orange into the pan and mix with the vegetables. Sprinkle 3 Tablespoons toasted sesame seeds (see "Toasting Seeds and Nuts", page 36) over the cooked vegetables before serving.

• Mix cooked pieces of halibut, cod, tuna, salmon or chicken with the cooked vegetables and serve over a cooked grain to make a complete meal.

Jade Spear Sauté

This is an elegant and delicious way to serve asparagus.

SERVES 4

½ cup leeks, chopped
1 Tablespoon fresh ginger, finely chopped or grated
2 Tablespoons cold-pressed extra-virgin olive oil
3 carrots, sliced on the diagonal
1 teaspoon salt
½ teaspoon white pepper
1 Tablespoon curry powder (optional)
½ cup water
1 bunch asparagus spears, cut on the diagonal, woody ends removed
½ cup toasted almonds, chopped (see "Toasting Seeds and Nuts", below)

1. In large frying pan, sauté the leeks and ginger in olive oil until leeks soften.

2. Add carrots, sprinkle with salt and pepper and sauté 3 minutes. If using curry powder, add it to the pan now and sauté 1 minute more.

3. Add water, cover and cook on medium heat until carrots are almost tender, about 8 minutes.

4. Mix in asparagus and cook until it turns bright green, about 5 minutes.

5. Sprinkle with toasted almonds and serve.

COOK'S TIP: TOASTING SEEDS AND NUTS

The intention here is to heat the seeds and nuts just long enough that they begin to expand and release their natural flavors (which is right about when they start to brown), without going over that quantum edge when they burn. Accordingly, your nose and eyes are your best guides here. Two additional notes: do not grease the toasting surface, and never overcrowd the seeds or nuts. Trust us. Large, whole nuts, like almonds, take longer to heat through (up to 10 minutes or so) than chopped or small nuts. Small seeds, like sesame or poppy seeds, take almost no time.

Skillet Method: Place nuts or seeds in heated, heavy, **ungreased** skillet. Stir over medium heat until heated through and you begin to smell their fragrance. Remove from pan (or they'll keep cooking, sometimes past that quantum edge.)

Oven method: Preheat oven to 350° F, spread seeds or nuts in one layer on an **ungreased** baking sheet. Bake, stirring occasionally, until you begin to smell their fragrance. Remove from oven and baking sheet.

Steamed Artichokes with Creamy Lemon Sauce

Enjoy this treat! Artichokes are at their peak from March through May. They are an excellent source of natural antioxidants. Select artichokes that feel heavy and hard when squeezed. The inner leaves should be wrapped tightly around the choke and heart inside.

To eat artichokes, pull the leaves, one at a time, from the base and use them to scoop the dressing. The fleshy end of each leaf is eaten as well as the base of the choke and the heart.

Artichokes are wonderful served hot or cold as an appetizer, or as an accompaniment with a meal.

SERVES 4

4 fresh artichokes

1. Wash artichokes and cut off stems flush with the base. Slice ½-inch off the top of each artichoke. Remove small bottom leaves and trim sharp tips of remaining leaves with scissors.

2. Cut each artichoke in half or quarters. Scoop out fuzzy part ("hair") on the base.

3. Place artichokes in a 4-quart pan and add water to cover about half of pot. Bring to a boil then lower heat to medium. Cover and cook approximately 25 minutes or until the base can be easily pierced with a fork.

4. Eat plain, use Vegenaise™ dressing for dipping, or use Creamy Lemon Sauce (see recipe below.)

Creamy Lemon Sauce

¾ cup Vegenaise™ dressing
1 Tablespoon fresh dill, finely chopped
1 Tablespoon lemon juice

1. Combine all ingredients and serve as a dip for the artichokes.

Greek Style Dandelion Greens

A delicious way to prepare dandelion greens. Eat them alone, or serve them as a side dish.

SERVES 4

1 bunch dandelion greens
½ teaspoon salt
¼ cup lemon juice

1. Wash dandelion greens and coarsely chop them. Place greens in a medium-size sauce pan.

2. Add salt and cover with water.

3. Bring to a boil.

4. Turn heat to medium-low and cook for approximately 10 minutes. Greens should be very tender and the amount reduced by half.

5. Pour greens into a strainer and drain the water.

6. Place in a serving bowl and toss with the lemon juice.

7. Serve as a vegetable accompaniment with any meal.

BODY BALANCING TIP: DANDELION GREENS

Consider this: all those dandelions that come up in your yard each spring are a gift. They signal that it is time to shift your food choices with spring, and they are the plant to help you do just that. The whole dandelion plant has been used for centuries as a body balancing herb - roots, leaves and flowers. The leaves are one of the most vitamin-rich foods available, and the whole plant is rich in calcium, potassium, iron, Vitamin A, and other nutrients. Traditionally, dandelion leaves are eaten as a spring tonic, to gently cleanse the body with the change of seasons. That distinct, slightly bitter taste signals the presence of compounds that stimulate and support the liver and kidneys, which can otherwise become burdened by the breakdown of cells as the warmer weather thins our blood and mucosal linings.

You can buy dandelion greens in the spring at your local farmers' market or natural foods stores. Better yet, go pick your own. Find plants in areas away from heavily travelled roads and which have not been sprayed. Pick the young, tender leaves. Wash them well and use them quickly. They are great raw, steamed or sautéed. Your body will thank you!

spring FISH & SEAFOOD

CONTENTS

Pan-Seared Tuna Steaks with Creamy Horseradish Sauce

These steaks are easy to prepare and the horseradish sauce adds a gourmet touch to the tuna. The sauce can be used as an accompaniment with any type of fish. It can also be used as a salad dressing when thinned with a little water.

SERVES 4

3 Tablespoons cold-pressed extra-virgin olive oil, divided
4 tuna steaks, 4–5 ounces each. Select ahi (sushi grade quality) or yellowfin tuna steaks
1 teaspoon salt
½ teaspoon white pepper

1. Spread 1 Tablespoon olive oil on both sides of tuna steaks. (The olive oil helps keep the steaks tender when cooking.) Sprinkle salt and pepper on both sides.

2. Spread remaining olive oil over bottom of large frying pan and turn heat to medum-high.

3. When pan is hot, place steaks in pan, cover and let cook. For ahi steaks: cook 3–4 minutes per side. Steaks will be rare. For less rare, or to cook through entirely, cook 6 minutes more on each side. For yellowfin tuna steaks: cook 2–3 minutes per side. (Yellowfin tuna steaks are thinner than ahi steaks. They will cook through in this time.)

4. Spread a dollop of Creamy Horseradish Sauce (see recipe below) on each steak before serving. Serve remaining sauce in a bowl. Everyone will love this spicy, creamy sauce.

Creamy Horseradish Sauce

1 cup Vegenaise™ dressing
¼ cup lemon juice
2 Tablespoons horseradish, grated, fresh or prepared (salt-brined, e.g. Bubbies™)
3 green onions, finely chopped, including green tops

1. In a small bowl, mix Vegenaise™ with lemon juice.

2. Add the horseradish and green onions and mix well.

3. Add more horseradish if you want a stronger taste.

VARIATIONS:

• Use 1 Tablespoon wasabi powder (or more to taste) in place of horseradish.

• Cut cooked tuna in large pieces. Serve with Nori seaweed sheets, sliced into pieces. To eat, tear off pieces of Nori slices, wrap them around tuna pieces, and dip them into sauce.

spring POULTRY & EGGS

CONTENTS

Thai Chicken Stir Fry

This tasty, easy-to-prepare dish is delicious, light and satisfying. Served with Basmati rice, millet or rice noodles, it makes a complete meal.

SERVES 4

2 Tablespoons dark sesame oil or cold-pressed extra-virgin olive oil
1 carrot, cut into ½-inch strips
½ cup leeks, chopped
1 Tablespoon chili flakes
3 boneless, organic chicken breast halves, 5 ounce each, cut into strips
1 cup snow peas
1 teaspoon salt or to taste
¼ cup lime juice
3 green onions, chopped, including green tops
⅓ cup cilantro leaves, chopped
2 limes, sliced in quarters (optional)

1. Heat oil in a wok or large non-stick skillet over high heat.

2. Add carrots and leeks and cook 1–2 minutes, tossing occasionally.

3. Add chili flakes, chicken, snow peas and salt.

4. Cook for another 2 minutes or until chicken has browned.

5. Pour lime juice over mixture.

6. Cook for another 3 minutes or until chicken is cooked through.

7. Mix in green onions and cilantro.

Monterey Chicken

This is great served over cooked rice noodles.

SERVES 4

2 whole, boneless, organic chicken breasts,
    cut in 1-inch strips
½ teaspoon salt
¼ teaspoon white pepper
2 Tablespoons cold-pressed extra-virgin olive oil
½ cup organic chicken broth
1 can artichokes, in water, quartered
Grated rind of 1 lemon, divided
1 avocado, sliced

1. Preheat oven to 350°F.

2. Sprinkle chicken strips with salt and pepper and
   brown them in olive oil in a skillet.

3. Arrange strips in bottom of medium-size casserole.
   Add chicken broth, cover and bake for 30 minutes.

4. Spread artichokes over top with half of grated
   lemon rind.

5. Cover and bake 10–15 minutes more until
   chicken is done.

6. Serve garnished with sliced avocado and rest of
   lemon rind.

BODY BALANCING TIP: WHITE PEPPER

White pepper is the naked seed of
a ripe peppercorn, the berry of the
pepper plant, native to Southern Asia.
Ripe berries are soaked in water until
the skin and flesh softens and comes off,
leaving the seed, which is then dried.

Black pepper is the dried whole
berry, and is made from unripe green
peppercorns (ripe peppercorns are
red) which are picked, cooked briefly to
break open the skin, and sun-dried. As
the berry dries, oxidation causes the flesh
to wrinkle and turn black.

We favor using white and red
peppercorns, and abstain from using
black pepper for several reasons.

- First, white pepper comes from a
  ripe berry, black pepper comes
  from an unripe berry. Unripe fruit
  and vegetables are unripe for
  a reason: in the eyes of Mother
  Nature, they're not ready for
  distribution. Generally, there's some
  mechanism for deterring premature
  consumption: a disagreeable
  taste or smell, for example, or a
  compound that provokes our
  immune system into action in some
  way when we eat the unripe item.
  Whether we notice it or not, it still
  impacts our system.

- Second, the sun-dried, wrinkled
  flesh of black pepper is susceptible
  to accumulating mold or other
  fungus, further provoking our
  chronically over- stimulated immune
  systems. (See "A Word About...
  Allergens," page 7)

Creamy Chicken Over Rice Noodles

The blending of the Vegenaise™ dressing and spices makes this a nurturing and mouth-watering dish.

SERVES 4

1 box (16 ounces) rice pasta
1 teaspoon salt
½ teaspoon white pepper
2 chicken breasts, boneless and skinned
2 Tablespoons cold-pressed extra-virgin olive oil
⅔ cup organic chicken broth
2 heaping Tablespoons Vegenaise™ dressing
½ teaspoon cayenne pepper (add more if hotter taste is desired)
1 Tablespoon arrowroot
1 pound asparagus, cut into ½-inch pieces (woody ends removed)
2 cups spinach
2 Tablespoons fresh dill, chopped
2 Tablespoons fresh basil, chopped

1. Cook rice pasta as directed on box, drain and set aside.

2. Rub salt and pepper on chicken breasts and cut into 1-inch pieces. In large pan, brown chicken pieces in olive oil. Remove from pan and set aside.

3. Blend chicken broth, Vegenaise™ and cayenne pepper into pan and heat. Mix arrowroot in 3 Tablespoons cold water. Add to chicken broth and cook, stirring constantly until sauce thickens slightly and becomes shiny.

4. Add asparagus and cook until bright green and can be pierced with a fork, 3–4 minutes. Add spinach, chicken pieces, dill, and basil. Cook until spinach, dill, and basil wilt. Serve over rice noodles.

VARIATION:

• Serve over rice, millet, or quinoa.

Scrambled Eggs with Vegetable Medley

This dish is an excellent choice for breakfast and is just as wonderful for lunch or dinner.

SERVES 4 – 6

2 Tablespoons cold-pressed extra-virgin olive oil
1 carrot, chopped in ¼-inch pieces
2 stalks celery, cut in ¼-inch pieces
2 green onions, chopped, including green tops
½ teaspoon salt
¼ teaspoon white pepper
1 cup spinach, chopped
6 eggs, lightly beaten with a pinch of salt and white pepper
2 Tablespoons fresh cilantro, chopped

1. Heat olive oil in a large skillet. Add carrots, celery, and green onions. Sprinkle with salt and pepper and sauté for 8 minutes or until vegetables are tender when pierced with a fork.

2. Mix in the spinach until it wilts, about 3 minutes.

3. Add eggs and cilantro into vegetable mixture and cook until eggs are slightly firm, about 3–4 minutes, stirring frequently. Serve immediately.

VARIATIONS:

• Substitute leeks for green onions.

• Add asparagus or snow peas.

• Substitute chard or kale or any other greens, for spinach.

• Substitute dill for cilantro.

spring BEANS

CONTENTS

Chickpea Burgers with Artichoke Hearts

These tasty burgers are great served on gluten-free buns spread with Vegenaise™ dressing, avocado slices, and sprouts.

MAKES 5 PATTIES

½ cup parsley, coarsely chopped
½ cup dill, coarsely chopped
½ cup green onions, coarsely chopped, including green tops
4 cups organic chickpeas, drained, canned or cooked
      (see page 21 for instructions on cooking dried beans)
1 cup artichoke hearts, frozen, or canned (in water), drained
½ teaspoon salt
½ teaspoon white pepper
1 teaspoon ground cumin
2 Tablespoons lemon juice
1 teaspoon chili flakes
½ cup cooked brown Basmati rice (see cooking instructions, page 53, brown Basmati variation)
½ cup rice flour
2 Tablespoons cold-pressed extra-virgin olive oil

1. Place all ingredients, except rice, rice flour and olive oil, in a food processor. Pulse until mixture is coarsely mixed, then blend for 1 minute. Mixture should be a little chunky.

2. Place into a medium-size bowl. Mix in the rice and rice flour.

3. Form into patties about ½-inch thick.

4. Spread olive oil over bottom of large frying pan.

5. Heat to medium-high and fry burgers on both sides until lightly browned, about 2–3 minutes on each side.

VARIATIONS:

• Add 1 beaten egg.

• Substitute cilantro for parsley.

spring GRAINS & PASTA

CONTENTS

Steamed Basmati Rice

Basmati rice has a delightful, nut-like flavor and aroma. This small, long-grained rice has been grown in the foothills of the Himalayas for thousands of years. The name literally translates as "queen of fragrance."

SERVES 6

2 cups white Basmati rice, uncooked
4 cups water
¼ teaspoon salt

PREPARING THE RICE:

1. Place rice in a deep bowl.
2. Add enough water to cover generously and gently rub the rice between your palms for about 5 seconds.
3. Pour into strainer.
4. Run water through the strainer, rubbing the rice between your palms.
5. Rinse the rice and drain well.

COOKING THE RICE:

1. Bring water to a boil in a 2½-quart sauce pan.
2. Add salt and rinsed rice.
3. Bring back to a boil, cover, turn heat to low.
4. Cook for 20 minutes.
5. Turn off heat and let stand covered for 15 minutes.
6. Fluff and serve.

VARIATIONS:

- Substitute brown Basmati rice for white and cook for 1 hour.
- Add several Tablespoons watercress and parsley to water before boiling.
- Add 3 Tablespoons each rosemary, oregano, and dill to water before boiling.
- For additional protein, add up to ¼ cup chopped almonds or sesame seeds. These can be added to boiling water with the rice, or mixed in with cooked rice when it is fluffed.
- Add ¼-inch slice of fresh ginger to water before boiling. Remove ginger before serving rice.
- Add 1 vegetable broth cube to water before boiling.

Steamed Millet

Millet, native to Asia and Africa, is an easily digested, gluten-free grain with a delightful nutty flavor. Because it does expand more than rice, millet requires a little more water when cooking. Try it! It makes an excellent accompaniment to any meal.

SERVES 6 - 8

2 cups millet, uncooked
4½ cups water
¼ teaspoon salt

PREPARING THE MILLET:

1. Place millet in a deep bowl and add water to cover generously.
2. Gently scrub the millet between your palms until water gets dark.
3. Dump out water and repeat 2 or 3 times until water appears mostly clear. (Millet can have more residual dirt than other grains and can require more rinsing.)

COOKING THE MILLET:

1. Bring water to boil in a 2½-quart sauce pan.
2. Add the rinsed millet and salt, bring back to a boil, cover and turn heat to low.
3. Cook for 1 hour.
4. Let set for 15 minutes.
5. Fluff and serve.

VARIATIONS:

- Add 1 vegetable broth cube, 1 Tablespoon chopped fresh dill or cilantro, and ½ teaspoon ground cumin or coriander to water before boiling.
- Add 1 bay leaf and 3 Tablespoons fresh chopped dill to boiling water when adding the rinsed millet.

Rice Pasta with Swiss Chard and Pine Nuts

The combination of ingredients in this dish gives it a gourmet touch.

SERVES 4

1 pound rice pasta, uncooked
2 Tablespoons cold-pressed extra-virgin olive oil
½ cup leeks, chopped
1 bunch Swiss chard (5 cups), leaves and stems cut into ½-inch pieces
2 Tablespoons lemon zest (optional)
1 teaspoon salt
½ teaspoon red pepper flakes
⅓ cup Vegenaise™ dressing
⅓ cup pine nuts

1. Bring a large pot of water to a boil and cook pasta as directed on package. Drain and set aside.

2. Heat olive oil in large skillet over medium heat.

3. Add leeks and stir until soft, about 2 minutes.

4. Stir in chard, lemon zest, salt and red pepper flakes.

5. Cook covered, stirring occasionally, until chard has wilted, about 2–3 minutes.

6. Stir in pasta, Vegenaise™, and pine nuts.

7. Cook, stirring occasionally for approximately 2 minutes until all ingredients are well mixed.

8. Divide among serving dishes.

VARIATIONS:

• Substitute spinach, kale, or bok choy for Swiss chard.

• Substitute chopped toasted almonds for pine nuts.

• Substitute hemp nuts for pine nuts.

Herbed Pasta

Here is a simple, light pasta dish. The addition of herbs gives it a pleasing flavor that works well as an accompaniment to any meal.

SERVES 4

1 box (16 ounce) rice spaghetti noodles
6 green onions, chopped, including green tops
2 Tablespoons cold-pressed extra-virgin olive oil
2 Tablespoons each: fresh chives, rosemary, and oregano, or 1 Tablespoon each, dried
1 teaspoon salt
½ teaspoon white pepper

1. Cook pasta according to directions on package, drain and set aside.

2. In a skillet, sauté green onions in olive oil for about 2 minutes or until soft.

3. Mix in herbs, salt and pepper, and stir for 1 minute.

4. Stir in pasta and mix well.

ABOUT: ROSEMARY

Native to the Mediterranean, this perennial evergreen herb is a potent aromatic, providing a flavor that tastes somewhat like lemon and pine. It is fabulous in breads, dressings, soups and stews, and combines well with eggs, fish and poultry. Rosemary leaves can be used fresh or dried, ground, chopped, or whole. You can dry your own rosemary by hanging a whole sprig upside down in a cool dark place. To release the flavor of dried whole rosemary leaves, crush them in the palm of your hand.

A member of the mint family, rosemary is extremely high in iron, calcium, Vitamin B6 and various antioxidants and has a long history as an herbal medicinal. Like so many other culinary herbs, rosemary has a large number of biologically active compounds that support balancing the body's systems in myriad gentle ways, even though we humans have yet to figure out exactly how they do this.

spring DESSERTS

CONTENTS

Strawberries and Cream Frozen Dessert

This is a simple, elegant dessert. Let the rice milk "ice cream" soften a bit before serving and it tastes like strawberries and cream.

SERVES 4 - 6

1 pint vanilla rice milk-based frozen dessert (e.g. Rice Dream™)
1 pint organic strawberries, washed, stems removed and sliced

1. Scoop frozen dessert in individual bowls and top with sliced strawberries and serve.

VARIATION:

• Use vanilla coconut milk-based frozen dessert.
• Top the dessert with this Cooked Strawberry Sauce (see recipe below).

> BODY BALANCING TIP:
> EATING STRAWBERRIES
>
> We recommend eating strawberries only during their natural season, late May through mid-July. The body does not digest strawberries easily at other times of the year.

Cooked Strawberry Sauce

1 pint fresh strawberries, sliced
½ cup agave nectar or honey

1. Mix strawberries with sweetener in a sauce pan.

2. Cook on medium heat for about 10 minutes or until strawberries are cooked into a sauce. Serve warm or cold.

Lavender Lemon Sorbet

The sweet and tart flavor of this sorbet, mixed with a hint of lavender, makes this a light and elegant, cleansing dessert you will want to make often.

SERVES 6

½ cup raw agave nectar or honey
2 organic lemons, washed, juiced, and peels chopped
2½ cups water
1 Tablespoon dried lavender

1. Add sweetener, lemon juice, and lemon peel to water in a sauce pan. Bring to boil and stir until boiling. Lower heat and simmer for 6 minutes.

2. Add lavender, remove saucepan from heat and allow to cool approximately 6–10 minutes.

3. Pour liquid into strainer and drain so only the lemon juice liquid is left. This is now your "sorbet mix."

4. Place sorbet mix in ice cream maker and follow directions to make the sorbet.

DIRECTIONS FOR FREEZING IF YOU DON'T HAVE AN ICE CREAM MAKER:

1. Freeze sorbet mix in a glass container for 2–3 hours.

2. When the mixture is mushy and still half-frozen, remove from the freezer and blend in a blender.

3. Freeze again until firm.

4. Allow to soften slightly before serving.

ABOUT: LAVENDER

A member of the mint family and native to the Mediterranean, tropical Africa and southern India, lavender lends a floral and slightly sweet flavor to most dishes. For most cooking applications the dried buds or flowers are used, though some chefs experiment with the leaves as well. Only the buds contain the essential oil of lavender, which is where the scent and flavor of lavender are best derived.

A tea made from lavender buds is a gentle digestive aid and is generally soothing to the whole body..

Creamy Orange Custard

This custard has a creamy orange flavor and is delicious and nurturing.

SERVES 8 – 10

4 cups apple juice
½ cup agave nectar or honey
½ cup tahini (optional)
1 teaspoon grated orange rind
1 teaspoon juice from grated fresh ginger (see below)
4 Tablespoons agar flakes
2 cups orange juice
2 Tablespoons arrowroot
Almonds, chopped for garnish (optional)

1. In a large sauce pan, combine first five ingredients.

2. Place pan over medium heat and sprinkle agar flakes over top of mixture. Let simmer for 3 minutes.

3. Stir agar flakes into mixture; simmer and stir until all agar flakes are melted, approximately 5 minutes. It may take up to 15 minutes for agar to melt.

4. Pour orange juice into a small bowl and mix in arrowroot.

5. Add to apple juice mixture, cook and stir until mixture becomes thickened and clear.

6. Let mixture cool. Just before it sets, whip in blender or use a whisk to blend it.

7. Pour into serving glasses or small bowls.

8. Place bowls in refrigerator and allow to cool and get firm.

9. Garnish with chopped almonds before serving, if desired.

ABOUT: AGAR

Agar (aka 'agar-agar' or 'kanten') is a gelatinous substance derived from red algae, a form of seaweed. Traditionally used throughout Asia as an ingredient in desserts, it can be substituted for gelatin (which typically is derived from the collagen inside animals' skin and bones.)

Agar actually sets stronger than gelatin, so not as much of it is needed to achieve the required effect.

TO MAKE GINGER JUICE:

1. Grate 1 Tablespoon fresh ginger. Place grated ginger in a tablespoon and press to release juice to fill one teaspoon.

Strawberry Mousse

Enjoy a light, healthful mousse made with the season's first berries to top off a spring meal. Strawberries are an early season berry. The body responds best to eating them only in their natural growing season: late May–mid July. Note: This recipe requires four hours for mousse to set.

SERVES 6 – 8

4 cups apple juice, divided
4 Tablespoons agar flakes
1½ Tablespoons arrowroot
1 teaspoon vanilla
1 pint organic strawberries, washed, stems removed and sliced in halves

1. Pour 3¾ cups apple juice in large sauce pan.

2. Place pan over medium heat and sprinkle agar flakes over top of mixture. Let simmer for 3 minutes.

3. Stir agar flakes into juice. Continue simmering about 5 minutes or until flakes have melted. (It may take up to 15 minutes for agar to melt.)

4. Mix arrowroot into remaining apple juice.

5. Pour into simmered mixture and stir constantly until thickened and clear, approximately 3 minutes.

6. Remove from heat, mix in vanilla, and pour into large bowl.

7. Place in refrigerator for 1–2 hours until mixture begins to thicken.

8. When mixture is cool and thickened, fold in sliced strawberries.

9. Continue to refrigerate until mousse is completely thick, about 2 hours.

10. Serve in small bowls.

VARIATIONS:

• Substitute any fruit juice for apple juice (mixed berry, apricot, etc.).

• Finely chop 1 Tablespoon fresh mint and fold in mousse with strawberries.

• Substitute blueberries for strawberries.

summer SEASON

Shifting your food choices with summer | gluten-free & dairy-free recipes

CONTENTS

Harmony with Summer

Summer is a time of growth and movement, a time of expansion and maturation. It is also a time of great heat.   The best way to keep our body cool in this season is by staying hydrated three different ways:

· drink water

· eat a light diet which requires less effort by the body to digest

· eat foods with a high water content

The heart and small intestine are considered most active during summer. One of the heart's main functions is to regulate blood circulation, the process by which nutrients get delivered to all the body's cells. During this season of high physical activity, the body is constantly processing food to fuel muscles and make new tissue. The small intestine has the ability to expand during these summer months, allowing a more effective processing and delivery of nutrients from the abundance of fruits and vegetables that are available in this season.

In addition to keeping the body cool, eating a light diet with lots of foods that have a high water content supports keeping the small intestine clear and flexible, allowing for easy digestion and assimilation. An imbalance in the heart or small intestine may cause a build-up of toxins in the body, resulting in sluggish blood flow and less nutrients being absorbed. This may result in experiencing one or more of the following symptoms:

· Observing difficulty tolerating heat

· Experiencing excessive sweating

· Feeling lethargic and sluggish

· Noting heaviness in the body

· Having low stamina

· Encountering slowness in action and thought

· Experiencing cold hands and feet

· Noting difficulty relaxing, feeling a need to keep busy all the time

· Feeling stiffness in sections, or all over the body

Eating in the following way supports the heart and small intestine. Also, it will assist the body to tolerate heat and to feel light and energetic:

- Eliminate baked desserts, breads, and roasted vegetables or protein foods.

- Prepare lighter meals unless extremely active or doing hard physical labor.

- Eat simpler foods such as light salads and dressings, cool soups, meals made of grains and vegetables, and cooling drinks.

- Consume large amounts of fresh organically-grown vegetables and fruit.

- Eat plenty of green leafy vegetables and fresh herbs. In addition, cucumbers and citrus fruits assist the body in cooling.

- Cook more gently. Use lower heat and cook vegetables until they are tender/crisp. Steaming, gentle stewing, and low oil sautéing are the best techniques to use in cooking at this time.

- Cut vegetables in small pieces when making soup to create less cooking.

- When using salt, we recommend using an unrefined sea or rock salt rather than regular table salt. Unrefined salts are rich in minerals and trace elements. See "A Word About... Salt," page 11.

- Eat a little less protein. At least once daily, use a sprinkling of freshly roasted seeds, almonds or pine nuts over whole grains to replace heavier protein foods such as beans, eggs, fish, seafood or poultry.

- Prepare heavier meals during the cooler parts of the day (i.e., early morning or early evening) to avoid overworking the digestive system.

- Eat dinner no later than 8 p.m. or no less than three hours before going to bed.

- Avoid fried foods, processed foods, alcohol, and excessive caffeine as they overtax the body.

- Drink at least two quarts of water each day. If doing heavy exercise (i.e., hiking running, biking) more water is required — three quarts or more.

- Relax, take days off whenever possible and have fun. Get a wide variety of exercise outdoors.

- During summer, enjoy the wonderful array of fresh foods, herbs, and edible flowers available locally to help create enjoyable meals, picnics, and barbecues.

summer

harmony

SUMMER FOODS LIST

A wide array of fresh foods are available in summer. The list below describes those we particularly recommends as supporting your body's desire for foods with a higher water content. Generally, we recommend eating foods grown locally whenever possible, so that your body's rhythm matches that of your environment. While some of the foods on this list are not local to all locations, they still have valuable balancing properties at this time of the year and we recommend them during this season even if they come to you from other locations.

BEANS
Aduki beans
Black-eyed peas
Cannelini beans
Fava beans
Chickpeas
Lentils *(brown, green, red)*
Lima beans
Navy beans
Pinto beans
Red beans
White beans

GRAINS
Corn meal
Millet
Oats, rolled
(certified gluten-free)
Quinoa
Rice
*(Basmati: white,
Brown: long grain)*

HERBS TO EAT MOST OFTEN
Anise hyssop
Basil
Bay leaf
Bee balm
Chamomile
Chervil
Chicory
Chives
Cilantro
Dill
Fennel fronds
Ginger
Lavender
Marjoram
Mint
Oregano
Parsley
Penny royal
Sage
Savory *(summer, winter)*
Spearmint
Rosemary
Tarragon
Thyme

VEGETABLES
Artichoke
Arugula
Beets
(chioggia, golden, red)
Bok choy
Burdock root
Chickweed
Chicory
Collard greens
Broccoli
Broccoli rabe *(or rapini)*
Cabbage *(green, Napa, red)*
Carrots
(burgundy, cream, orange)
Cauliflower
Celery
Chili pepper
Corn
Cucumber
Daikon radish
Endive
Escarole
Green onion
Jicama
Green beans
Kale *(all types)*
Kohlrabi
Lambsquarter
Leek

Lettuce greens
*(all types except iceberg,
which the body does not
tolerate in any season)*
Mustard greens
Nettles
Okra
Peas *(English, snap, snow)*
Radicchio
Radish
Sorrel greens
Spinach
Sprouts
Sweet potato
Swiss chard
Summer squash *(all types)*
Turnip
Turnip greens
Watercress

FRUITS

Apricot
Apple
Avocado
Banana
Berries
(*blackberry, blueberry, black currant, boysenberry, raspberry, strawberry*)
Cherries
Coconut
Figs, fresh
Guava
Grapefruit
Kiwi
Lemon
Lime
Mango
Melons
(*casaba, Crenshaw, honeydew, musk, Persian, watermelon*)

Only eat melons alone, and only in their natural season: July–late August. The body does not tolerate melons in combination with other foods or at other times of the year. See "A Word About...Food Combining," page 9.

Nectarine
Orange
Papaya
Passion fruit

Peach
Pineapple
Plum
Pluot
(*cross between a plum and an apricot*)
Rhubarb

EDIBLE FLOWERS

Arugula
Bachelor's button
Borage
Broccoli
Calendula
Chamomile
Chives
Chrysanthemum
Daisy
Day lily
Dianthus
Marigold
Nasturtiums
Pansy
Scented geranium
Squash blossom
Stock

We offer the following recipes as suggestions for enhancing your summer meals.

ENJOY!

A Note on Edible Flowers...

The vibrant colors of flowers are a wonderful addition to summer meals. They add an elegant touch to meals and many edible flowers are high in vitamin C and/or vitamin A, along with other essential nutrients. The colors of the flowers also assist in energizing the body.

Here are some fun and fanciful ways to use flowers in your summer meals:

- Sprinkle them in any type of salad for a splash of color and taste.

- Freeze whole small flowers (i.e., Johnny jump-ups, gem marigolds, pansies) into ice pieces for a pretty addition to punches, water, and other beverages.

- Use as a garnish on dips, grain dishes, or on a plate of food.

- Whatever inspires you in the moment!

It is best to use only organic flowers, collected in the wild, away from roadsides, or purchased from an organic farm. Flowers purchased from commercial green houses typically are heavily sprayed with chemicals and are not grown for human consumption. Alternatively, you can grow your own! Growing edible flowers can be fun and rewarding.

Select flowers that are newly-opened, perky (not wilting) and free of any bug-eaten or diseased spots. Normally, the petals are the only portions to be eaten. Flowers can be refreshed by dropping them in a bowl of ice water for 30 seconds and then draining them on a paper towel. Pick home-grown flowers in the morning or late afternoon when their water content is higher.

Only use flowers recommended on the summer food list because other flowers can be inedible and cause digestive distress. It is possible that people with asthma and pollen allergies could have an allergic reaction to certain edible flowers, particularly calendula, chicory, chrysanthemum, daisy, English daisy, or marigold. It is a good idea to check with your guests before serving flowers.

summer APPETIZERS

CONTENTS

Green Goddess Dip

This flavorful and luscious dressing keeps well and can be used as a salad dressing or as a sauce for cooked fish or vegetables. We suggest making a double or triple batch to have extra on hand! It keeps well in the refrigerator up to five days.

We recommend using fresh herbs in the dip for optimum flavor.

MAKES 3 CUPS

2 green onions, coarsely chopped, including green tops
2 cups Vegenaise™ dressing
Juice of ½ medium-size lemon
½ cup water
⅓ cup fresh dill, coarsely chopped
½ cup fresh parsley, coarsely chopped
½ cup fresh basil, coarsely chopped

1. Place all ingredients in blender or food processor and blend until smooth.
2. Place in bowl and surround with an array of vegetables for dipping (see below).

Vegetables for Dipping

Use any combination of the following vegetables:

Carrots, cut in 2-inch slices
Celery, cut in 2-inch slices
Green beans, whole
Whole snap peas
Broccoli, cut in 2-inch pieces
Any other vegetable(s) of your choice

Deviled Eggs with Curry

These colorful eggs can be served as an appetizer or as a protein accompaniment with a meal. Fresh eggs can be difficult to shell cleanly. Adding a little salt to the water before boiling will make them easier to peel. Another hint is to roll the cooled eggs between the palms of your hands before trying to shell them.

SERVES 6 – 8

6 hard-cooked organic eggs (see instructions below)
¼ cup Vegenaise™ dressing
1 teaspoon curry powder (optional)
½ teaspoon salt
¼ teaspoon white pepper
Paprika for garnish

PREPARING HARD-COOKED EGGS:

1. Place unshelled, uncooked eggs in sauce pan.
2. Cover with water and pinch of salt and bring to rolling boil. Be careful water doesn't boil over.
3. Turn off heat and leave them on burner 12 minutes.
4. Carefully pour out hot water from pan and replace with cold water to cover eggs. Cool 5–8 minutes.
5. Pour out water. (Cooking eggs this way eliminates a green ring from forming around the yolk.)

PREPARING THE DEVILED EGGS:

1. Shell the hard-cooked eggs.
2. Cut eggs in half lengthwise and remove yolks carefully. Place yolks in bowl and mash with a fork.
3. Add Vegenaise™, curry powder, salt, and pepper. Mix well. Add more Vegenaise™ if a creamier consistency is desired.
4. Carefully spoon egg yolk mixture back into egg white halves.
5. Sprinkle a little paprika over top of each egg for color and serve.

Garlic & Tahini-Free Hummus

This recipe is light and creamy and contains no garlic or tahini. It's great on rice crackers, rice cakes, or as a sandwich filling on gluten-free bread with sprouts, avocado, and lettuce. It also is a tasty dip for chips or raw vegetables.

MAKES 6 CUPS

6 cups organic chickpeas, drained, canned or cooked
    (see page 21 for instructions on cooking dried beans)
⅓ cup cold-pressed extra-virgin olive oil
1½ cups fresh parsley, coarsely chopped
1½ cups fresh cilantro, coarsely chopped
⅓ cup lime juice
½ teaspoon cayenne pepper
1½ teaspoons salt
½ Tablespoon white pepper
1 teaspoon ground cumin

1. Blend all ingredients in food processor or blender. Blend to smooth consistency.

2. Taste for seasoning, add more salt or lime juice if desired. (Note: Because flavors will expand and enhance with time, be cautious of over-seasoning.)

3. Place in air-tight container and refrigerate for at least 4 hours. Taste for seasoning before serving.

VARIATION:

• Substitute lemon juice for lime juice.

ABOUT: CILANTRO

This ubiquitous herb, a member of the carrot family, is native to southern Europe, and from northern Africa to southwest Asia. While all parts of the plant are edible, the fresh leaves and the dried seeds (known as coriander) are the parts most commonly used in cooking. The leaves have citrus overtones, different from the seeds. Today, cilantro (and coriander) are common ingredients in cultural dishes all around the world.

The leaves make wonderful pestos, salsas and chutneys, and also accent soups, salad dressings, stews and salads well. As heat diminishes their flavor quickly, cilantro leaves are often used raw or added to the dish immediately before serving.

COOK'S TIP: CILANTRO

Picked cilantro leaves lose their freshness quickly. Keeping freshly cut stems in about an inch of water in the refrigerator can help. Changing the water every other day, and keeping stems freshly cut can preserve the herb for about a week. Alternatively, you can pack clean, dry cilantro leaves into ice cube trays, cover with water, and seal the cubes in plastic bags when ready.

Creamy White Bean Artichoke Dip/Sauce

This flavorful bean dip tastes wonderful with raw or partially cooked vegetables or gluten-free crackers. It can be a whole meal when served over steamed vegetables. Also, it makes a creamy pasta dish when tossed with rice pasta, or a creamy salad tossed with slightly cooked green beans, sweet potatoes, or carrots.

MAKES 2 CUPS

1 cup artichoke hearts, frozen or canned (in water), drained
⅓ cup organic white beans, drained, canned or cooked, (see page 21 for instructions on cooking dried beans)
½ cup Vegenaise™ dressing
2 Tablespoons lemon juice
½ teaspoon salt
2 teaspoons lemon zest
1 Tablespoon fresh dill, chopped
1 pinch cayenne pepper

1. Place all ingredients in food processor and blend until smooth.

2. This stores well in refrigerator up to 5 days.

COOK'S TIP: ZESTING

Zest is the outer, colored peel of the citrus fruit, free of the thick, white pith below the outer surface of the fruit's skin. The easiest way to zest fruit is with a zester, which looks like a channel knife with a series of parallel openings along the channel, just sharp enough to scrape the zest from the fruit. However, you can collect zest easily using a paring knife or cheese grater. Here's how:

Cheese Grater Method

Use the side of a cheese grater with the smallest holes (the one for Parmesan cheese) and gently scrape the washed, dried surface of the citrus fruit against it. Make sure you avoid grating any of the white, spongy pith into your zest, as it adds a bitter taste.

Paring Knife Method

1. Scrub the fruit surface thoroughly with warm, soapy water. Rinse and dry well.

2. Use a sharp paring knife to cut the peel away from the pith.

3. Lay the peel flat on a cutting board, flesh-side-up, slicing it into two or three pieces if needed to lay it flat. If you've included any pith with the peel, slice it away now.

4. Now slice the clean peel into thin strips.

5. Turn the long thin strips perpendicular and slice again, making tiny confetti of peel.

summer SOUPS

CONTENTS

Minted Pea Soup

The addition of mint to this simple summer soup provides a delightful zest.

SERVES 5

2 Tablespoons cold-pressed extra-virgin olive oil
½ cup leeks, chopped in small pieces
2 cups fresh shelled or frozen peas
4 cups water
2 vegetable broth cubes
1 cup mint leaves, finely chopped, divided
4 Tablespoons Vegenaise™ dressing (optional)
¼ teaspoon white pepper

1. Heat olive oil in large deep sauce pan over medium heat. Add leeks and cook, stirring for 5 minutes or until softened.

2. Add peas and stir until coated with olive oil.

3. Add water, vegetable broth cubes and bring to boil.

4. Lower heat to medium and cook 8 minutes or until peas are tender.

5. Add ¾ cup mint leaves. Cook about 2 minutes.

6. Blend with hand blender or food processor to a thick purée. If soup seems too thick, add more water to make the consistency you like.

7. Divide soup among 4 soup bowls. If you choose, swirl 1 Tablespoon Vegenaise™ on the top of each.

8. Sprinkle with white pepper and remaining mint and serve.

ABOUT: MINT

This cool, refreshing, perennial herb is part of a large family of plants naturalized around the world. Traditionally, this plant has been valued for a host of different uses since ancient times, most of them due to the potency and flavor of its aromatic, essential oils. The leaves have a pleasant warm, fresh, aromatic, sweet flavor with a cool aftertaste, making them a wonderful ingredient for teas, beverages and desserts. Chop or crush fresh mint leaves, and/or use a small sprig as garnish. Mint tea is a wonderfully soothing tea, particularly for settling upset stomachs, and just generally quieting the body.

The most common mints are peppermint and spearmint, and there are a host of others that your local farmers' market will likely carry. Better yet, grow your own - mint is an easy, hardy plant. Then all you have to do is pluck a few leaves when you want them. Here are some of the mint variety options to explore: apple mint, orange mint, pineapple mint, chocolate mint, licorice mint, ginger mint and mountain mint. Each have their own distinctive taste.

summer SALADS

CONTENTS

Mixed Greens with Honey Orange Dressing and Edible Flowers

The edible flowers in this salad enhance the table with their elegance and color.

SERVES 6

6 – 8 cups mixed greens
½ cup chopped fresh basil, chopped
1 cup assorted pesticide-free edible flowers such as pansies, nasturtiums, borage, gem marigolds, calendula petals, chive blossoms, or rose petals (See "A Note on Edible Flowers," page 67.)
½ cup pine nuts
2 green onions, chopped in small pieces, including green tops

1. Toss together mixed greens, basil, and flowers. Reserve a few flowers for garnish.

2. Toss with Honey Orange Dressing (see recipe below) and garnish with green onions, remaining flowers, and pine nuts.

Honey Orange Dressing

MAKES ¾ CUP

½ cup fresh orange juice
¼ cup cold-pressed extra-virgin olive oil
2 Tablespoons agave nectar or honey
1 Tablespoon chive blossoms, small pieces (optional)

1. Place orange juice, olive oil, and sweetener in small bowl. Whisk until well mixed.

2. Mix chive blossoms into dressing and toss with salad.

VARIATIONS:

• Substitute lime or lemon juice for orange juice in dressing.

• Substitute fresh cilantro or thyme for basil.

• Substitute sunflower seeds for pine nuts.

Crunchy Romaine Salad with Spicy Honey Mustard Dressing

This is an elegant salad that will dress-up any meal.

SERVES 4

4 cups romaine lettuce, torn in small pieces
1 carrot, grated
3 Tablespoons raisins
2 Tablespoons toasted almonds, chopped

1. Combine all ingredients in large salad bowl.

2. Toss with Spicy Honey Mustard Dressing (see recipe below).

Spicy Honey Mustard Dressing

MAKES ½ CUP DRESSING

2 Tablespoons fresh tangerine or orange juice
2 Tablespoons lime juice
2 Tablespoons cold-pressed extra-virgin olive oil
1½ Tablespoons agave nectar or honey
1 teaspoon mustard powder
⅛ teaspoon cayenne pepper

1. Mix all ingredients until dressing is smooth and creamy.

2. Pour ingredients over salad and toss.

Green Bean Salad with Pumpkin Seed Dressing

This pumpkin seed dressing is rich and creamy and complements the green beans wonderfully. Add water to thin, and it makes a delightful salad dressing!

SERVES 4

½ cup green hulled pumpkin seeds
¼ cup cold-pressed extra-virgin olive oil
¼ cup water
1½ Tablespoons fresh lemon juice
½ teaspoon ground cumin
½ teaspoon salt
2 Tablespoons fresh cilantro, finely chopped, divided
½ pound green beans, cut in 2-inch pieces

1. Place seeds in blender with olive oil, water, lemon juice, ground cumin, salt and 1 Tablespoon cilantro. Blend until smooth. If too thick, add more water.

2. Bring 3 cups water to boil in 2½-quart sauce pan. Add green beans and cook until tender and can be pierced with a fork, about 3 minutes. Drain in colander and rinse under cold water.

3. Toss cooked beans with dressing and garnish with remaining cilantro. Serve as is, or on a bed of salad greens.

VARIATIONS:

•   Use a combination of pumpkin and sunflower seeds or only sunflower seeds or pine nuts.

ABOUT: SUNFLOWER SEEDS

We actually eat sunflower seed kernels, and they are delicious raw or toasted. (See "Toasting Seeds & Nuts," page 36.) They also are highly nutritious, being an excellent source of dietary fiber, vitamins (particularly the B and E vitamins), minerals, and a host of compounds that balance cholesterol levels. The kernel also produces sunflower oil, a vegetable oil valued for thousands of years. Sunflower butter, made from ground roasted kernels, is a wonderful, nutritional alternative to peanut butter, to which more and more people seem to be developing food sensitivities. (See "A Word About...Allergens," page 7.)

ABOUT: PUMPKIN SEEDS

Also known as pepitas, these seeds have been eaten since at least the time of the Aztecs and probably much earlier. The pumpkin seed kernels are green in color, inside a chalky white hull. The kernels are a key ingredient in Mexican cooking, and also are eaten plain, as a snack. Folks eat them raw, roasted and/or salted. The seed kernels also can be ground into a butter, or pressed to produce pumpkin seed oil. Pumpkin seed kernels are a good source of protein, essential minerals, and essential fatty acids.

Sweet Potato Salad

Sweet potatoes are an excellent alternative to white potatoes, and are rich in vitamins and minerals. They are creamy white in color. Moreover, sweet potatoes are not members of the nightshade family (potatoes, tomatoes, eggplant and peppers are all nightshades) and so tend to be easier on the digestive system.

SERVES 6

3 medium sweet potatoes, cut in medium pieces
1 medium carrot, grated
2 stalks celery, cut in small pieces
4 green onions, chopped, including green tops
1 cup peas (optional)
½ cup fresh dill, chopped or two tablespoons dried

DRESSING:

¾ cup Vegenaise™ dressing
½ teaspoon salt
3 Tablespoons lime or lemon juice

1. Place sweet potatoes in medium-size sauce pan. Cover with lightly salted water. Cover pot and bring to boil, reduce heat to medium and cook sweet potatos until they can be pierced with a fork, about 20 minutes. Drain and cool.

2. When sweet potatoes are cool, add remaining ingredients and combine.

3. Blend dressing ingredients in small bowl.

4. Mix dressing into sweet potato mixture until well coated.

5. Cover and place in refrigerator for an hour or more to let flavors blend.

6. Taste for seasoning and serve.

VARIATIONS:

• Add 3 Tablespoons chopped chives.

• Add ¼ cup toasted almonds.

• Add ¾ cup chopped olives.

Creamy Pea Salad with Honey Mustard Dressing

This salad is easy to make and quite satisfying. Enjoy it for lunch or a light dinner. (Note: Some dairy-free cheese contains casein, a milk protein. Check ingredient list on the package if this is a concern.)

SERVES 8

8 hard-cooked organic eggs, chopped (see below)
6 cups fresh or frozen peas
1 cup celery, chopped in 1-inch pieces
4 ounces vegan rice cheese, cut in ½-inch pieces
1 cup Honey Mustard Dressing

PREPARING HARD-COOKED EGGS:

1. Place unshelled, uncooked eggs in sauce pan.

2. Cover with water and pinch of salt and bring to rolling boil. Be careful water doesn't boil over.

3. Turn off heat and leave them on burner 12 minutes.

4. Carefully pour out hot water from pan and replace with cold water to cover eggs. Cool 5–8 minutes.

5. Pour out water. (Cooking eggs this way eliminates green ring from forming around the yolk.)

PREPARING THE SALAD:

1. Shell and chop hard-cooked eggs. Place in large mixing bowl.

2. Add all remaining ingredients to bowl.

3. Blend with Honey Mustard Dressing (see recipe below) until thoroughly combined.

4. Serve as is, or on a bed of salad greens.

Honey Mustard Dressing

MAKES ABOUT 1 CUP

1 cup Vegenaise™ dressing
1 Tablespoon organic Dijon mustard
3 Tablespoons agave nectar or honey

1. Mix all ingredients until creamy.

summer VEGETABLES

CONTENTS

Cabbage Carrot Sauté

The combination of cabbage, carrots, and dill is delicious and makes an excellent accompaniment to any fish or chicken dish.

SERVES 6

2 Tablespoons cold-pressed extra-virgin olive oil
½ cup leeks, chopped
2 cups carrots, cut in ¼-inch pieces
4 cups green cabbage, cut in small pieces
½ teaspoon salt
½ teaspoon white pepper
2 Tablespoons fresh dill, chopped or 1 Tablespoon dried

1. Combine olive oil, leeks, carrots, cabbage, salt and pepper in skillet.

2. Sauté 5–8 minutes or until vegetables are soft and leeks are slightly brown.

3. Mix in dill and cook 1–2 minutes.

4. Remove from heat and serve.

Baby Bok Choy with Carrots and Ginger

This is a tasty way to enjoy summer carrots and garden greens. It is easy to prepare and goes well with any fish or poultry dish. Ginger is a wonderful digestive aid.

SERVES 4

1 Tablespoon fresh ginger, cut in thin strips, 1–2 inches long
1 cup carrots, cut in thin strips, 1–2 inches long
2 Tablespoons cold-pressed extra-virgin olive oil
½ teaspoon salt
½ teaspoon white pepper
3 bunches baby bok choy
2 Tablespoons fresh cilantro, coarsely chopped

1. Chop bok choy into large pieces.

2. In frying pan, sauté ginger and carrots in olive oil 3 minutes.

3. Mix in salt and pepper.

4. Add bok choy and cook 3–5 minutes or until bok choy is wilted and carrots can be pierced with a fork.

5. Mix in cilantro and serve.

VARIATION:

• Substitute 3 cups chopped regular bok choy for the baby bok choy.

Herb Marinated Grilled Vegetables

Grilling vegetables is fun and easy. The flavor is unbeatable! If using an outdoor grill, we recommend using a grilling basket as this makes the vegetables easier to manage on the grill.

SERVES 6

MARINADE

⅓ cup cold-pressed extra-virgin olive oil
3 Tablespoons lime juice
2 teaspoons lime zest (optional)
½ teaspoon agave nectar or honey
½ teaspoon salt
1 teaspoon fresh rosemary, chopped or ½ teaspoon dried
1 teaspoon fresh thyme leaves, chopped or ½ teaspoon dried
1 teaspoon fresh oregano, chopped or ½ teaspoon dried
1 teaspoon fresh basil, chopped or ½ teaspoon dried
⅛ teaspoon cayenne pepper or more for a hotter taste

VEGETABLES

2 zucchinis sliced lengthwise
¼ pound green beans, whole
1 large fennel bulb, cut in quarters
5 medium-size carrots, cut in four pieces each
2 sweet potatoes, cut in quarters

1. In small bowl, whisk together marinade ingredients.

2. Place vegetables in self-sealing plastic bag and pour in marinade. Seal and toss lightly to coat vegetables. Refrigerate 10 minutes or up to 2 hours.

3. Remove vegetables from bag and reserve marinade.

4. Preheat grill to medium-high. Place vegetables in grilling basket.

5. Lay vegetables in basket on grill. Grill on both sides, 4–5 minutes each, until vegetables have grill marks and are tender.

6. Place vegetables on serving plate and pour marinade over top.

COOK'S TIP: GRILLING VEGETABLES

- When chopping your vegetables, keep your pieces on the large size, as they are easier to handle on the grill this way.

- If you can, use a grilling basket to hold your vegetables. It really makes your vegetables easy to manage on the grill.

- Skewers are another way to manage the vegetables easily.

If you don't have a grill: Broiling vegetables in the oven is the next-best thing. Set the broiler on medium-high, place vegetables on backing sheet, and place sheet on rack 2–3 inches below the broiler. Broil for 5 minutes each side, or until vegetables are browned and tender.

summer FISH & SEAFOOD

CONTENTS

Fresh Poached Cod with Lemon Sauce

This recipe is easy and rewarding to prepare. Reducing the liquid yields a sauce with a delicate lemon flavor.

4 wild cod fillets (½ pound each)
½ teaspoon salt
Juice of 2 medium lemons
¼ cup cold-pressed extra-virgin olive oil
2 teaspoons agave nectar or honey
¼ cup capers (optional)
2 Tablespoons fresh dill, chopped or 1 teaspoon dried

1. Place cod fillets in large skillet. Sprinkle with salt.

2. In a small bowl, mix together lemon juice, olive oil, and sweetener. Pour evenly over fish.

3. Sprinkle capers and dill over fish.

4. Cover skillet. Turn heat to medium-low and let simmer until cod flakes with fork, about 10–15 minutes. (As the fish cooks, more liquid will come from the fish.)

5. Remove fish from pan and place on platter in 200°F oven.

6. Pour liquid from skillet into small sauce pan — this will become your sauce. Bring to boil and continue boiling until liquid is about ¼ the original amount.

7. Place fish on individual plates and pour sauce over each portion.

VARIATION:

•   Substitute halibut for cod.

ABOUT: CAPERS

Culinary capers refers to the pickled bud of a perennial spiny bush (a caper bush), native to the Mediterranean. The plant is best known for the edible bud and fruit (caper berry) which are usually consumed pickled. (Unripe nasturtium seeds can be substituted for capers; they have a similar texture and flavor when pickled.) Capers are ubiquitous in Mediterranean cuisine and are a key ingredient in tartar sauce.

Pickling the caper bud, traditionally in salt, produces the unique, intense caper flavor, as mustard oil is released by the processing. The crystallized white spots often seen on the surfaces of individual pickled caper buds, is rutin, a powerful antioxidant in the body. In fact, capers have some of the highest concentrations of preferred antioxidants of any plant.

Salmon Patties with Creamy Dill Sauce

The addition of curry powder makes these salmon patties extra flavorful. Serving with the Creamy Dill Sauce makes them irresistible. They can be prepared on the grill or in a pan, and served with a salad or on a gluten-free bun.

MAKES 7 MEDIUM-SIZE PATTIES

1 pound fresh wild sockeye or coho salmon,
   or 14½ ounce canned pink or wild sockeye salmon
½ teaspoon salt (if using fresh salmon)
½ teaspoon white pepper (if using fresh salmon)
3 Tablespoons lemon juice (if using fresh salmon)
1 stalk celery, cut in ¼-inch pieces
½ cup leeks, chopped
5 Tablespoons cold-pressed extra-virgin olive oil, divided
2 Tablespoons curry powder
1 egg
3 Tablespoons lemon juice
1 teaspoon salt
½ teaspoon white pepper

Creamy Dill Sauce

MAKES ABOUT 1½ CUPS

1½ cups Vegenaise™ dressing
6 Tablespoons lemon juice
   (or more for a stronger lemon flavor)
2 Tablespoons fresh dill, finely chopped

1.   Place all ingredients in a small
     bowl and mix well.

When using fresh salmon, start with step #1, below. If using canned salmon, start with step #2.

1.   Sprinkle fresh salmon with salt, pepper, and 3 Tablespoons lemon juice. Place in a baking dish. Bake at 350°F for 15 minutes or until it flakes. Remove from oven and cool.

2.   Flake salmon into small pieces and place in large mixing bowl.

3.   Sauté leeks and celery in 2 Tablespoons olive oil in medium-size skillet until softened, about 3–4 minutes. Add to salmon.

4.   Add rest of ingredients, except remaining olive oil. Mix thoroughly.

5.   Form mixture into patties about 2 inches in diameter.

6.   Heat remaining olive oil in large skillet. Sauté patties 3–4 minutes on each side or until golden brown. For grilling, cook approximately 4 minutes on each side or until golden brown.

7.   Serve topped with Creamy Dill Sauce (see recipe above.)

VARIATIONS:

•   Substitute lime juice for lemon juice.

•   Use a combination of lemon and lime juices.

•   Substitute cilantro for dill in both the salmon patties and sauce.

Grilled Halibut with Avocado Papaya Salsa

Grilling fish enhances its flavor. The Avocado Papaya Salsa makes it an extra-special treat.

SERVES 4

4 halibut fillets, 4 ounces each
¼ cup cold-pressed extra-virgin olive oil
¼ cup lemon juice
1 Tablespoon salt
2 teaspoons white pepper
3 Tablespoons fresh chives, chopped
2 Tablespoons fresh dill, chopped

1. Turn grill to high for about 15 minutes

2. Rub fillets on both sides with olive oil, lemon juice, salt and pepper.

3. Press chives and dill onto both sides of halibut fillets.

4. Place fillets on grill, turn heat to medium. Grill 4–5 minutes each side. Fish will be done when it flakes. Thicker cuts of fish take longer to cook. If you prefer, the fish can be cooked under the broiler using the same instructions as for grilling.

5. Remove fish from grill and serve topped with Avacado Papaya Salsa (see recipe below).

VARIATIONS:

• Leave out chives and dill.

• Substitute salmon for halibut.

• Substitute lime or orange juice for lemon juice.

Avocado Papaya Salsa

MAKES ABOUT 1½ CUPS

1 avocado, peeled and seeded
1 papaya, peeled and seeded, or one 15-ounce can
2 green onions, coarsely chopped, including green tops
¼ cup fresh cilantro, chopped
¼ cup lemon juice

1. Place avocado, papaya, green onions, cilantro, and lemon juice in food processor. Pulse a few times until mixture is chunky.

2. Serve over grilled halibut fillets.

Pan-Seared Salmon with Cucumber Chutney

The cucumber chutney is cooling and refreshing, and provides a wonderful contrast to the salmon. Note that you will want to make the chutney at least an hour before you cook the fish, so the flavors can blend.

SERVES 4

3 Tablespoons cold-pressed extra-virgin olive oil, plus extra to brush
4 pieces wild sockeye or coho salmon with skin on (about 4 ounces each)

1. Heat olive oil in a non-stick skillet over medium-high heat.

2. Add salmon, skin side down, and cook covered 4 minutes or until skin is crisp.

3. Reduce heat to medium, turn salmon fillets and continue to cook covered, for another 4 minutes or until just cooked through.

4. Salmon will flake when it is done. Serve with Cucumber Chutney.

Cucumber Chutney

MAKES ABOUT 1½ CUPS

1 Tablespoon lime juice
1½ teaspoons cold-pressed extra-virgin olive oil
1 teaspoon agave nectar or honey
½ teaspoon red pepper flakes
1 teaspoon salt
1½ cucumber, peeled and seeded, cut in ¼-inch pieces
2 green onions, chopped in small pieces, including green tops
1 Tablespoon fresh cilantro, chopped

> **BODY BALANCING TIP: CHUTNEYS**
>
> Chutneys are a class of condiments that have been a part of East Indian cooking literally for millenia. They form an integral part of the East Indian Ayurvedic tradition of body balancing through food.
>
> Chutneys typically comprise a fruit or a cooling vegetable, such as cucumber, in combination with seasonings and spices that access all five major taste sensations: salty, sweet, bitter, sour and savory.
>
> Key ingredients include salt and some form of sweetener, often raw honey. The combination of ingredients in a freshly-made chutney is soothing to the digestive system and supports the body in digesting heavy proteins such as poultry and fish, as well as grains and legumes.
>
> Chutneys also can be allowed to pickle, releasing valuable enzymes and other compounds that support balanced digestion

1. Combine lime juice, olive oil, sweetener, pepper flakes, and salt in a medium-size bowl and mix well. Set aside.

2. Add cucumbers, green onions, and cilantro to dressing and mix well. Cover and refrigerate for 1 hour or longer so flavors can blend.

summer POULTRY & EGGS

CONTENTS

Grilled Herb Chicken with Chipotle Orange Marinade

Chicken always tastes great when prepared on the grill. The chipotle marinade gives this recipe a special flavor.

SERVES 4 – 6

4 organic chicken breasts, 4 ounces each, skin removed

3. Prepare Chipotle Orange Marinade (see recipe below).

4. Place chicken breasts in zip top plastic bag. Pour in marinade. Seal and toss to coat chicken, then allow to marinate at least 15 minutes or longer for extra flavor.

5. Remove chicken from marinade. Broil or grill chicken over medium-high heat until cooked through, turning frequently, about 6–8 minutes per side. Cooking time will depend on thickness of chicken breasts. Allow longer cooking times for thicker pieces.

6. Pour remaining marinade over each breast and serve.

Chipotle Orange Marinade

MAKES ABOUT 1 CUP MARINADE

1 cup fresh orange juice
¼ cup lime juice
1 Tablespoon fresh oregano, chopped (optional)
2 teaspoons orange zest
2 teaspoons chipotle chili powder
1 teaspoon cumin seeds, crushed or 1 teaspoon ground cumin
½ teaspoon salt

1. Combine orange juice and lime juice in small sauce pan and boil until ½ cup liquid remains.

2. Mix the rest of ingredients into reduced juice mixture.

3. Refrigerate at least 15 minutes or longer so marinade can cool and flavors can blend.

Turkey Burgers with Avocado Salsa

These versatile, flavorful burgers can be served in a variety of ways: as the main entrée with a salad, or on a gluten-free bun.

MAKES 7 OR 8 MEDIUM-SIZED BURGERS.

½ cup leeks, chopped in small pieces
3 green onions, chopped in small pieces,
    including green tops
½ cup celery, finely chopped
3 cups ground, organic turkey or chicken
1 teaspoon salt
1½ cups gluten-free bread crumbs
¾ cup organic organic chicken broth
2 eggs, beaten
½ cup Kalamata olives, chopped (optional)
½ cup pine nuts
½ teaspoon chili powder
3 Tablespoons cold-pressed extra-virgin olive oil
    (for cooking on stove top)

1. Place all ingredients except olive oil in large mixing bowl and mix until well blended. (You can mix ingredients with your hands to get a smooth texture.)

2. Form into patties 2 inches in diameter.

Avocado Salsa

1 ripe avocado, finely chopped
2 Tablespoons lemon juice
2 Tablespoons lime juice
2 Tablespoons fresh cilantro,
    chopped
1 Tablespoon Vegenaise™ dressing
½ cup leeks, finely chopped
1 teaspoon ground cumin
⅛ teaspoon cayenne pepper
    (add more for a hotter flavor)
½ teaspoon salt

Thoroughly mix all ingredients in medium-size bowl and serve over burgers.

COOK PATTIES:

3. On a stove: Heat olive oil in large skillet, at medium-high heat. Place patties in skillet, cover and cook on both sides until brown, about 4 minutes on each side.

4. On a gas grill: Turn on high for 15 minutes, then turn to medium and cook patties 4 minutes on each side or until browned.

5. Top burgers with Avocado Salsa (see recipe above) and serve with a salad or on a gluten-free bun.

Chicken Penne Salad with Green Beans

Using a combination of pasta, green beans, and chicken makes this a tasty, refreshing meal for lunch or a light dinner.

SERVES 4

2 cups uncooked penne rice pasta
2 cups raw green beans (about ½ pound), cut in 2-inch pieces
2 cups cooked chicken breast, shredded
½ bunch green onions, chopped, incuding green tops
¼ cup fresh basil, chopped
2 Tablespoons fresh Italian parsley, chopped
1 teaspoon salt
1 teaspoon white pepper

1. Cook pasta according to directions on box, adding green beans 4 minutes before pasta is done.

2. Allow beans to cook with pasta. Drain pasta and green beans and rinse with cold water. Drain again.

3. Combine pasta and green beans, chicken, green onions, basil, parsley, salt and pepper in large bowl, toss gently to combine.

DRESSING

2 Tablespoons cold-pressed extra-virgin olive oil
3 Tablespoons lemon juice
1 Tablespoon water

1. Combine olive oil, lemon juice and water in a small bowl, stirring with a whisk or fork.

2. Drizzle over pasta mixture, toss gently to coat.

VARIATION ON THE DRESSING:

• Mix ½ cup lemon juice with ½ cup Vegenaise™.

Egg Salad

This simple egg salad tastes great served over mixed greens. It makes a delicious sandwich with gluten-free bread and sprouts, or as a snack on rice crackers or rice cakes.

SERVES 4

4 hard-cooked organic eggs (see directions below)
1 stalk celery, chopped in small pieces
¼ cup fresh dill, cilantro, or parsley, finely chopped
2 green onions, chopped in small pieces, including green tops
½ cup Vegenaise™ dressing (use more if you like a creamier salad)

PREPARING HARD-COOKED EGGS:

1. Place unshelled, uncooked eggs in sauce pan.

2. Cover with water and pinch of salt and bring to rolling boil. Be careful water doesn't boil over.

3. Turn off heat and leave them on burner for 12 minutes.

4. Carefully pour out hot water from pan and replace with cold water to cover eggs. Cool 5–8 minutes.

5. Pour out water and peel eggs. (Cooking eggs this way eliminates a green ring from forming around the yolk.)

PREPARING EGG SALAD:

1. Place hard-cooked eggs in small bowl. Mash eggs with fork.

2. Add celery, dill, and green onions to mashed eggs and mix.

3. Mix in Vegenaise™.

summer BEANS

CONTENTS

Summer Bean Salad

This salad has a delightful "Southwest" flavor.

SERVES 6

4 cups organic kidney beans, drained, canned or cooked
   (see page 21 for instructions on cooking dried beans)
1 cup celery, chopped
1 cup carrot, grated
½ cup fresh cilantro, finely chopped
⅓ cup lime juice
1 teaspoon ground cumin
1 teaspoon salt
½ teaspoon white pepper
Pinch of cayenne pepper pepper or more for a hotter taste (optional)
½ bunch green onions, chopped, including green tops
1 avocado, cut in ¼-inch pieces

1.   Combine all ingredients in large bowl. Toss until well mixed.

2.   Put in refrigerator 1 hour or more to let flavors blend.

3.   Taste for seasoning and serve at room temperature.

BODY BALANCING TIP: CAYENNE PEPPER

This very hot, intense red chili pepper often is used in ground form as a spice. Its species are native to the Americas, where they have been cultivated for thousands of years. The hot, biting flavor of cayenne is utilized in cultural dishes around the world, including Mexican, Caribbean and Szechuan cuisines.

It is possible that cayenne may be valued more as a medicinal than as a culinary ingredient. In addition to being a rich source of vitamins and minerals, cayenne contains capsaicin, the compound responsible for the pepper's "heat." Capsaicin stimulates blood circulation and metabolism, both of which properties balance blood pressure levels and help "cool" the body. It also stimulates the digestive system, particularly the stomach and digestive tract, and has been used as a 'spring cleanse' tonic ingredient for centuries (see recipe in Harmony With Spring, under suggestions for assisting the body in cleansing.) The pepper also has a long history for use in treating infections, particularly fungal infections, and recently has been found to support triggering cell death of certain cancer cells. We invite you to consider including this spice into your diet from time to time ...a little bit goes a long way!

Chickpea Cucumber Salad with Fresh Mint

This light, refreshing salad makes a great lunch or a light dinner. It keeps well and makes a wonderful dish for picnics.

SERVES 6

3 cucumbers
1¼ cups organic chickpeas, drained, canned or cooked
    (see page 21 for instructions on cooking dried beans)
½ cup mint leaves, roughly chopped
2 medium carrots, grated
½ cup raisins
1½ teaspoons fennel seeds, crushed or 1 teaspoon ground fennel
3 green onions, chopped, including green tops
4 Tablespoons lemon juice
1½ Tablespoons cold-pressed extra-virgin olive oil
½ teaspoon salt
½ teaspoon white pepper

1. Cut cucumbers in half lengthwise. Scoop out seeds with spoon and discard.

2. Cut cucumbers into ¼-inch pieces. Place in medium bowl.

3. Add chickpeas, mint, carrots, raisins, fennel, and green onions.

4. In separate bowl, whisk together lemon juice, olive oil, salt, and pepper until well mixed.

5. Toss salad ingredients with dressing.

6. Serve at room temperature.

ABOUT: CHICKPEAS

Also known as garbanzo beans, these members of the legume family are native to the Middle East and have been cultivated for over 7,000 years. Tan in color and with a nutty flavor, chickpeas are a nutrient-dense food. They comprise about 20% protein, are chock-full of minerals and vitamins, and they are high in dietary fiber, making them an attractive nutrient source for folks with diabetes or insulin sensitivity.

Curried Red Lentil Burgers

This burger has a robust flavor for a delicious entrée. It can be served on a gluten-free bun with Vegenaise™ dressing and sprouts, or inside a gluten-free wrap with salad greens and Vegenaise™.

1¼ cups red lentils
2 cups water
1 cup quinoa flakes
⅓ cup shredded carrots
⅓ cup celery, finely chopped
3 green onions, finely chopped, including green tops
½ cup fresh cilantro, finely chopped
1 Tablespoon curry powder
¼ teaspoon cayenne pepper
2 Tablespoons lime juice
2 Tablespoons Bragg Liquid Aminos™
3 Tablespoons cold-pressed extra-virgin olive oil

1. Rinse lentils under running water.

2. Add lentils and water to a medium-size sauce pan.

3. Bring to boil, turn heat to medium-low and cook until all water has been absorbed and lentils are soft and a little moist (about 10–15 minutes).

4. In a medium-size bowl, blend cooked lentils, quinoa flakes, carrots, celery, green onions and cilantro.

5. Add curry powder, cayenne pepper, lime juice, and Bragg Liquid Aminos™ to mixture and blend with your hands. If mixture is too thin, add more quinoa flakes. If mixture is too firm, add 1–2 Tablespoons lime juice.

6. Place in refrigerator 15–30 minutes.

7. Form into 2-inch patties. Cook patties in olive oil in a skillet on medium-high heat 3–4 minutes on each side until browned. Serve with a dollop of Vegenaise™ dressing.

VARIATIONS:

- Substitute finely chopped asparagus for celery.
- Substitute dill for cilantro.

summer GRAINS & PASTA

CONTENTS

Pasta Tossed in Fresh Herbs

The addition of fresh herbs to this simple recipe enhances the flavor, putting it a touch above the ordinary. Served with toasted almonds or pine nuts and a salad makes it a light summer meal, perfect for hot summer days.

SERVES 4

1 box (16 ounce) rice spaghetti noodles
2½ teaspoons salt, divided
2 Tablespoons cold-pressed extra-virgin olive oil
6 green onions, chopped, including green tops
2 Tablespoons each fresh parsley and oregano, chopped
1 Tablespoon fresh mint, chopped
½ teaspoon white pepper

1. Fill 4-quart soup pot with 8 cups water and bring to boil.

2. Add pasta and 1 teaspoon salt.

3. Cook pasta according to directions on package. Drain.

4. In skillet, sauté green onions in olive oil for 2 minutes or until soft. Mix in parsley, oregano, remaining salt and pepper, and stir for 1 minute.

5. Stir in cooked, drained pasta and mix well. Mix in more olive oil if desired.

VARIATION:

•   Substitute basil for parsley.

Pasta Tossed with Pesto Sauce

It is hard to recognize that this delicious pesto sauce is made without garlic. Try this tasty sauce on poultry, fish, grains, or vegetables.

SERVES 4

1 box (16 ounce) rice spaghetti noodles
1½ teaspoons salt, divided

1. Fill 4-quart soup pot with 8 cups water and bring to boil. Add 1 teaspoon salt and pasta. Cook according to directions on package. Drain.
2. Mix with Pesto Sauce (see recipe below) and serve.

Pesto Sauce

MAKES 1 CUP

3 cups fresh basil, coarsely chopped
2 Tablespoons fresh parsley
1 green onion, coarsely chopped, including green tops
½ teaspoon salt
¼ teaspoon cayenne pepper
½ cup cold-pressed extra-virgin olive oil

1. Place basil, parsley, green onion and salt in a food processor and blend until herbs are mashed.
2. Add cayenne pepper. Blend until well mixed.
3. Gradually pour in olive oil and blend until sauce is smooth.

summer DESSERTS

CONTENTS

Luscious Fruit Cup

This refreshing summer fruit combination makes a delightful dessert or snack. The fresh basil provides a wonderful counterbalance to the sweetness of the fruit. There are a number of different basil varieties, each with its own unique flavor: cinnamon basil, Genovese basil, lemon basil, Thai basil. We invite you to experiment with the different varieties.

SERVES 6

4 peaches, pit removed and sliced
2 apricots, sliced
1 cup blueberries
½ cup raspberries
¼ cup fresh basil, chopped
2 Tablespoons agave nectar or honey
¼ cup lemon juice

1. Place fruit in large bowl.

2. Add basil and mix.

3. In small bowl, combine sweetener and lemon juice. Blend together with fruit.

4. Chill ½–1 hour before serving to allow the flavors to blend.

VARIATIONS:

- Substitute nectarines for peaches.

- Substitute lime or orange juice for lemon juice.

BODY BALANCING TIP: EATING FRUIT WITH MEALS

After a full meal do enjoy a piece of fruit or a whole fruit cup. We just recommend waiting at least a half hour before you indulge. If you can wait longer, so much the better. It will support your whole system to do this, and you will feel more satisfied.

We love fruit. A whole host of them have fabulous vitamins, minerals, antioxidants and other beneficial goodies to support our bodies. And fresh fruit is delicious! However, if we eat fruit right after a heavy meal of starches and/or protein, our body can't properly digest the fruit, and all those goodies go to waste. Moreover, it stresses the system to try to digest both fruit and starches or protein simultaneously, the effort often causing a gassy or bloated feeling. So, if you are done with your main meal, take a walk or drink a slow cup of green or herbal tea and visit with a friend before reaching for that bowl of cherries. Your body will thank you. (See "A Word About...Food Combining", page 9)

Peach Coconut "Ice Cream"

Using coconut milk as a base for this ice cream makes it rich and creamy. The fresh peaches make it delectable!

MAKES APPROXIMATELY 1 QUART

2 cups light coconut milk
2 cups pitted and sliced fresh peaches, packed
½ cup Medjool dates, pitted and packed

1. Combine coconut milk, peaches, and dates in blender. Blend at high speed until mixture is smooth.

2. Place the blender in freezer for 40–60 minutes, until well chilled, or place in refrigerator overnight.

3. Pour the mixture into an ice cream maker and freeze according to the manufacturer's instructions.

4. Serve immediately or transfer to an airtight container and store in the freezer until ready to serve.

VARIATIONS:

- Substitute 1 cup of blueberries for 1 cup peaches.
- Substitute pitted cherries for peaches.
- Substitute almond milk for coconut milk.

Vanilla "Ice Cream" with Fresh Raspberries

It can be hard to believe this elegant dessert is so simple to make. Let the frozen dessert or "ice cream" soften before serving and it tastes like raspberries and cream!

SERVES 4 – 6

1 pint vanilla rice milk-based frozen dessert
1 pint organic raspberries, washed

1. Place scoops of frozen dessert in a bowl. Let soften.

2. Top with raspberries and serve.

VARIATIONS:

- Substitute blackberries, blueberries, or boysenberries for the raspberries, alone, or in combination.
- Substitute a coconut milk-based frozen dessert, such as Coconut Bliss™, for the rice milk-based frozen dessert.

Raspberry Mousse

Enjoy a light, healthful mousse to top off a summer meal. This mousse is made with succulent raspberries.

SERVES 6 – 8

4 cups apricot juice, divided
4 Tablespoons agar flakes
1½ Tablespoons arrowroot
1 teaspoon vanilla
1 pint fresh raspberries, washed

1. Pour 3¾ cups apricot juice in large sauce pan.

2. Place pan over medium heat and sprinkle agar flakes over top of juice. Let simmer for 3 minutes.

3. Stir agar flakes into mixture; simmer and stir until all agar flakes are melted, approximately 5 minutes. It may take up to 15 minutes for agar to melt.

4. In separate bowl, mix arrowroot with remaining apricot juice.

5. Pour into simmered mixture and stir constantly until thickened and clear, approximately 3 minutes.

6. Remove from heat, mix in vanilla and pour into large bowl.

7. Place in refrigerator 1–2 hours until mixture begins to thicken. When mixture is cool and thickened, fold in raspberries.

8. Continue to refrigerate until mousse is completely thick, about 2 hours.

9. Serve in small bowls.

ABOUT: ARROWROOT

The starch of this tropical root vegetable native to the Americas is valued because of its easy digestibility and high fiber content. For this reason, arrowroot flour is often used in breads and biscuits for children.

Ground into a fine powder, the starch is used in cooking as a thickener and makes a great substitute for cornstarch or flour. Unlike cornstarch, it doesn't develop a chalky taste if undercooked, and it has about 50% more thickening power than wheat flour. Moreover, it is gluten-free and not a known allergen as many corn-based products have become. When cooked, it is tasteless and becomes transparent, making it a good thickener for clear fruit sauces. Because it can be cooked at low temperatures it also works well with egg-based sauces.

VARIATIONS:

• Substitute any fruit juice for apricot nectar (mixed berry, apple, etc.).

• Substitute blueberries, blackberries, and/or boysenberries for raspberries.

• Finely chop 1 Tablespoon fresh mint and fold into mousse together with raspberries.

Peach Raspberry Blueberry Pie

The combination of the date almond crust and fresh fruit in this uncooked pie satisfies anyone's sweet tooth. It is always a favorite!

SERVES 8-10

CRUST

2 cups raw almonds, unsalted
1 cup Medjool dates, pitted
1 teaspoon vanilla

1. Place ingredients in food processor and blend until well mixed. If mixture is too dry, add ½–1 cup water. Mix with your hands. It should be moist and hold together.

2. Oil a pie plate with small amount of olive oil.

3. Press almond mixture into pie plate.

4. Place in refrigerator for ½–1 hour, if time permits.

FILLING

1 cup Medjool dates, pitted
6 peaches or nectarines, pits removed, divided
1 cup raspberries
1 cup blueberries

1. Blend Medjool dates and 2 peaches in blender or food processor until puréed.

2. Cut remaining peaches or nectarines into ½ inch pieces. (Reserve a few slices, uncubed, for garnish.)

3. Place cubed peaches, raspberries, and blueberries in medium-size bowl. (Reserve a few berries for garnish.)

4. Mix in date-peach purée. Spread into pie shell.

5. Garnish with remaining fruit and serve.

VARIATIONS:

• Substitute apricots or mango for peaches.

• Substitute strawberries for raspberries.

• Finely chop 1 Tablespoon fresh mint and fold into fruit mixture.

Refreshing Drinks

Fresh Lemonade

Enjoy this refreshing and cleansing drink on a hot summer day.

MAKES 1 QUART

1 cup fresh lemon juice
1 cup agave nectar
4 cups filtered water
Flower ice pieces (optional)

1. Combine lemon juice, agave, and water in quart pitcher.
2. Pour into glasses filled with ice pieces and serve with a sprig of fresh mint.

VARIATION:

• Substitute lime in place of lemon.

Root Beer Float

This treat may rekindle some wonderful childhood memories!

SERVES 4

8 scoops vanilla rice milk-based or coconut milk-based frozen dessert
4 cups chilled root beer

1. Place frozen dessert in 8 or 12 ounce glasses.
2. Pour chilled root beer over frozen dessert or "ice cream".
3. Serve immediately, with a straw (optional).

Banana Blueberry Smoothie

Use frozen bananas to make a colder, thicker smoothie.

SERVES 4

2 bananas, frozen or fresh
3 cups apple juice
1 cup blueberries

1. Place ingredients in food processor or blender and blend until smooth. (Add more juice for thinner consistency.)
2. Serve in glasses garnished with a mint leaf or pansy.

VARIATIONS:

• Substitute raspberries, blackberries, 2 peaches, or a mango for the blueberries.

• Substitute almond or hemp milk for the apple juice.

COOK'S TIP: MAKING FLOWER ICE CUBES

Place petals or whole edible flowers such as Johnny Jump-ups, violets, gem marigold, nasturtiums or borage flowers in ice cube trays filled with water and freeze.

late
summer SEASON

shifting your food choices with late summer | gluten-free & dairy-free recipes

CONTENTS

Harmony with Late Summer

Late summer, which occurs near the middle of August, is a short season, lasting about four weeks. This interim season signals the transition from the seasons of outward expression and growth: spring and summer, to the seasons of inward focus and cycle completion: autumn and winter.

Weather swings are common in late summer, fluctuating between hot and dry, and cold and damp. In cultures that mark their personal cycles by the seasons, late summer indicates a time to begin moving inward and become more introspective.

During this interim season, our bodies are strengthening themselves for the harvest to come. A good harvest is essential for a graceful and easy winter, during which we rest and rely on food stores until we can plant again in spring.

The organs that are considered most active for late summer are the stomach, pancreas, and spleen. These three organs are essential to our digestive process, which we can consider analogous to the harvest season. The stomach can be viewed as a granary, processing food and preparing it for absorption. The spleen and pancreas provide necessary constituents for the body to absorb the nutrients and translate them into muscle, blood and food stores. Strengthening the stomach, spleen and pancreas then is like preparing the granary and sharpening the harvest tools, providing you with a strong, vital and grounded digestive system, ready for the autumn harvest and the processing of food for winter.

If there is an imbalance in the stomach, pancreas or spleen, the following symptoms may occur:

- Indigestion, bloating, belching or intestinal discomfort
- Acid stomach
- Swelling, cracking or peeling of the lips
- Pain or stiffness in muscles
- Low energy
- Constipation or diarrhea
- A cold or some type of infection
- Low blood sugar
- Excessive worry or forgetfulness
- Feeling ungrounded, sad, depressed, lonely, melancholy or unsettled.

The following suggestions will support your body to begin the transition into colder weather:

- In a limited way, start baking again. Bake some vegetables, protein foods, quick breads and light cakes.
- Eat more protein: poultry, fish, beans, nuts and seeds.
- Add more grains to meals; millet is especially nourishing to the stomach, pancreas and spleen.
- Continue eating plenty of fresh, organic fruits and vegetables. Local organic farmers offer the most ideal selections.
- Eat dates to nourish the stomach, pancreas and spleen.
- Eat less salads and raw foods, particularly on cold days. A bowl of soup is warming on those days.
- Use a little more oil in cooking.
- Take time to eat, and chew food well.
- Eat simple food combinations. Avoid eating several food combinations at the same time.
- Continue to spend time outdoors. Begin strengthening exercises (i.e., working with weights, calisthenics and isometrics) to prepare for the upcoming cold weather. Stretching out muscles as they begin to contract with the cold is helpful in keeping the body and joints loose and supple.

late summer

harmony

LATE SUMMER FOODS LIST

A wide array of fresh foods are available in late summer. The list below describes those we particularly recommend as in alignment with your body's desire for foods that are more warming. Generally, we recommend eating foods grown locally whenever possible, so that your body's rhythm matches that of your environment. While some of the foods on this list are not local to all locations, they still have valuable balancing properties at this time of the year and we recommend them during this season even if they come to you from other locations.

BEANS
Aduki beans
Black-eyed peas
Cannelini beans
Fava beans
Chickpeas
Lentils (*brown, green, red*)
Lima beans
Navy beans
Pinto beans
Red beans
White beans

GRAINS
Corn meal
Millet
Oats, rolled
(*certified gluten-free*)
Quinoa
Rice
(*Basmati: white,
Brown: long grain, wild*)

EDIBLE FLOWERS
Arugula
Bachelor's button
Borage
Broccoli
Calendula
Chamomile
Chives
Chrysanthemum
Daisy
Day lily
Dianthus
Marigold
Nasturtiums
Pansy
Scented geranium
Squash blossom
Stock

See "A Note on Edible Flowers" page 67.

FRUITS
Apricot
Apple
Avocado
Banana
Berries
(*blackberry, blueberry, black currant, boysenberry, raspberry, strawberry*)
Cherries
Coconut

Figs, fresh
Guava
Grapefruit
Kiwi
Lemon
Lime
Mango
Melons
(*casaba, Crenshaw, honeydew, musk, Persian, watermelon*)

Only eat melons alone, and only in their natural season: July–late August. The body does not tolerate melons in combination with other foods or at other times of the year. See "A Word About...Food Combining," page 9.

Nectarine
Orange
Papaya
Passion fruit
Peach
Pineapple
Plum
Pluot (*plum/apricot cross*)
Rhubarb

HERBS
Anise hyssop
Basil
Bay leaf
Bee balm
Chamomile
Chervil
Chicory
Chives
Cilantro
Dill
Fennel fronds
Ginger
Lavender
Marjoram
Mint
Oregano
Parsley
Penny royal
Sage
Savory (*summer, winter*)
Spearmint
Rosemary
Tarragon
Thyme

All other fresh herbs are appropriate to eat as well, but not as often as these listed.

VEGETABLES

Artichoke
Arugula
Beets
(chioggia, golden, red)
Bok choy
Burdock root
Chickweed
Chicory
Collard greens
Broccoli
Broccoli rabe *(or rapini)*
Cabbage *(green, Napa, red)*
Carrots
(burgundy, cream, orange)
Cauliflower
Celery
Chili pepper
Corn
Cucumber
Daikon radish
Endive
Escarole
Green onion
Jicama
Green beans
Kale *(all types)*
Kohlrabi
Lambsquarter
Leek
Lettuce greens
*(all types except iceberg,
which the body does not
tolerate in any season)*

Mustard greens
Nettles
Okra
Peas *(English, snap, snow)*
Radicchio
Radish
Sorrel greens
Spinach
Sprouts
Sweet potato
Swiss chard
Summer squash
(all types)
Turnip
Turnip greens
Watercress

We offer the following recipes
as suggestions for enhancing
your late summer meals.

ENJOY!

late
summer APPETIZERS

CONTENTS

Chickpea Sweet Potato Dip

Sweet potato adds a creamy richness to this unusual dip. Serve it with broccoli flowerets, baby carrots, celery strips or rice crackers for dipping, or spread it on a teff or rice tortilla, top with sprouts, and roll for a healthy wrap.

MAKES 2 CUPS

¾ cup sweet potato, peeled and cut in ½-inch pieces
2 cups organic chickpeas, canned or cooked
3 Tablespoons cold-pressed extra-virgin olive oil
½ cup Kalamata olives
1 teaspoon crushed red pepper flakes (add more for hotter taste)
½ cup tightly packed fresh basil leaves
¼ cup lemon juice
1 teaspoon salt

1. Steam sweet potatoes or place in sauce pan with water to cover. Cook until tender when pierced with a fork, about 10 minutes.

2. Place cooked sweet potatoes, chickpeas, olive oil, olives, red pepper flakes, lemon juice, and salt in a food processor and purée until smooth. If too thick, thin with water. Add basil and pulse until finely chopped. Add more lemon juice or salt if desired.

3. Place in bowl and serve garnished with one olive and basil leaves.

ABOUT: TEFF

Teff is a tasty, nutritious ancient gluten-free grain, native to Northeastern Africa and and Southwestern Arabia. It has a mild, nutty flavor and packs a serious nutritional punch. White teff in particular has an excellent balance of amino acids and is rich in protein, calcium, iron and a host of other minerals. It also is very high in dietary fiber, is easily digested by the body, and is thought to benefit people with diabetes as it has a low glycemic index and helps control blood sugar levels. Similar in cooking to quinoa and millet, teff can be steamed as a grain, made into a porridge, or ground into flour for baking. Teff makes a wonderful flour for tortilla wraps.

late
summer SOUPS

CONTENTS

Curried Vegetable Coconut Soup

The combination of the herbs and coconut milk in this soup make it unusual, delicious and satisfying. The lime leaves impart an exotic cooling flavor and can be found easily at natural foods stores, Asian specialty food stores and larger supermarkets.

SERVES 5

2 Tablespoons cold pressed cold-pressed extra-virgin olive oil
1 cup carrots, chopped in ½-inch pieces
1 cup celery, chopped in ½-inch pieces
1 cup fennel (include stock and fronds),
    chopped in ½-inch pieces
1 Tablespoon curry powder
4 cups water
1 vegetable broth cube
1 Tablespoon chives, finely chopped
3 lime leaves
1 Tablespoon lemon balm, finely chopped, or lemon zest
½ cup zucchini, chopped
1 cup light coconut milk

ABOUT: LIME LEAVES

Lime leaves provide a fresh citrus overtone in a variety dishes and are a well-known ingredient in Cambodian, Indonesian and Thai cooking, particularly in soups and curries. The Kaffir lime variety is the primary source for lime leaves. Lime leaves can be kept for up to six months in an airtight bag in the freezer. For shorter periods of storage, keep them in your refrigerator, in an airtight bag.

1. Sauté olive oil, carrots, celery, and fennel in a soup pot until a glaze forms on vegetables. Add curry powder and sauté a few seconds, until there is an aroma.

2. Add water, vegetable broth cube, chives, lime leaves, and lemon balm or zest to the pot. Bring to a boil then lower heat to medium-low and cook 10 minutes or until vegetables are tender when pierced with a fork.

3. Add zucchini and coconut milk and cook for five minutes or until zucchini is tender.

4. Remove lime leaves and blend soup with a hand blender or in a food processor until vegetables are small chunks.

Beet Borscht

Refreshing, beautifully colored and especially good served cold on a hot day or warm on a cool day.

2 cups beets, cut in ½-inch pieces
2 cups carrots, cut in ½-inch pieces
5 cups water
1 vegetable broth cube
¼ teaspoon pepper
½ cup green onions, chopped in small pieces, including green tops
1 Tablespoon lemon zest
3 Tablespoons fresh dill, chopped or 1 Tablespoon dried
¼ cup lemon juice
3 Tablespoons agave nectar or honey
6 Tablespoons Vegenaise™ dressing
Chopped chives and chive blossoms for garnish (optional)

1. Bring beets, carrots, water and vegetable broth cube to a boil in soup pot. Lower heat to medium. Add pepper, green onions and lemon zest.

2. Cook for 8–10 minutes or until beets and carrots are tender. Add dill.

3. Blend with hand blender until vegetables are slightly chunky. Mix in lemon juice and sweetener. Taste for seasoning. Add more lemon or sweetener as desired.

4. Serve warm, or place in refrigerator until chilled. Serve in individual bowls topped with 1 Tablespoon Vegenaise™ and sprinkled with chives and chive blossoms.

VARIATIONS:

- Substitute beets for carrots.
- Substitute golden beets for red beets.

Chickpea Soup with Arugula

This is a perfect soup for arugula lovers. The nutty flavor goes well with the chickpeas.

SERVES 4 - 6

½ cup leeks, chopped in small pieces
1 cup carrots, cut in ½-inch pieces
1 cup celery, cut in ½-inch pieces
1 bay leaf
2 Tablespoons cold-pressed extra-virgin olive oil
4 cups water
1½ vegetable broth cubes
2 cups organic chickpeas, cooked, drained (see page 21 for instructions on cooking dried beans)
½ teaspoon white pepper
8 cups loosely packed arugula, chopped in small pieces

1. In soup pot, sauté leeks, carrots, celery, and bay leaf in olive oil until they are glazed, 1–3 minutes.

2. Add water with vegetable broth cubes, chickpeas, and pepper. Bring to a boil. Cook on medium-low heat until vegetables are tender.

3. Mix arugula into soup and cook until soft, 1–2 minutes. Discard bay leaf and blend soup with a hand blender or in a food processor until chunky.

late
summer SALADS

CONTENTS

Quinoa Salad with Sweet Potatoes on Mixed Greens with Orange Honey Dressing

All the ingredients in this dish combine to create a delicious whole meal.

SERVES 4

1 cup quinoa
2 cups water
1 vegetable broth cube
½ teaspoon salt
1 cup sweet potato, finely diced
½ cup chives, cut in small pieces (optional)
2 Tablespoons toasted almonds, chopped (see "Toasting Seeds and Nuts", page 36)
3 cups mixed greens

1. Wash quinoa in a bowl of water, rubbing the grains together with your hands for 1–2 minutes. Place in strainer and rinse.

2. Bring water and salt to boil in 2½-quart sauce pan. Add quinoa and vegetable cube to boiling water. Resume boiling, cover and turn heat to low. Cook 30–40 minutes, or until all water has been absorbed and small white rings have formed. Turn off heat and let sit (covered) 15 minutes.

3. Steam or boil sweet potatoes 5 minutes or until sweet potatoes can be pierced with a fork. Rinse sweet potatoes under cold water. Set aside.

4. Fluff quinoa and in a large bowl, mix 2 cups cooked quinoa with sweet potatoes, chives and toasted almonds. Add 6 Tablespoons Orange Honey Dressing (see recipe below) and refrigerate for at least one hour to allow the flavors to blend.

5. When ready to serve, toss mixed greens with remaining dressing and arrange equal portions of each on four plates. Place equal amounts of quinoa salad on mixed greens and serve immediately.

Orange Honey Dressing

MAKES 1 CUP

2 Tablespoons cold-pressed extra-virgin olive oil
2 teaspoons agave nectar or honey
4 teaspoons grated fresh ginger, grated
⅔ cup orange juice

1. Mix all ingredients in a small bowl.

Corn, Rice and Bean Salad with Chili Vinaigrette

This Southwest-style salad is very satisfying and refreshing.

SERVES 8

4 cups cooked white Basmati rice (see cooking instructions, page 53)
3 cups pinto or red beans, drained, canned or cooked (see page 21 for instructions on cooking dried beans)
2 cups corn kernels, fresh or frozen
1 cup green onions, finely chopped, including green tops
1 cup cilantro, finely chopped

1.   Combine cooked rice, beans and corn. Toss with green onions and cilantro.

2.   Drizzle Chili Vinaigrette (see recipe below) over rice and bean mixture and mix thoroughly.

3.   Cover and let sit in refrigerator for an hour to let flavors blend.

4.   For maximum flavor, return to room temperature before serving.

Chili Vinaigrette

¼ cup cold-pressed extra-virgin olive oil
¼ cup fresh lime juice
2 Tablespoons agave nectar or honey
1 teaspoon salt
2 jalapeño peppers, seeded and chopped in small pieces or ¼ teaspoon cayenne pepper to taste
2 teaspoons chili powder
1 teaspoon ground cumin

1.   Mix olive oil, lime juice, sweetener, salt, jalapeño peppers or cayenne pepper, chili powder and ground cumin in small bowl.

Creamy Coleslaw

Red and green cabbage with bright orange carrots create a colorful presentation in this refreshing salad.

<u>SERVES 5</u>

½ cup Vegenaise™ dressing
1 Tablespoon lemon juice
1 teaspoon ground celery seed (optional)
¼ teaspoon salt
¼ teaspoon pepper
2 cups red cabbage, grated or cut in small pieces
2 cups green cabbage, grated or cut in small pieces
1 cup carrots, grated
¼ cup green onion, thinly sliced, including green tops
2 Tablespoons fresh dill, chopped or 1 Tablespoon dried

1. Combine Vegenaise™, lemon juice, celery seed (if using), salt and pepper in large mixing bowl.

2. Toss red and green cabbage, grated carrots, green onion and dill with dressing until well coated. Add more Vegenaise™ if a creamier consistency is desired.

ABOUT: CABBAGE

The cultivated cabbage is derived from the wild mustard plant. Native to the Mediterranean, the wild mustard was praised for its medicinal properties by the ancient Greeks and Romans. The 'modern' cabbage, while different in shape, is just as nutritionally potent. It is richer in vitamin C than oranges, has a unique fiber concentration that promotes proper digestion, stimulates the immune system, and promotes good blood circulation. Not to mention that its abundance of antioxidants are causing quite a stir in the cancer research field. Its no wonder this vegetable is widely used throughout the world. Enjoy it raw or cooked.

Green Bean Salad with Sesame Vinaigrette

The lovage in this recipe provides the salad with a delightful bouquet and flavor, reminiscent of both celery and anise. You can find fresh lovage at your local farmers' market or natural foods store. If lovage is not available, substitute fresh cilantro, chervil or tarragon.

SERVES 4 - 5

3 cups green beans, with ends trimmed and cut in half
⅓ cup leeks, chopped in small pieces
⅓ cup fresh lovage, chopped
½ cup Sesame Vinaigrette dressing

1. Bring a large pot of salted water to boil. Add beans and cook 2–3 minutes until bright green and slightly crisp.

2. Drain and rinse under cold running water.

3. In medium-size bowl, combine green beans, leeks and lovage. Toss with Sesame Vinaigrette dressing (see recipe below).

Sesame Vinaigrette

MAKES ½ CUP

2 Tablespoons lemon juice
⅛ teaspoon dry mustard powder
⅛ teaspoon salt
2½ Tablespoons Bragg Liquid Aminos™
¼ cup cold-pressed extra-virgin olive oil
⅛ teaspoon toasted sesame oil
¼ teaspoon white pepper
½ teaspoon fresh tarragon, chopped

1. Whisk lemon juice, mustard powder, salt, Bragg Liquid Aminos™, olive oil, toasted sesame oil, and pepper in small bowl.

2. Mix in tarragon. Toss with green bean mixture.

ABOUT: LOVAGE

This perennial herb, native to the Mediterranean, is a member of the parsley family. LIke its cousins celery, dill and fennel, the whole plant is edible: seeds, stalks and leaves. Lovage's unique aromatic flavor, a combination of celery and anise, makes a wonderful salt substitute. Use chopped leaves and stalks to flavor salads, soups, stews, breads, biscuits and pickles. The lovage flavor is potent, so a little bit goes a long way. The seeds, when ground, make a wonderful substitute for pepper. Freeze lovage stalks for a long-term supply as dried lovage is not particularly flavorful.

Lovage has a long history as a medicinal. Brewed as a tea, it has been used as a digestive aid and overall body tonic since the days of early Greece. It also has strong antiseptic properties and is second only to capers in quercetin, a powerful flavonol.

late summer VEGETABLES

CONTENTS

Honey Curried Kale

The flavors of this kale dish are a delicious blend of sweet, tart and spicy.

SERVES 6

½ cup leeks, chopped
1 Tablespoon cold-pressed extra-virgin olive oil
1 Tablespoon curry powder
1 Tablespoon agave nectar or honey
1 teaspoon lemon juice
6 cups kale, chopped (with tough stems removed)
2 Tablespoons Bragg Liquid Aminos™
¼ cup water

1. In large skillet, sauté leeks in olive oil on medium heat until lightly browned, about 8–10 minutes.

2. Stir in curry powder, agave nectar or honey, and lemon juice.

3. Add kale, Bragg Liquid Aminos™ and water. Cook 8–10 minutes, tossing repeatedly until kale is chewy and tender.

Beets with Lemon Glaze

This recipe is easy to make, and the combination of sweet with sour creates a flavor explosion with every bite.

SERVES 4

8 very small beets or 4 medium-size, quartered
2 Tablespoons cold-pressed extra-virgin olive oil
4 Tablespoons lemon juice
1 Tablespoon agave nectar or honey
Zest of 1 lemon
1 Tablespoon parsley, chopped

1. Steam or boil beets until tender when pierced with a fork. Set aside.

2. Mix oil, lemon juice and agave nectar or honey in medium-size sauce pan. Cook over moderate heat about 5 minutes or until slightly syrupy.

3. Mix in cooked beets and heat through.

4. Garnish with lemon zest and chopped parsley and serve.

Green and Yellow Beans Cooked with Savory

Savory's flavor resembles a cross between mint and thyme, and goes well with these green beans. There is a summer and winter variety. Either one can be used.

SERVES 6

½ cup leeks, finely chopped
3 Tablespoons cold-pressed extra-virgin olive oil
3 cups green beans, trimmed and cut in thirds
3 cups yellow beans, trimmed and cut in thirds
¾ cup water
2 Tablespoons fresh savory, chopped
½ teaspoon salt
½ teaspoon white pepper
¼ teaspoon cayenne pepper (more if a hotter flavor is desired)

1. In medium-size skillet, sauté leeks in olive oil until soft, about 2–3 minutes. Add green and yellow beans and sauté 2 minutes. Add water, savory, salt, pepper and cayenne pepper.

2. Cover and cook on medium heat 8–10 minutes or until beans can be pierced with a fork.

3. Taste for seasoning. Add more salt, pepper or cayenne pepper if desired.

VARIATION:

• Substitute purple beans for green beans.

ABOUT: SAVORY

A member of the mint family, this delicate, aromatic herb is a staple in eastern European cuisine. Its slight peppery and tangy taste blends well with other herbs, and provides spice to soups, sauces and marinades. Of the two varieties, summer and winter, summer is more commonly known and used in cooking.

Medicinally, the plant has a long history as a digestive aid. Brewed as a tea, it is used to balance an array of internal health issues, especially those relating to the intestines, lungs, and kidneys. Like other mint-family herbs, savory also has valuable aromatherapeutic properties

late summer

vegetables

Summer Squash Sauté

Late summer is an excellent time of the year to make this dish because of the wide array of summer squash available in this season. Use small squashes as these have a better flavor and less water than the larger ones.

SERVES 6

3 cups small zucchini, cut in rounds ½-inch thick
3 cups small yellow zucchini or crookneck squash, cut in rounds ½-inch thick
2 cups small patty pan squash, cut in half, then crosswise into pieces ½-inch thick
2 Tablespoons cold-pressed extra-virgin olive oil
½ teaspoon salt
½ teaspoon pepper
3 Tablespoons fresh basil, chopped
1 teaspoon fresh oregano, chopped
½ teaspoon fresh marjoram, chopped

1. Sauté all squashes in olive oil in medium-size skillet over medium-high heat. Sprinkle with salt and pepper. Cover and cook, stirring occasionally, until tender when pierced with a fork, 10 – 12 minutes.

2. Stir in basil, oregano and marjoram and serve.

VARIATIONS:

• Substitute 1 Tablespoon chopped chives for marjoram.
• Substitute 1 Tablespoon chopped mint for oregano and marjoram.

ABOUT: SUMMER SQUASH

Native to the Central Americas, summer squashes are a soft-shelled vegetable with thin edible skins and seeds. With a tender flesh that requires only a short amount of cooking time, summer squash are low in calories, and high in vitamin C, minerals, and fiber. The name "summer squash" refers to the short storage life of these squashes, unlike that of winter squashes, which have a thick, hard skin that allows them to be stored over winter. Common varieties of summer squash include crookneck, pattypan, yellow squash, and zucchini. Enjoy them raw, steamed or sauteed.

Oriental Stir Fry

This is a quick and easy way to prepare vegetables. The addition of arugula adds a nutty flavor. This stir fry is fabulous served with rice or rice noodles.

SERVES 6

½ cup leeks, finely chopped
3 Tablespoons cold-pressed extra-virgin olive oil
2 cups carrots, cut in thin strips, 1-2 inches long
1 cup broccoli flowerets, cut in 2-inch pieces
1 cup yellow zucchini, cut in 2-inch pieces
1 cup arugula, finely chopped
3 Tablespoons Bragg Liquid Aminos™
2 Tablespoons fresh cilantro, chopped

1. Sauté leeks in olive oil in medium-size skillet on medium-high heat 3 minutes, until leeks have softened. Add carrots and broccoli. Sauté 4–5 minutes.

2. Add zucchini and cook, stirring frequently, until vegetables can be pierced with a fork. Mix in arugula and cook until it softens, 2–3 minutes.

3. Stir in Bragg Liquid Aminos™ and cilantro and serve.

VARIATIONS:

• Substitute chopped Napa cabbage or kale for arugula.

• Substitute celery for zucchini.

late
summer FISH & SEAFOOD

CONTENTS

Curried Fish Salad

The curry flavor enhances this creamy, crunchy salad. Serve it together with a sweet potato salad or a salad of fresh summer greens, for a simple, delightful late summer meal.

SERVES 5 – 6

2 cups cooked flaked halibut, cod, orange roughy
    or wild salmon
½ cup celery, chopped in ¼-inch pieces
¼ cup leeks, finely chopped
2 Tablespoons fresh dill, chopped
1½ Tablespoons curry powder
1 teaspoon salt
1 Tablespoon lime or lemon juice
¼ cup Vegenaise™ dressing
    (add more if creamier texture is desired)

1. In medium-size bowl, mix fish, celery, leeks and dill.

2. In small bowl mix curry powder, salt and lime or lemon juice with Vegenaise™. Add to fish mixture.

3. Chill at least an hour to bring out flavors.

VARIATION:

•   Substitute chopped fresh fennel bulb for chopped celery.

COOK'S TIP:
MAKE YOUR OWN CURRY POWDER

Curry powder is a valued spice mixture in Indian cooking, both for the flavor and aroma it provides, and for its body-balancing properties. The term 'curry powder,' aka 'masala powder,' refers to a spice mixture of widely varying composition. It literally varies from family to family throughout India. That being said, the spices typically included in curry powder (e.g., cumin, coriander, peppercorn, turmeric, fenugreek, allspice, cinnamon) all support the body's digestive and immune systems. While there are some wonderful packaged organic curry powders available, we invite to you experiment and make your own. It's easy!

Buy small quantities of high quality, organic dried spices in bulk. Here are some samples to choose from, as well as a sample recipe below: turmeric, coriander, cumin, white or red peppercorn, allspice, cinnamon, fenugreek, mustard, mace, ginger, nutmeg, cloves.

Toast the spices together gently over medium heat in a dry skillet - just long enough for the spices to begin releasing their fragrance and darkening in color.

Grind the toasted spices in a dedicated coffee mill-type grinder or with a mortar and pestle. When cooled, store powder in a glass jar in a cool, dry, dark space. Use often! (P.S. This makes a great gift.)

SAMPLE RECIPE: ⅛ cup peppercorns, ⅛ cup cardamom pods, ¼ cup coriander seeds, ¼ cup cumin seeds, 1 stick cinnamon, 4 cloves, ¼ teaspoon fennel seeds, ¼ teaspoon turmeric.

late summer

fish & seafood

Pan-Seared Orange Roughy with Ginger Lime Sauce

This simple cooking method brings out the delicious flavor of orange roughy.

SERVES 4

Juice of ½ lemon
1 pound orange roughy
Salt to taste
White pepper to taste
2 Tablespoons fresh dill, chopped or 1 Tablespoon dried
3 Tablespoons cold-pressed extra-virgin olive oil

1. Squeeze lemon juice over both sides of fish. Sprinkle salt, pepper and dill on both sides of fish.

2. In a large skillet, sauté fish in olive oil on medium-high heat 5 minutes on both sides or until browned and fish can be flaked with a fork.

3. Serve plain or with Ginger Lime Sauce (see recipe below.)

Ginger Lime Sauce

1 cup Vegenaise™ dressing
2 Tablespoons lime juice
1 green onion, finely chopped, including green tops
1 Tablespoon fresh ginger, grated
1 Tablespoon ground cumin
1 Tablespoon lime zest (optional)
¼ cup water
3 Tablespoons fresh cilantro, finely chopped

1. Blend all ingredients together until creamy. Add more water if too thick.

ABOUT: GINGER

The root, or tuber, of the subtropical ginger plant is both a spice and a medicinal. It has a tan skin and its flesh ranges in color from ivory to light green. Ginger is available in a variety of forms, including: fresh, dried (ground), juiced, crystallized (candied), and pickled. While used in cultural dishes around the world, ginger, which is related to cardamom and turmeric, is particularly popular in Asian and Indian cooking.

Ginger has a long history as a valued medicinal, particularly as a digestive aid, to reduce or settle nausea, and to alleviate flu-like symptoms. In traditional Chinese Medicine's 'Five Elements' nutritional philosophy, ginger has the unique property of being considered both a cooling and a warming spice.

In summer, fresh ginger's tangy, slightly sweet and spicy flavor is recommended as a cooling spice for balancing the system, whereas the dried spice, which produces a sharper, somewhat more bitter flavor, balances the body in winter as a warming spice.

Tuna Patties with Remoulade Sauce

These tuna patties are fun to cook. They can be served on a gluten-free bun or plain with Remoulade Sauce. Note: Chilling the patty mixture for at least one half hour helps the patties hold together when sautéed. Similarly, chilling the Remoulade Sauce for a half hour allows the flavors in the sauce to blend.

MAKES 10 MEDIUM-SIZE PATTIES

5 Tablespoons cold-pressed extra-virgin olive oil, split
3 cups cooked, fresh sushi-grade tuna steak (¾ pound)
    or canned albacore tuna
½ teaspoon white pepper
1½ teaspoons salt, split
3 Tablespoons fresh dill, chopped or 1 Tablespoon dried
1 cup celery, cut in ¼-inch pieces
1 cup leeks, finely chopped
3 Tablespoons lemon juice
1 teaspoon salt
½ teaspoon white pepper
½ cup fresh spinach, arugula or Italian parsley,
    finely chopped
2 eggs, beaten

Remoulade Sauce

MAKES ¾ CUP

½ cup Vegenaise™ dressing
2 Tablespoons water
¼ teaspoon salt
2 teaspoons organic Dijon mustard
⅛ teaspoon cayenne pepper
    or more for hotter taste
1 Tablespoon capers (optional)
1 Tablespoon fresh tarragon, chopped
    or 1½ teaspoons dried
¼ cup green onions, chopped,
    including green tops

In a small bowl, combine all ingredients. Add water if a thinner consistency is desired. Refrigerate for one half hour or more to allow ingredients to blend.

1. Preparing fresh tuna (if using canned, go to step 3): Spread 1 Tablespoon olive oil on both sides of tuna steaks. Sprinkle with pepper and ½ teaspoon salt.

2. In large skillet cook tuna steaks in 2 Tablespoons olive oil four minutes on both sides or until browned and almost cooked through.

3. Flake cooked fresh tuna or canned tuna into small pieces and place in large mixing bowl.

4. Mix all remaining ingredients, except eggs, into tuna mixture. Mix in eggs. Refrigerate for one half hour or more if possible. This will help bind patty mixture. Form mixture into patties about 2 inches in diameter.

5. Heat remaining olive oil in large skillet. Sauté patties on both sides for approximately 3–4 minutes on medium-high heat or until browned.

6. Serve topped with Remoulade Sauce. (see recipe above.)

late
summer POULTRY & EGGS

CONTENTS

Chicken Salad with Caraway Seed

The addition of caraway seeds adds extra flavor to this salad. It makes an excellent sandwich with fresh greens and/or sliced avocado or served simply on a bed of greens.

SERVES 4

2 cups cooked chicken, cut in small pieces
¼ cup celery, cut in small pieces
3 green onions, chopped, including green tops
1 Tablespoon chives, chopped (optional)
2 teaspoons caraway seeds, slightly crushed
1½ teaspoons salt
½ teaspoon white pepper
2 Tablespoons fresh cilantro, finely chopped
½ cup Vegenaise™ dressing

1. Mix cooked chicken, celery, green onions, chives, caraway seeds, salt, pepper and cilantro in a medium-size bowl.

2. Stir in Vegenaise™ and serve. Add more Vegenaise™ if creamier consistency is desired.

late summer

poultry & eggs

ABOUT: CARAWAY

Native to western Asia and Northern Africa, this relative of dill and fennel is valued for its aromatic seeds. Caraway seeds have a pungent anise-like aroma and flavor that stands out well in soups, stews, curries, casseroles, and baked goods. The seeds and the oil inside them also have long been valued as a medicinal. Brewed as a tea, caraway has been used to balance the digestive system, calm colic, and as a tonic for stimulating balanced kidney function. The tea also calms the nauseating and griping effects of some modern medicines.

Egg Foo Young with Oriental Honey Sauce

A light version of this favorite Chinese dish. Delicious with a pot of steaming rice and a salad.

SERVES 4

6 eggs
3 Tablespoons rice flour
½ teaspoon salt
½ teaspoon white pepper
6 green onions, thinly sliced, including green tops
¼ cup bean sprouts
½ cup snow peas, finely chopped
2 teaspoons sesame or cold-pressed extra-virgin olive oil

1. Make Oriental Honey Sauce (recipe below.)

2. Beat eggs in a small bowl. Set aside.

3. In a medium-size bowl, mix together flour, salt, and white pepper. Add green onions, bean sprouts and snow peas and toss to coat. Stir in eggs.

4. In a medium-size skillet, heat ½ teaspoon sesame or olive oil over medium heat. Ladle ½ cup of egg mixture into skillet and cook 2–3 minutes or until bottom is lightly browned. Flip eggs and cook 2–3 minutes more or until eggs are firm and lightly browned.

5. Transfer to a warm platter. Repeat process with remaining oil and egg mixture.

6. Serve topped with Oriental Honey Sauce (see recipe below.)

Oriental Honey Sauce

1 Tablespoon arrowroot
¾ cup vegetable broth (¾ cup water mixed with ¼ vegetable broth cube)
1 teaspoon agave nectar or honey
1 teaspoon Bragg Liquid Aminos™
1 teaspoon toasted sesame oil
½ teaspoon red pepper flakes

1. Mix arrowroot and vegetable broth in a small sauce pan. Stir and heat until smooth. Whisk in sweetener, Bragg Liquid Aminos™, toasted sesame oil and red pepper flakes. Cook over medium heat 2–3 minutes, until smooth and thickened, stirring constantly. Taste for seasoning. Cover and set aside.

late
summer BEANS

CONTENTS

Falafel Wrap with Tahini Lemon Dressing

These wraps are flavorful, nutritious, and fun to eat. This recipe is a variation on a well-known Middle Eastern dish. "Falafel" is derived from the Arabic word for nourishment.

MAKES 6 WRAPS

3¾ cups organic chickpeas, canned or cooked, drained
   (see page 21 for instructions on cooking dried beans)
¼ cup water
½ cup leeks, chopped in small pieces
1¼ Tablespoons ground cumin
1 Tablespoon ground coriander
2 teaspoons curry powder
1 teaspoon baking powder
1 teaspoon salt
2 Tablespoons Bragg Liquid Aminos™
¼ teaspoon white pepper
⅓ cup chickpea flour
3 Tablespoons fresh parsley, finely chopped
3 Tablespoons fresh cilantro, finely chopped
3 Tablespoons cold-pressed extra-virgin olive oil
6 teff tortillas (dark or ivory)
Mixed greens

Tahini Dressing

MAKES 1¼ CUPS

½ cup tahini
4 Tablespoons lemon juice
3 Tablespoons Bragg Liquid Aminos™
½ cup water
¼ teaspoon cayenne pepper
2 Tablespoons parsley, finely chopped

1. Mix tahini, lemon juice and Bragg Liquid Aminos™ in small mixing bowl until smooth.

2. Stir in water, cayenne pepper and parsley. Add more water if too thick. Set aside.

1. Place chickpeas and water in food processor and blend until smooth.

2. Add leeks, ground cumin, coriander, curry powder, baking powder, salt, Bragg Liquid Aminos™ and pepper. Blend until well mixed.

3. Place chickpea mixture in a large mixing bowl. Mix in chickpea flour, parsley and cilantro. Mixture should be the consistency of cookie dough.

4. Heat olive oil in large skillet on medium-high heat. Form chickpea mix into 2-inch patties. Add to skillet and cook on both sides until browned, about 3 minutes each side.

TO ASSEMBLE WRAP:

1. Place 2 falafels in 1 teff tortilla. Place mixed greens over falafels. Pour Tahini Dressing (see recipe above) over mixed greens. Fold bottom of tortilla and fold one side of tortilla over the other side and serve.

VARIATION:

• Substitute rice flour wraps for teff wraps.

Summer Succotash Salad

This variation of succotash salad is bright and refreshing.

<u>SERVES 6</u>

2 cups baby lima beans, drained, canned or cooked (see page 21 for instructions on cooking dried beans)
2 cups fresh or frozen organic corn kernels, uncooked
1 cup cucumber, peeled, seeded and cut into 1-inch pieces
½ cup celery, cut in 1-inch pieces
½ cup carrot, grated
¼ cup leeks, chopped in small pieces
2 Tablespoons lemon juice
2 teaspoons agave nectar or honey
1½ teaspoons curry powder
½ teaspoon ground cumin
3 Tablespoons cold-pressed extra-virgin olive oil
2 Tablespoons fresh cilantro, chopped

1. Combine lima beans, corn, cucumber, celery, carrot and leeks in a large bowl.

2. Mix lemon juice, sweetener, curry powder and ground cumin in a small bowl. Slowly drizzle in the oil, whisking constantly. Pour over vegetables and mix well. Refrigerate for at least one hour before serving, to enhance flavor.

3. Toss with cilantro, taste for seasoning and serve.

<u>ABOUT: LIMA BEANS</u>

These are the beans of a legume, originating in the Andean region of South America and domesticated over 5,000 years ago. The beans, which typically are cream or green in color, are sometimes called "butter beans" because of their starchy yet buttery texture. They have a delicate flavor that complements a wide variety of dishes. Look for fresh beans in summer and fall at your local farmers' market — they are especially delectable and worth the hunt.

Lima beans are high in dietary fiber, which supports keeping cholesterol and blood sugar levels balanced and, when eaten together with a grain, make a complete, high-quality protein. In addition, lima beans are high in vitamins and minerals, including the trace mineral molybdenum, which supports detoxifying sulfites, a common preservative in prepared foods.

Lentils with Fennel Bulb

The sweet fennel and lentils combine to create a delicate, slightly sweet flavor.

SERVES 6

1 cup lentils
4½ cups water
1½ teaspoons salt, divided
2 cups fennel bulb, cut into ¼-inch pieces, discard stalks, chop and save fronds
½ cup leeks, cut in small pieces
1 cup carrots, cut in 1-inch pieces
3 Tablespoons cold-pressed extra-virgin olive oil
1 teaspoon fennel seeds, lightly crushed
1 vegetable broth cube
3 Tablespoons fresh flat leaf parsley, chopped
½ teaspoon white pepper

1. In 2-quart pot, bring lentils, water and 1 teaspoon salt to a boil. Reduce heat to medium-low and simmer uncovered until lentils are tender, 30–45 minutes.

2. In medium-size skillet, combine chopped fennel bulb, leeks and carrots, and sprinkle with ½ teaspoon salt. Sauté in olive oil on medium-high heat 10–12 minutes or until vegetables can be pierced with a fork. Stir in fennel seeds and cook with vegetables for a few seconds. Set aside.

3. Drain cooked lentils in strainer over bowl, reserving cooking water. In large skillet, add ½ cup cooking water and vegetable broth cube. Cook on medium heat until cube is dissolved. Mix in lentils, sautéed vegetables, and parsley. Cook over moderate heat until heated through. If mixture is too dry, add more cooking liquid.

4. Mix in ¼ cup chopped fennel fronds.

ABOUT: LENTILS

Lentil beans are the seeds of a legume that originated in what is now considered the Middle East, and have been part of the human diet since Neolithic times. Lentil beans, which come in colors that range from yellow to red-orange to green, brown and black, have one of the highest protein concentrations of any plant-based food. They also are high in vitamins, folate and minerals, particularly iron, and are an excellent source of fiber, making lentils a valued resource for vegetarians.

late
summer GRAINS & PASTA

CONTENTS

Quinoa Pilaf with Creamy Curried Dressing

The combination of curry and lime juice gives this dish an unusual and rich taste. Serve it as a side dish or as a whole meal.

SERVES 6

1½ cups quinoa
3 cups plus 2 Tablespoons water, divided
1 teaspoon salt
½ cup leeks, chopped in small pieces
1 carrot, cut in ¼-inch pieces
1 cup celery, cut in ¼-inch pieces
2 Tablespoons cold-pressed extra-virgin olive oil
2 cups spinach, cut in coarse pieces
3 Tablespoons fresh cilantro, finely chopped
½ cup toasted almonds, chopped
    (see "Toasting Seeds and Nuts", page 36)

Creamy Curry Dressing

⅓ cup Vegenaise™ dressing
1 Tablespoon fresh lime juice
2 teaspoons curry powder
1 teaspoon fresh ginger, grated
¼ teaspoon white pepper
2 Tablespoons water

Whisk together all ingredients until well combined.

1. Wash quinoa in a bowl of water, rubbing the grains together with your hands for 1–2 minutes. Place in strainer and rinse.

2. Bring 3 cups water to boil in 2½-quart sauce pan. Add salt and quinoa to boiling water. Return to boil, cover and turn heat to low. Cook 30–40 minutes, until all water has been absorbed and small white rings have formed. Turn off heat and let sit (covered) for 15 minutes. Fluff before using.

3. While quinoa is cooking, sauté leeks, carrots and celery in olive oil until glazed. Add ¼-inch water to pan. Cover and cook five minutes or until vegetables are almost tender and all water is absorbed.

4. Add spinach and cook 2–3 minutes or until spinach is wilted.

5. Mix in cilantro, cooked quinoa and Creamy Curry Dressing (see recipe above.) Sprinkle with almonds and serve.

VARIATIONS:

* Substitute broccoli flowerets for celery.

* Substitute Napa cabbage for spinach.

* Substitute sunflower, pumpkin, sesame seeds, or pine nuts for almonds.

Dilled Millet

The combination of dill and bay leaf gives this millet dish a wonderful aroma and added flavor.

SERVES 6

1 cup millet
2¼ cups water
½ teaspoon salt
1 Tablespoon fresh dill, chopped or ½ teaspoon dried
1 bay leaf

1. Place millet in a strainer. Run water over it and wash by scrubbing the grains lightly between the palms of your hands for about a minute, or until water is almost clear. Drain and rinse.

2. Bring water to boil in medium sauce pan. Add millet, salt, dill and bay leaf. Return to boil, then cover and lower heat to low. Cook for 1 hour. Turn off heat and let sit (covered) for 15 minutes.

3. Remove the bay leaf, fluff and serve.

ABOUT: MILLET

A small-seeded grain that grows well in arid and semi-arid regions of the world, it has been cultivated in East Asia for at least 10,000 years. Both millet porridge and steamed millet are traditional cultural dishes in Russian and Chinese cuisine, and millet flour is a staple ingredient in Indian baking. The grain has a light, nutty flavor and is high in protein, minerals and vitamins, making it an attractive and nutrient-rich gluten-free alternative.

Rice with Spinach and Green Onions

This aromatic rice dish is excellent served with any meal.

<u>SERVES 6</u>

1 cup white Basmati rice
2 cups water
1 vegetable broth cube
3 green onions, chopped in small pieces, including green tops
4 cups spinach, coarsely chopped
2 Tablespoons fresh cilantro, finely chopped
1 Tablespoon lemon zest (optional)
¼ teaspoon white pepper
¼ teaspoon cayenne pepper

1. Place rice in strainer. Run water over it and wash by rubbing the grains lightly with your hands for about one minute. Drain and rinse.

2. Bring water and vegetable broth cube to a boil in 2½-quart sauce pan. Add rice. Resume boiling, reduce heat to low, cover and cook 20 minutes. Turn off heat. Place green onions, spinach and cilantro on top of cooked rice. Allow to sit (covered) for 15 minutes.

3. Add lemon zest (if using), pepper and cayenne pepper to rice and blend all with a fork (using a fork helps keep the rice from clumping.)

<u>VARIATIONS:</u>

*   Substitute 3 cups chopped Swiss chard or kale for spinach.
*   Add toasted chopped almonds or sunflower seeds (see "Toasting Seeds and Nuts," page 36.)

Soba Noodles with Sesame Sauce

This noodle dish is delicious, satisfying and easy to make.

SERVES 4

1 8-ounce package of 100% buckwheat noodles
3 Tablespoons fresh ginger, grated
3 Tablespoons lemon juice
2 Tablespoons tahini
2 Tablespoons almond butter
¼ cup water
2 Tablespoons Bragg Liquid Aminos™
2 teaspoons agave nectar or honey
1 teaspoon dark sesame oil
⅛ teaspoon cayenne pepper or more if hotter taste desired
4 green onions, coarsely chopped, including green tops

1. Cook noodles according to directions on package. Set aside.

2. Place ginger in a medium-size bowl and mix with lemon juice.

3. Mix in tahini, almond butter and water. Add remaining ingredients except green onions and mix well.

4. Stir in green onions.

5. Add noodles to sauce and toss until well coated, and serve.

VARIATION:

• Substitute tahini for almond butter.

ABOUT: BUCKWHEAT

Native to Russia, this fast-growing, naturally pest-resistant plant is not a true grain but rather an herb related to rhubarb and sorrel. The seed kernels have an earthy, grassy flavor with a slight cocoa overtone and taste best when the kernels are roasted (aka 'kasha'), producing a hearty, flavorful winter-worthy comfort food. Buckwheat flour is the main ingredient in traditional Japanese soba noodles.

Buckwheat is a rich source of lysine, and has high levels of protein, calcium, magnesium, phosphorous, B vitamins, and iron. Because it contains no gluten, it is an excellent wheat substitute for people who are gluten-sensitive.

Orange-Glazed Vegetables with Rice Pasta

The combination of colors and flavors in this recipe makes an lively and sophisticated dish.

SERVES 4 – 5

⅓ cup orange juice
½ cup water
3 Tablespoons Bragg Liquid Aminos™
1 heaping Tablespoon arrowroot
¼ package brown rice linguini
½ cup leeks, chopped in small pieces
1 Tablespoon fresh ginger, grated
1 cup celery, cut in ¼-inch pieces
2 Tablespoons cold-pressed extra-virgin olive oil
½ teaspoon salt
¼ teaspoon white pepper
2 cups bok choy, chopped in 1-inch pieces
½ cup fresh basil, chopped
2 Tablespoons toasted pine nuts (see "Toasting Seeds and Nuts," page 36)

1. Mix orange juice, water, Bragg Liquid Aminos™ and arrowroot in a small bowl and set aside.

2. Cook pasta according to directions on package. Set aside.

3. In a large skillet, sauté leeks, ginger and celery in olive oil on medium-high heat one minute or until slightly glazed. Sprinkle with salt and pepper. Cover and cook 3–4 minutes or until vegetables are slightly tender when pierced with a fork, stirring occasionally.

4. Stir in bok choy, cover and cook 2 more minutes or until greens are wilted and white part of bok choy can be pierced with a fork.

5. Add basil. Pour in orange juice mixture. Stir until liquid thickens and is clear, approximately 2 minutes. Mix in cooked pasta and top with toasted pine nuts. Serve immediately.

VARIATIONS:

*   Substitute spinach for bok choy.

*   Substitute Swiss chard for bok choy.

*   Substitute toasted chopped almonds or sunflower seeds for pine nuts.

Curried Bean Thread Noodles with Vegetables

This satisfying dish is a variation on Asian cooking styles. Bean thread noodles, which are made from mung beans, are readily available in natural food stores, Asian specialty-food stores and larger supermarkets.

SERVES 4

4 ounces bean thread noodles
4 cups boiling water
1½ Tablespoons curry powder
4 Tablespoons Bragg Liquid Aminos™
½ teaspoon salt
¼ teaspoon agave nectar or honey
½ cup leeks, finely chopped
1 Tablespoon fresh ginger, grated
1 cup carrots, cut in thin strips or ¼-inch pieces
½ cup green beans, cut in ¼-inch pieces
2 Tablespoons cold-pressed extra-virgin olive oil
2 cups bok choy, cut in ¼-inch pieces
1 cup bean sprouts
2 Tablespoons fresh cilantro, finely chopped

1. Place bean thread noodles in a medium-size bowl. Cover with boiling water and let sit 20 minutes. Drain, rinse and set aside.

2. In a small bowl, mix curry powder, Bragg Liquid Aminos™, salt and sweetener and set aside.

3. Sauté leeks, ginger, carrots and green beans in olive oil 3–4 minutes or until almost tender, stirring frequently. Mix in bok choy and cook another two minutes or until bok choy is tender.

4. Mix in bean sprouts and cilantro. Toss curry mixture with bean thread noodles and serve.

ABOUT: MUNG BEANS

These are the seed of a legume native to Bangladesh, India and Pakistan. In the East Indian Ayurvedic tradition of body balancing through food, the mung bean is revered as competent to balance all three 'doshas' (bodily humours that make up one's constitution.) Mung beans generally are eaten either whole (with or without skins) or as bean sprouts. Mung bean starch also is extracted to make jellies and "transparent/cellophane" noodles, common in Asian cooking.

Mung beans are rich in protein, minerals and vitamins, and are a good source of dietary fiber, helping to keep blood sugar and cholesterol levels balanced in the body. Sprouting the bean makes more of the vitamins and minerals available, and produces vitamin C, which is not present in the dry bean. See "A Word About ...Beans," page 7, for instructions on sprouting beans.

VARIATIONS:

• Substitute rice vermicelli noodles for bean thread.

• Substitute snow peas or Chinese cabbage for bok choy.

• Add cooked shrimp or any type of fish before mixing in curry mixture.

late
summer BREADS

CONTENTS

Zucchini Bread

This is a moist, lemon-flavored bread. While the flours used in this recipe may sound exotic, they are readily found in natural foods stores and larger supermarkets. The same is true for xanthan gum.

MAKES ONE LOAF

¾ cup sorghum flour
½ cup brown rice flour
¼ cup tapioca flour
1 teaspoon xanthan gum
2 teaspoons baking powder
½ teaspoon baking soda
1 teaspoon powdered ginger
½ teaspoon salt
¼ teaspoon nutmeg
¼ cup cold-pressed extra-virgin olive oil
½ cup maple or plain agave nectar or maple syrup
1 egg
2 teaspoons lemon zest
1 Tablespoon fresh lemon balm, chopped (optional)
⅔ cup almond milk
1 teaspoon vanilla

1. Preheat oven to 350°F. Grease 8 x 4 x 2-inch loaf pan.

2. In large bowl, mix sorghum, rice, and tapioca flours, xanthan gum, baking powder, baking soda, ginger, salt and nutmeg.

3. In medium-size bowl, mix olive oil, agave nectar or maple syrup, egg, lemon zest, lemon balm, almond milk and vanilla.

4. Stir wet ingredients into dry ingredients. Pour into loaf pan and bake for 50–60 minutes or until a toothpick inserted in the center comes out clean.

5. Place on cooling rack 20 minutes or until bread has cooled. Remove from loaf pan. Bread is easier to cut when cool.

ABOUT: LEMON BALM

A minty green herb with a citrus aroma, this plant, native to the Mediterranean, is a member of the mint family. The sweet citrus flavor resembles the taste of lemon. Lemon balm leaves are used to enhance the taste of fruit salads and beverages. The herb also goes well with seafood, poultry, pasta and rice dishes.

Lemon balm has been used as an herbal medicinal in the traditional Middle Eastern and Tibetan cultures for thousands of years. As a tea, it helps relax and calm the body's systems, particularly the digestive and nervous systems. Its essential oil, aka Melissa, is also highly valued as an aromatherapeutic oil.

late summer

breads

Raspberry Peach Crisp

The combination of raspberries and peaches in this recipe is scrumptious. Serve topped with vanilla coconut ice cream, rice milk frozen dessert or vanilla coconut yogurt.

SERVES 10 – 12

TOPPING

3 cups gluten-free rolled oats
½ teaspoon salt
⅓ cup cold-pressed cold-pressed extra-virgin olive oil
½ cup maple syrup
⅓ cup apple juice
2 teaspoons vanilla

FILLING

6 cups raspberries
3 organic peaches, cut in ½-inch pieces
½ teaspoon salt
¾ cup agave nectar or honey
1 teaspoon vanilla

1. Preheat oven to 400°F degrees.

2. In medium-size bowl, mix oats, salt, olive oil, maple syrup, apple juice, and vanilla. Mixture will be very moist. Set aside and let sit at least 10 minutes to allow the oats to absorb the liquid.

3. In large bowl, mix raspberries, peaches, salt, sweetener, and vanilla. Place in 9 x 13-inch baking dish.

4. Spread topping over mixture. Place in oven and bake 30–40 minutes or until topping is lightly browned and raspberry mixture is bubbling.

5. Remove from oven. Place on a cooling rack 5–10 minutes. Serve warm or at room temperature.

VARIATIONS:

• Substitute nectarines for peaches.

• Substitute blueberries or huckleberries for raspberries.

Grilled Nectarines Topped with Almond Cream

An elegant and easy dessert. The Almond Cream topping is an excellent substitute for whipped cream. If you do not wish to grill outdoors, the nectarines are easily broiled in the oven.

SERVES 6

3 large ripe nectarines, halved and pitted
½ cup extra-virgin olive or sunflower oil
2 cups fresh or frozen blueberries
½ cup toasted almonds, chopped

1. Lightly oil grill with olive oil and preheat to high.

2. Brush nectarine halves with oil. Grill nectarines, cut side down, 3 minutes or until grill marks form. Turn and grill an additional 3 minutes.

3. Remove from grill and place nectarine halves on plate. Spoon a dollop of Almond Cream (see recipe below) into each center. Top with blueberries and garnish with toasted almonds. Serve warm.

Almond Cream

MAKES 2 CUPS

1 cup blanched almonds or almond meal
½ cup water
4 Tablespoons agave nectar or honey
1 teaspoon vanilla
1 teaspoon orange zest (optional)

1. Combine almonds or almond meal in blender with water. Blend until smooth and creamy. If too thick, add more water. Add sweetener, and continue blending until smooth and creamy.

2. Mix in vanilla and orange zest (if using) and set aside.

VARIATIONS:

- Substitute peaches for nectarines.

- Substitute coconut milk or rice milk frozen dessert for Almond Cream.

- Substitute raspberries for blueberries.

- Use a combination of raspberries and blueberries.

Lemon Cake with Seven-Minute Frosting

Lemon balm and lemon thyme give this simple cake an unusual lemon flavor. The addition of applesauce makes a moister cake.

1¾ cups sorghum flour
½ cup tapioca flour
¼ cup arrowroot
2 teaspoons baking powder
½ teaspoon baking soda
½ teaspoon salt
½ cup cold-pressed extra-virgin olive oil
¾ cup agave nectar or honey
½ cup applesauce
2 eggs
½ cup almond milk
1 teaspoon vanilla
3 Tablespoons lemon zest
2 Tablespoons lemon juice
1 Tablespoon lemon balm, chopped (optional)
2 teaspoons lemon thyme (optional)

1. Preheat oven to 350°F degrees. Oil 9 x 13-inch baking dish.

2. In large mixing bowl, combine sorghum and tapioca flour, arrowroot, baking powder, baking soda, and salt.

3. In medium-size bowl, mix olive oil, sweetener, applesauce, eggs, almond milk and vanilla. Stir in lemon zest and juice, lemon balm, and lemon thyme.

4. Combine liquid ingredients into dry ingredients. If batter is too thick, add more almond milk.

5. Pour batter into baking dish and bake 30–40 minutes or until a toothpick inserted into cake center comes out clean.

6. Remove from oven.

7. Place on cooling rack and let cool before frosting cake with Seven Minute Frosting (see recipe next page.)

VARIATION:

• Substitute ¼ cup poppy seeds for lemon thyme and lemon balm. Add poppy seeds to dry ingredients.

Seven-Minute Frosting

MAKES 1½ CUPS

2 egg whites (room temperature)
½ cup agave nectar or honey
Pinch of salt
1 teaspoon vanilla

1. In top of double boiler, combine egg whites, sweetener and salt. Beat with electric mixer on low speed 30 seconds.

2. Heat water in bottom of double boiler to boiling and place top of double boiler over bottom pan (upper pan should not touch water).

3. Cook, beating constantly with the electric mixer, 7 minutes or until frosting forms stiff peaks.

4. Remove from heat. Blend in vanilla with mixer.

5. Spread on cake.

ABOUT: LEMON THYME

This hardy perennial plant is a variety of the herb thyme with a taste and smell reminiscent of lemons. Lemon thyme can be used in any recipe that calls for lemons, and as an accent in chicken dishes, salads, sorbets, and salmon.

As an herbal medicinal, lemon thyme has been valued throughout the centuries for its ability to relax and calm the body, and to soothe an irritated throat, among other uses. Its essential oil has many properties useful in aromatherapy.

ABOUT: AGAVE NECTAR

This sweetener is made from the juice of the agave cactus, native to the Central Americas. Raw agave juice, expressed from the core or heart of the agave cactus plant, is filtered and processed, typically by heating, to break down the primary carbohydrate and sweetener source, fructan (aka inulin), into fructose and some glucose. The resulting liquid syrup is slightly thinner and lighter in color than honey, and generally has a more neutral taste. "Raw" agave nectar is produced at a temperature below 118 °F to protect the naturally-occurring enzymes in the juice.

Among natural sweeteners, agave nectar is valued as having a naturally low glycemic index. In addition, like other natural sweeteners, agave nectar also contains trace minerals, including calcium, potassium, magnesium, and iron. (See "A Word About...Sugars," page 12)

autumn SEASON

shifting your food choices with autumn | gluten-free & dairy-free recipes

CONTENTS

Harmony with Autumn

Autumn is a time of transition from the warmth of summer to the cool of winter. This is a time when you may find your attention turning more inward, becoming more contemplative and focused on family, work and projects in the home. That natural rhythm you experience in your outer life is the same rhythm your body is experiencing inside. For example, just as you will naturally start to wear more clothing to keep your body warm, your blood vessels will contract somewhat during this season, to assist in keeping your blood warm.

Autumn is characterized by colder temperatures and a change in the air's moisture content. The lungs and large intestine are primarily engaged during autumn because of their roles in mediating air and water absorption in the body. In addition, the two organs communicate with one another through a common energy pathway, or meridian, that connects them. What affects one organ impacts the other, and the rest of our body.

An imbalance in the lungs or large intestine may cause excess mucous production, and slower intestinal function, which can cause a build-up of toxins in the body. Common experiences in the body of an imbalance in our lung or large intestine function or may cause one or more of the following symptoms:

- Awakening with sinus congestion, back stiffness, abdominal discomfort, or cramps
- Feeling sluggish in the morning
- Experiencing "the common cold" symptoms – headaches, sore throats, runny nose or coughs (really just one of the body's way of eliminating excess toxins)
- Feeling groggy and having difficulty thinking clearly
- Experiencing skin rashes, eczema, or asthma symptoms
- Acquiring a pale complexion
- Feeling crabby or dwelling on melancholy

Eating in the following way supports the lungs and large intestine. It will also support the body to feel warm and nurtured:

- Cut vegetables in large pieces when preparing them. Cook them at moderate heat until tender, giving them a longer cooking time.

- Add more oil in cooking and baking.

- Eat heavier sources of protein (e.g., beans, eggs, fish, seafood, poultry).

- Eat a higher proportion of whole grains to vegetables. Brown rice strengthens the lungs and large intestine. Whole gluten-free grains in general, assist in good elimination and keep the intestine well-toned.

- Use warming spices in cooking (e.g., cinnamon, allspice, nutmeg, cloves, ginger, coriander, curry, and cayenne pepper). Ginger, in particular, is stimulating to the lungs.

- Eat warming foods, such as soups, warm beverages, and warm meals.

- Cook foods by baking or roasting more often.

- Eat less raw foods, replacing them with cooked vegetables and fruit.

- Replace zucchini and raw tomatoes with winter squashes and fennel.

- Include a large number of root vegetables, such as sweet potatoes, yams, parsnips, carrots, celery root, Jerusalem artichokes, burdock root, turnips and rutabaga.

- When using salt, we recommend using an unrefined sea or rock salt rather than regular table salt. Unrefined salts are rich in minerals and trace elements. See "A Word About Salt" page 11.

- Keep warm and dry, particularly your head, neck, chest and feet.

- Hiking, walking, running, stretching and yoga all assist muscles to stay stretched. Lifting weights and isometric exercise helps strengthen the body in preparation for winter.

autumn

harmony

AUTUMN FOODS LIST

Autumn provides an abundant array of colorful foods. This list describes those foods we particularly recommend as in alignment with your body's desire for warming foods that support the lungs and large intestine. Generally, we recommend eating foods grown locally whenever possible, so that your body's rhythm matches that of your environment. While some of the foods on this list are not local to all locations, they still have valuable balancing properties at this time of the year and we recommend them during this season even if they come to you from other locations.

BEANS
Aduki
Black-eyed peas
Carob
Cannelini
Chickpea
Fava
Great northern
Kidney
Lentil *(all types)*
Lima
Navy
Pinto
Red
Split pea
White

GRAINS
Amaranth
Buckwheat
Millet
Oats
Quinoa
Rice
(basmati: brown, brown: long or short grain, red, wild)
Teff

HERBS
Anise - Hyssop
Chervil
Chives
Cilantro
Epizote
Fennel
Lavender
Lovage
Oregano
Parsley
Rosemary
Sage
Savory
Tarragon
Thyme

A note about herbs and spices: We recommend buying organic herbs and spices in small amounts as they can start to become stale after about 6 months and lose their potency. It is worth investing in high quality fresh herbs. They enhance the flavors and vitality of the foods you cook.

FRUITS
Apples
Avocado
Bananas
Berries:
(blackberry, cranberry)
Currants
Dates
Elderberries
Figs
Grapes
Pears
Persimmon
Plum-Italian
Pomegranate
Prunes
Quince
Raisins

VEGETABLES
Artichokes
Arugula
Beets
(red, gold, chioggia)
Bok choy
Broccoli
Broccoli rabe
(Rapini)
Brussels sprouts
Burdock root
Cabbage
(green, Napa, red)
Carrots
Cauliflower
Celery
Celery root
Chicory
Collard greens
Corn
Daikon radish
Ginger root
Horseradish
Jerusalem artichoke
Kale *(all types)*
Kohlrabi
Leeks
Lettuce greens
(all types except iceberg, which the body does not tolerate in any season)
Mizuna
Mustard greens
Okra
Parsnips
Pumpkin
Romanesco
Rutabaga
Spinach
Sweet potato
Swiss chard
Turnip
Watercress
Winter squash *(all types)*
Yams

We offer the following recipes as suggestions for enhancing your autumn meals.

ENJOY!

autumn APPETIZERS

CONTENTS

Nachos with Cilantro Cream

If you are a nacho lover, this is a delicious and healthy choice. Use yellow corn chips or a combination of yellow, blue, and red chips for color and variety. (Note: Some dairy-free cheese contains casein, a milk protein. Check ingredient list on the package if this is a concern.)

SERVES 4 – 6

6 cups organic corn chips
2 cups organic pinto or red beans, drained, canned or cooked (see page 21 for cooking dried beans)
1½ cups shredded rice or almond cheese (yellow, white, and/or jalapeno)
½ cup Kalamata olives, chopped in large pieces
1 cup spinach, chopped

1. Spread corn chips on 11-inch or 12-inch oven-proof platter or baking sheet and set aside.

2. Spoon beans over chips.

3. Spread olives and spinach over beans and sprinkle with shredded cheese.

4. Bake at 350°F 5–7 minutes, or until cheese melts.

5. Spoon Cilantro Cream (see recipe below) over warm nachos and serve immediately.

Cilantro Cream

MAKES ½-¾ CUP

½ cup Vegenaise™ dressing
2 Tablespoons fresh cilantro or parsley, chopped
¼ - ½ teaspoon cayenne pepper or chipotle pepper powder

1. In a small bowl, combine all ingredients.

VARIATIONS:

- Add any one, or a combination of, the following ingredients to the nachos. Spoon over chips before adding cheese.

  – 4 green onions, chopped, including green tops
  – 2 Tablespoons organic capers
  – ¼ cup fresh or canned jalapeño peppers, chopped
  – ¼ cup broccoli, chopped

Broccoli Spinach Spread

This is a delicious topping for crackers or bread. It also makes a wonderful dip for chips.

MAKES 2 CUPS

¼ cup cold-pressed extra-virgin olive oil
1 teaspoon cumin seeds or ½ teaspoon ground cumin
½ teaspoon crushed red pepper flakes
2 Tablespoons fresh lime juice
½ teaspoon salt
½ cup water
1 bunch broccoli, cut into ¼-inch pieces (including stems and leaves)
4 cups fresh spinach, chopped

1. Heat oil in non-stick skillet over medium-low heat.

2. Add cumin and pepper flakes. Sauteé for 1–2 seconds or until there is a fragrance.

3. Stir in lime juice, salt, and water.

4. Stir in broccoli and spinach, cover and simmer until vegetables are reduced to a chunky purée (45–60 minutes). Check mixture and stir frequently so it doesn't stick.

ABOUT: SPINACH

Thought to have originated in ancient Persia, this green annual is related to amaranth. Used in cuisines around the world as a cooked vegetable or a salad green, the leaf taste has a characteristic bite, due to the oxalic acid in the leaf. Spinach is rich in potassium, iron, riboflavin, vitamin A (particularly lutein), vitamin C, a host of trace minerals and omega-3 fatty acids. It also is an exceptional source of antioxidants.

Explore the different varieties of fresh spinach available today at your local farmers market, natural foods store or larger supermarket. Fresh spinach will maintain its vitality stored in a plastic bag in the refrigerator for about three days. Spinach has a tendency to be gritty so rinse it thoroughly before serving or cooking.

autumn

appetizers

Creamy White Bean Spread

The beans in this creamy spread are briefly simmered with herbs to infuse them with a subtle herbal flavor. Serve as a spread with rice bread or crackers, or as a sandwich filling with sprouts and avocado.

MAKES 1⅓ CUPS

2 cups great northern white beans, drained, canned or cooked
   (see page 21 for instructions on cooking dried beans)
1 cup water
¼ cup Italian parsley, chopped
1 bay leaf
2 teaspoons fresh ginger, grated
½ teaspoon dried thyme
½ teaspoon dried basil (1 Tablespoon fresh)
½ teaspoon ground fennel
¼ teaspoon dried sage
¼ teaspoon crushed rosemary (1 Tablespoon fresh)
½ - 1 teaspoon salt
½ teaspoon ground white pepper
¼ teaspoon cayenne pepper
1 teaspoon cold-pressed extra-virgin olive oil
1 teaspoon lemon juice

1. Drain and rinse beans.

2. Place beans in medium-size sauce pan and cover with water.

3. Add remaining ingredients, except olive oil and lemon juice.

4. Bring to boil over medium heat. Reduce heat to low and simmer uncovered 15 minutes.

5. Remove bay leaf. Drain and reserve 2 Tablespoons of cooking liquid.

6. In food processor or with hand blender, coarsely purée beans with 2 Tablespoons cooking liquid, olive oil, and lemon juice. For chunky texture, use a potato masher to mash beans.

7. Season to taste with salt and pepper.

autumn SOUPS

CONTENTS

Spinach and Lentil Soup

Your body will appreciate this full-bodied, robust soup as the days and evenings turn cooler.

SERVES 4

½ cup leeks, chopped
1 cup celery, cut into ¼-inch slices
1 cup carrots, cut into ¼-inch pieces
1 teaspoon fresh ginger, finely chopped or grated
1 Tablespoon cold-pressed extra-virgin olive oil
2 teaspoons fresh rosemary, chopped or 3 teaspoons dried
1 teaspoon ground cumin
½ teaspoon allspice
1 pinch red chili flakes
½ teaspoon white pepper
1 Tablespoon Bragg Liquid Aminos™
1 cup lentils (sorted, rinsed, and drained)
6 cups water
2 vegetable broth cubes
2 bay leaves
4 cups fresh spinach or Swiss chard, coarsely chopped
¼ cup fresh parsley, chopped (optional)

1. Sauté leeks, celery, carrots, and ginger in olive oil until vegetables are glazed.

2. Stir in rosemary, ground cumin, allspice, chili flakes, white pepper and Bragg Liquid Aminos™ for a few seconds.

3. Add lentils, 6 cups water, vegetable broth cubes and bay leaves. Bring soup to a boil, then reduce heat and simmer until lentils are tender, approximately 1 hour.

4. Thin soup, if desired, by adding more water.

5. Add spinach or Swiss chard and simmer 5 minutes, until greens are wilted. Remove bay leaves.

6. Ladle into soup bowls and garnish with fresh parsley (optional).

Split Pea Soup with Celery Root

This soup is warming, nurturing and delicious.

SERVES 6

2 cups split peas, picked over and washed well
7 cups water
½ cup leeks, chopped
1 medium-size celery root, peeled and cut into ½-inch pieces
3 Tablespoons cold-pressed extra-virgin olive oil
2 bay leaves
½ cup fresh dill, chopped or 3 Tablespoons dried
2 teaspoons salt
½ teaspoon white pepper
Chopped parsley for garnish (optional)

1. In 4-quart pot, add split peas to 7 cups water.

2. Bring to boil and simmer with lid ajar so it doesn't boil over.

3. Skim any foam off the surface. Simmer 10–15 minutes.

4. In medium-size skillet, sauté leeks and celery root in olive oil until leek softens and celery root glazes.

5. Add leek mixture and bay leaves to split peas.

6. Cook for 1½–2 hours until split pea mixture is smooth, creamy and shiny. Add dill in last ½ hour of cooking.

7. Add salt and pepper (add more if desired).

8. Ladle into soup bowls and garnish with chopped parsley (if using).

> ### ABOUT: CELERY ROOT
>
> Also known as celeriac, this member of the parsley family is native to the Mediterranean. Grown as a root vegetable, the bulb or 'root' has a knobby exterior, a creamy, white interior, and a flavor somewhere between celery and fennel, that can be sweet and slightly smoky.
>
> Peeled celery root can be eaten raw, boiled and mashed like potatoes, or cubed and added to soups and stews.
>
> The bulb is high in fiber, potassium, magnesium and vitamins B6, C and K. For a root vegetable, it also is uncharacteristically low in starch and thus has a low glycemic index.

VARIATIONS:

- Substitute ¾ cup each of chopped carrots and parsnips for celery root.
- Add 1 bunch chopped Swiss chard in addition to other vegetables.
- Substitute 1 Tablespoon curry powder for the dill.
- Add two vegetable broth cubes

Hearty Vegetable Soup

This is a hearty, flavorful soup that is warming on cool or rainy days. It is great for lunch or as a light dinner served with gluten-free crackers or toasted rice bread.

SERVES 6

½ cup leeks, chopped
2 stalks celery, chopped in small pieces
3 cups equal amounts :
  – carrots, cut in ¼-inch pieces
  – green beans, cut in ½-inch pieces
  – acorn or butternut squash, cut in ½-inch pieces
1 Tablespoon fresh ginger, grated or 2 teaspoons powdered ginger
3 Tablespoons cold-pressed extra-virgin olive oil
1 teaspoon dried dill, or 1 Tablespoon fresh
1 Tablespoon dried thyme
½ teaspoon nutmeg
1 Tablespoon Bragg Liquid Aminos™
5 cups water
2 vegetable broth cubes
1 bay leaf
½ teaspoon white pepper
1 cup kale or Swiss chard, chopped in small pieces

1. In 4-quart pot, sauté leeks, celery, carrots, green beans, squash and ginger in olive oil until vegetables are glazed and leeks are soft.

2. Add dill, thyme, nutmeg, and Bragg Liquid Aminos™. Sauté 1–2 seconds until vegetables are coated with the spices.

3. Stir in water, vegetable broth cubes, bay leaf and pepper. Bring to boil, cover and cook on medium heat about 20 minutes until vegetables are tender.

4. Add kale or chard and cook 5 minutes more until greens are wilted.

VARIATION:

• Add cooked fish or chicken at the end of cooking to make a complete one-dish meal.

Curried Pumpkin Soup with Coconut Milk

The curry adds a kick to this creamy, rich soup.

SERVES 4 - 6

½ cup leeks, chopped
½ cup carrots, chopped
½ cup celery, chopped
3 Tablespoons cold-pressed extra-virgin olive oil
2 teaspoons curry powder
1½ cups water
2 vegetable broth cubes
2 cups fresh or canned pumpkin purée
1 cup light coconut milk

1. In large sauce pan over medium heat, sauté leeks, carrots, and celery in oil until leeks soften and vegetables are glazed. Add curry powder and sauté 1 minute.

2. Add water, vegetable broth cubes and pumpkin purée to vegetable mixture.

3. Bring to boil, reduce heat to medium-low and cook 15 minutes or until carrots and celery are tender. Mix well.

4. Stir in coconut milk and simmer 5 minutes.

5. Purée with hand blender or food processor.

6. Add more coconut milk if a thinner consistency is desired.

VARIATION:

• Substitute any squash purée for pumpkin purée.

ABOUT: COCONUT MILK

This 'milk' is the liquid produced by grating fresh coconut 'meat' or 'flesh', boiling it in water, and straining the contents through cheesecloth. This process may be repeated once or twice to produce lighter coconut milks, which have lower oil or fat contents and lighter consistencies that may be preferred for different recipes. Coconut milk is a key ingredient in Southeast Asian cuisine, used in soups, curries, desserts and beverages.

Coconut milk is highly valued as a balancing liquid in the East Indian Ayurvedic tradition of body balancing through food. The milk has demonstrated anti-microbial properties, and the saturated fat in coconut milk is one of the most easily digested by the human body, possibly because one of its primary constituents is lauric acid, also found in mother's milk.

autumn

soups

autumn SALADS

CONTENTS

Steamed Greens with Tahini Dressing

The Tahini Dressing's robust flavor enhances the flavor of the mixed greens, making an outstanding combination.

SERVES 4 - 5

1 bunch red or green kale, chopped in medium-size pieces
   (include stems)
1 bunch Swiss chard, chopped in medium-size pieces
3 Tablespoons cold-pressed extra-virgin olive oil
2 cups red or green cabbage, chopped in medium-size pieces
3 Tablespoons cold-pressed extra-virgin olive oil
¼ cup water

> **BODY BALANCING TIP: COOKING FALL SALADS**
>
> In the fall we recommend eating cooked salads rather than salads made with raw vegetables. Cooked salads assist the body transition to the cooler, drier weather.

1. In large skillet, sauté kale, chard and cabbage in olive oil 1–2 minutes.

2. Add water, cover and let cook until greens are wilted.

3. Mix and cook a few minutes more until greens are tender.

4. Remove greens from pot and place in a salad bowl. Toss with Tahini Dressing (see recipe below.)

5. Serve warm or at room temperature.

Tahini Dressing

MAKES 1 CUP

½ cup tahini
½ cup water
¼ cup lemon juice
3 Tablespoons Bragg Liquid Aminos™
½ teaspoon salt
⅛ teaspoon cayenne pepper (use more for hotter flavor)
¼ cup fresh parsley, chopped

1. Mix all ingredients, except parsley, in medium-size bowl. If dressing is too thick, add more water until you have the desired consistency.

2. Add parsley, combine, and serve over steamed greens.

autumn VEGETABLES

CONTENTS

Roasted Sweet Potatoes and Yams

This combination is tasty and filling. The white sweet potatoes and orange yams also make this a colorful dish. In addition, the fennel aids digestion and adds a slightly sweet anise flavor.

SERVES 4 – 6

2 large yams, cut in ½-inch pieces
2 large sweet potatoes, cut in ½-inch pieces
½ fennel bulb, cut in ¼-inch pieces
⅓ cup cold-pressed extra-virgin olive oil
2 Tablespoons fresh dill, chopped or 1 Tablespoon dried
1 teaspoon salt
½ teaspoon white pepper

1. Toss yams, sweet potatoes, and fennel in large bowl with oil, dill, salt, and pepper. Add more oil if mixture seems a little dry. (Olive oil makes the potatoes and fennel crisp and brown.)

2. Place in 9 x 12-inch baking dish and bake at 415°F for 30–40 minutes, tossing mixture every 10–15 minutes. The vegetables are fully cooked when potatoes are slightly golden and tender.

VARIATIONS:

- Leave out fennel.

- Use either sweet potatoes or yams only.

ABOUT: SWEET POTATOES & YAMS

True yams and sweet potatoes are biologically unrelated plants. In the U.S. the terms are used interchangeably and typically refer to different varieties of sweet potatoes (the orange flesh variety being called yams, the white or yellow flesh variety being called sweet potatoes). Throughout this cookbook, all references to yams refer to the orange sweet potato variety.

True sweet potatoes are related to morning glories and, while native to South America, are now grown in the US. They have a moist mouth feel and sweet flavor. The tubers have a thin skin and can be short and blocky with round ends, like a potato, or longer, with tapered ends. True yams are native to Africa, and today are imported from the Caribbean. The mouth feel is dry with a starchy taste. These tubers have a thick, scaly skin, the flesh varies in color from white to yellow to purple, and their shape is long and cylindrical, often with off-shoots called 'toes'. True yams can grow to 7 feet, and weigh over 100 pounds.

Sweet potatoes are rich in vitamin A, beta-carotene and potassium. Yams are rich in vitamin C, vitamin B6, potassium, manganese and dietary fiber.

Medley of Sautéed Vegetables

The combination of vegetables in this recipe, particularly the broccoli rabe and artichoke hearts, is particularly helpful in assisting the body adapt to autumn. Broccoli rabe can be found at your local farmers market, natural foods stores and larger supermarkets.

SERVES 4-6

½ cup leeks, chopped
2 cups carrots, cut in ½-inch pieces
1 cup green beans, cut in 1-inch pieces
3 Tablespoons cold-pressed extra-virgin olive oil
1 teaspoon salt
½ teaspoon white pepper
4 cups broccoli rabe, coarsely chopped
½ cup artichoke hearts, frozen or canned (in water), drained
2 Tablespoons fresh Italian parsley, chopped
2 Tablespoons fresh dill, chopped or 1 Tablespoon dried
½ cup toasted almonds, chopped (optional, see "Toasting Seeds and Nuts," page 36)

1. Sauté leeks, carrots, and beans in oil in large skillet. Add salt and pepper, cover, and cook until vegetables are glazed and just tender when pierced with fork. Stir frequently to prevent sticking.

2. Mix in broccoli rabe, cover and cook 5–8 minutes until rabe is tender.

3. Mix in artichokes, parsley and dill. Cook until artichokes are warm and herbs are wilted. Mix in almonds if you choose.

VARIATION:

• Substitute broccoli for broccoli rabe.

ABOUT: BROCCOLI RABE

Broccoli Rabe (pronounced "robb" and aka broccoli raab, rapini), is related to both the broccoli and turnip family of vegetables,. This green-leafed vegetable or "cooking green" is a staple of Italian cuisine. The leaves have a peppery, radish-like flavor that becomes milder when blanched and cooked. When preparing, use only the leaves and broccoli-like flowerets, as the stems are quite bitter. Broccoli rabe is wonderful added to salads, mixed into soups and stews, or as the vegetable dish, sauteed with olive oil, salt, pepper and pine nuts. It is an excellent source of vitamins, particularly vitamins A and C.

Stewed Autumn Vegetables

The combination of burdock root and Jerusalem artichokes gives this colorful stew a rich and distinctive taste. This dish is full of vitamins and minerals and is deeply satisfying.

SERVES 5

½ cup leeks, chopped
½ cup burdock root (outer layer scraped off),
    and cut into ¼-inch pieces
3 Tablespoons cold-pressed extra-virgin olive oil
2 cups carrots, cut in ½-inch pieces
1 cup Jerusalem artichokes, cut in ½-inch pieces
1 teaspoon salt
½ teaspoon white pepper
1½ cups kale, chopped
½ cup water
1 Tablespoon fresh savory, chopped or 2 teaspoons dried

1. In large skillet, sauté leeks and burdock root in oil 3 minutes until leeks softens.

2. Add carrots and Jerusalem artichokes. Sprinkle with salt and pepper and sauté until vegetables are glazed.

3. Add kale and water. Cover and cook on medium heat until vegetables are tender when pierced with a fork and kale is wilted, about 10 minutes. There should be little or no water left in the pan. Turn off heat.

4. Mix in savory and serve.

VARIATIONS:

• Substitute sweet potato or squash for carrots.

• Substitute collard greens for kale.

ABOUT: BURDOCK ROOT

Also known as "gobo root", from the Japanese, this vegetable is the root of the burdock plant, a member of the thistle family. When dried, the root has a thin, tan colored, wrinkled outer skin covering a crisp and tender-textured, but chewy flesh. (In Japanese restaurants, it often is orange in color, traditionally dyed with a plant-based colorant.) When cooked, the flesh has a somewhat robust and earthy flavor, like that of artichoke hearts. A nutritious and delicious root vegetable high in fiber, the root also has long been used in herbal remedies around the world to assist with indigestion, arthritis, rheumatism, some skin or nervous disorders, and other ailments.

To prepare, wash under cold water and peel the thin outer skin away form the flesh, before cutting to size. Place slices in cold water until ready to use to prevent flesh from oxidizing and darkening in color.

autumn
vegetables

Steamed Squash

Here is a simple and delicious way to cook squash. This dish goes well with almost any fall meal. There are many wonderful varieties of squash and you can use your personal favorites. We are partial to buttercup squash, which is dark orange, rich, and sweet. Other squashes such as butternut or acorn also are good. Each has its own unique flavor.

SERVES 4

4 cups buttercup squash (or any other variety),
    cut in ½-inch pieces with skin on
½ teaspoon salt (if desired)

> ABOUT: SQUASH SKINS
>
> Skin is edible on most winter squashes except acorn squash.

1. Place squash pieces in a vegetable steamer over boiling water. Steam 10 minutes or until squash is soft.

2. Add salt (if desired).

3. Serve warm.

VARIATION:

To roast squash:

1. Cut squash in half or in quarters. Remove seeds.

2. Place face down in 9 x 13-inch baking dish. Add ½-inch water to dish.

3. Cover squash and bake at 400°F for 30 minutes or until squash can be easily pierced with a knife.

4. Remove from oven, scoop out squash and serve plain or lightly salted.

autumn FISH & SEAFOOD

CONTENTS

Baked Salmon with Maple Lime Sauce

Use wild sockeye or Coho salmon. Adding water to bottom of baking dish will make the fish more tender.

SERVES 4 – 5

4 salmon fillets (4 ounces), or 1½ pound whole fillet
½ teaspoon salt
½ teaspoon white pepper
Zest of 1 lime or lemon (optional)

1. Preheat oven to 350°F.
2. Place salmon in 9 x 13-inch baking dish and sprinkle salt and pepper over fish.
3. In small bowl make the Maple Lime Sauce (see recipe below.)
4. Spread sauce over salmon with pastry brush. Sprinkle zest (if using) over the top of fish.
5. Add ½ inch water to bottom of baking dish.
6. Cover and bake 15–20 minutes until fish flakes.
7. Serve with Maple Lime Sauce (see recipe below.)

Maple Lime Sauce

MAKES ½ CUP

1 Tablespoon cold-pressed extra-virgin olive oil
¼ cup maple syrup
2 Tablespoons Bragg Liquid Aminos™
1 Tablespoon lime or lemon juice

1. Mix all ingredients together in small bowl.

VARIATION:

• Omit Bragg Liquid Aminos™ and substitute 1 Tablespoon cinnamon.

Moroccan Style Whitefish

The aromas and combination of flavors in this tasty dish resemble Moroccan cooking. If whitefish is not available, substitute cod, halibut or orange roughy.

SERVES 4 – 5

4 cups water
¼ cup cold-pressed extra-virgin olive oil
½ cup leeks, chopped
½ cup fresh parsley, chopped
2 stalks celery, chopped in ¼-inch slices
2 Tablespoons capers
½ teaspoon turmeric or pinch of saffron
1 teaspoon salt or to taste
1 teaspoon ground cumin
2 pounds whitefish (thick pieces)

1. Combine all ingredients (except fish) in large sauce pan. Bring to boil, reduce heat to low and simmer 30 minutes.

2. Add fish and return to boil. Cover, reduce heat to low, and simmer until fish is tender, about 15–20 minutes.

3. Remove fish and arrange on a serving platter. Cover with foil. Place in oven at 250°F to keep fish warm.

4. Boil remaining liquid and vegetables on high heat until liquid is reduced by half, 10–15 minutes.

5. Pour liquid over fish and serve.

ABOUT: WHITEFISH

These are a species of freshwater fish found in cold water lakes throughout Canada and the northern United States. On average about 18 inches long, they have silvery sides, and a deeply forked tail. The flesh has a mild taste and is a good source of omega-3 fatty acids.

Cod Fish Stew

This dish is filling and warming. It's a whole meal in itself.

SERVES 4 - 5

½ cup leeks, chopped in large pieces
½ cup burdock root, scraped and cut in small pieces
6 Tablespoons cold-pressed extra-virgin olive oil, divided
1 Tablespoon fresh ginger, grated
1 small parsnip, cut in 2-inch pieces
2 small carrots, cut in 2-inch pieces
1 small bunch of kale
2 cups water
2 vegetable broth cubes
½ teaspoon salt
½ teaspoon white pepper
½ teaspoon paprika
¾ pound cod fillets
¼ cup toasted sesame seeds (optional, see "Toasting Seeds and Nuts," page 36)

1. In large skillet, sauté leeks and burdock root in 3 Tablespoons olive oil until leeks soften. Add ginger, parsnips and carrots and sauté until they glaze.

2. Add kale, water and vegetable broth cubes to mixture and cook on medium-low heat until vegetables are tender and kale is cooked down, about 15 minutes.

3. While vegetables are cooking, spread salt, pepper, and paprika on both sides of fish. Add rest of olive oil (3 Tablespoons) to medium-size skillet and sear fish on high heat (about two minutes on each side) until golden on both sides.

4. Cut fish in medium-size pieces and add to vegetable mixture.

5. Continue to simmer until fish is opaque, about 5 minutes.

6. Taste for seasoning and serve in soup bowls garnished with toasted sesame seeds.

VARIATION:

•   Substitute halibut for cod.

Almond Crusted Walleye

Serving this with Sweet Potato Wedges (see recipe page 233) makes a fun variation for fish and chips.

SERVES 4 – 6

1 cup ground almonds
Zest of 1 lemon
½ teaspoon salt
⅛ – ¼ teaspoon cayenne pepper
¼ teaspoon white pepper
¾ cup rice flour (for rolling fillets)
1 egg, beaten
1½ pounds walleye fillets
4 Tablespoons cold-pressed extra-virgin olive oil

1. Combine almonds, lemon zest, salt, cayenne pepper, and pepper in shallow bowl.

2. Roll fillets in flour, then dip them in the beaten egg. Press almond mixture into fillets, turning to coat both sides well.

3. In large skillet, sauté fillets in olive oil at medium-high heat until fillets are crispy and brown, approximately 4 minutes on each side.

VARIATIONS:

*   Substitute sole or red snapper fillets for walleye.
*   Substitute ¾ cup Vegenaise™ for eggs

ABOUT: WALLEYE

A freshwater lake fish native to most of Canada and the northern United States, it gets its name from the fact that its eyes, like that of a cat, reflect light. This lets walleyes see in low-light conditions like deep and/or turbid water. These fish have olive and gold-colored sides and grow to about 30 inches. The flesh is light and sweet, and is rich in vitamin D, trace minerals and omega-3 fatty acids.

autumn POULTRY & EGGS

CONTENTS

Roasted Chicken with Lemon and Rosemary

The combination of lemon and rosemary gives this dish a special and unique flavor.

SERVES 6 – 8

1 organic whole chicken (2½–3 pounds)
2 – 3 lemons, quartered
½ teaspoon salt
½ teaspoon white pepper
3 – 4 sprigs fresh rosemary
2 cups organic chicken broth or vegetable broth

1. Preheat oven to 350°F. Wash chicken skin with cold water. Also rinse the body cavity thoroughly under cold running water. Pat dry.

2. Rub whole chicken outside and inside cavity with 2 lemon wedges. Sprinkle salt and pepper on outside of chicken. Stuff cavity with remaining lemon wedges and 2 sprigs of rosemary.

3. Place chicken in roasting pan. Add broth to pan. Place 3 rosemary sprigs on top of chicken. Cover and bake 1½ hours or until drumsticks move easily in their sockets and chicken is no longer pink.

4. Arrange chicken on serving platter. Boil left-over liquid on medium-high heat for approximately 15 minutes or until it becomes thick. Serve as gravy.

VARIATIONS:

• Cook stuffed chicken in a crock pot on high for 4–5 hours, until chicken is tender.

• Rub 4 chicken breasts with 1 lemon wedge, salt and white pepper. Place chicken in large skillet, top with 1 quartered lemon and 4 sprigs rosemary. Add 1 cup organic chicken broth, cover and bake for 1 hour or until chicken is tender. Remove chicken to a serving dish and make gravy as described in recipe directions.

autumn

poultry & eggs

Chicken Fajitas with Creamy Southwest Sauce

These spicy fajitas make a delicious, fun meal.

SERVES 4-6

1 teaspoon salt, divided
¾ pound organic chicken or turkey breasts,
    cut into ½-inch strips
¼ cup cold-pressed extra-virgin olive oil
½ cup leeks, cut in small pieces
1 cup carrots, cut in thin strips
1 cup celery, cut in thin strips
½ teaspoon ground cumin
¼ teaspoon chili powder (optional)
¼ teaspoon cayenne pepper or chipotle pepper powder
¼ cup lime juice
½ cup fresh cilantro, chopped
½ cup green beans, cut in ½-inch pieces
8 teff or rice tortillas

> COOK'S TIP:
> WARMING TORTILLAS OR 'WRAPS'
>
> A key to easy wrapping is a soft, pliable tortilla or wrap. Often, store-bought wraps can be stiff, particularly if they have been frozen. This makes them subject to tearing when you start wrapping. Here's an easy and quick way to soften the wrap first:
>
> Place the tortilla on a hot, dry griddle or skillet for just a few seconds on each side. You'll know when the wrap is ready. Take care not to let them sit too long on the griddle, or you'll have a crisp, toasted wrap.

1. Sprinkle ½ teaspoon salt on chicken or turkey strips.

2. Heat oil in large skillet over medium-high heat.

3. Sauté leeks, carrot, celery, and green beans until leeks soften and vegetables are glazed.

4. Add remaining ingredients, except tortillas.

5. Sauté 8–10 minutes, stirring occasionally, until turkey or chicken is no longer pink and vegetables can be pierced with a fork.

6. Wrap in warm teff or rice tortillas with 1 or 2 dollops of Creamy Southwest Sauce (see recipe below.)

Creamy Southwest Sauce

MAKES 1¼ CUPS

1 cup Vegenaise™ dressing
1 Tablespoon fresh cilantro, chopped
3 green onions, chopped
⅛ teaspoon cayenne pepper or chipotle pepper powder

1. Mix all ingredients together in a medium-size bowl. Serve with fajitas.

VARIATION:

•   Substitute halibut for chicken or turkey.

Middle Eastern Chicken

The exotic combination of cinnamon and cumin in the sauce is divine!

SERVES 4

4 chicken breasts, 3–4 ounces each, skin removed

SAUCE

Juice of one lemon
1 teaspoon cinnamon
1 teaspoon ground cumin
½ teaspoon cayenne pepper
1 bay leaf
½ teaspoon salt
1 Tablespoon agave nectar or honey
1½ cups organic chicken broth

1. Place all sauce ingredients in small sauce pan.

2. Bring to boil and simmer 5 minutes.

3. Wash chicken breasts and place in medium-size baking dish. Spoon sauce over chicken, and marinate at room temperature 1 hour.

4. Bake at 350°F for 1 hour or until chicken is tender.

5. Place chicken on serving dish. Spoon sauce over chicken.

ABOUT: CINNAMON

This sweet spice with a slightly hot bite is derived from the inner bark of an East Indian evergreen tree of the laurel family. A related species from the cassia tree also can be used as cinnamon. The tree's inner bark is removed and laid out to dry, causing it to curl into long sticks. The sticks are cut and sold as is or the bark can be ground into a fine powder. Native to Sri Lanka and used since ancient times, the spice is a key ingredient in Middle Eastern cuisine, and in Mexican recipes that call for chocolate. Elsewhere it is a common and valued dessert spice.

Cinnamon has a rich history of uses dating back at least 5,000 years. Used by the Egyptians in their embalming ceremonies and by the Romans as an aphrodisiac, it was once valued as highly as gold. It is rich in antioxidants, and it balances the digestive system and the body generally. Its essential oil has a host of valuable aromatherapeutic properties, including as a food preservative and anti-microbial agent.

Vegetable Frittata

This frittata is great for brunch, lunch or dinner. It also works well baked without the crust in a well-oiled pie plate. It may seem like a lot of eggs in this recipe, but each portion contains only 1–1½ eggs.

<u>SERVES 8</u>

This recipe can be made with or without a crust. If using crust, make it first (see Savory Crust recipe next page.)

FILLING

10 organic eggs
2½ teaspoons salt divided
½ teaspoon white pepper, divided
½ cup leeks, chopped
3 Tablespoons cold-pressed extra-virgin olive oil
4 cups spinach, chopped
¾ cup artichoke hearts, frozen or canned (in water), drained
⅓ cup Kalamata or green olives, salt brined
¼ cup fresh Italian parsley, chopped
2 Tablespoons fresh thyme, chopped or 1 Tablespoon dried

1. Whip eggs, ½ teaspoon salt, and ¼ teaspoon pepper in a medium-size bowl and set aside.

2. In large skillet, sauté leeks in oil until soft and lightly brown, about 3 minutes. Add spinach, artichoke hearts, olives, parsley, thyme, and remaining salt and pepper. Sauté 1–2 minutes until spinach has wilted.

3. Place spinach mixture into crust or oiled pie plate. Pour egg mixture over vegetables and mix slightly. Bake 35–40 minutes at 350°F or until egg mixture has puffed up and is firm on top. Remove from oven and cool 10 minutes. The top will fall about one inch.

4. Cut in pie-shaped slices and serve warm.

1½ cup gluten-free rolled oats (ground in blender to make flour)
¾ cup brown rice flour
1 teaspoon dried thyme
2 teaspoons fresh rosemary, chopped or 1 teaspoon dried
1 teaspoon salt
¼ cup cold-pressed extra-virgin olive oil
⅔ cup water

1. In medium-size bowl, mix oat flour, rice flour, thyme, rosemary, and salt.

2. In small bowl, mix olive oil and water. Pour wet ingredients into dry ingredients. Mix together, then knead with hands to blend.

3. Press dough into oiled pie plate. Bake at 350°F for 5 minutes. Remove from oven and set aside.

VARIATIONS:

- Substitute 2 cups chopped broccoli for spinach.

- Add 1 Tablespoon chopped fresh rosemary to vegetables when sautéing.

- Substitute 1 Tablespoon curry powder for thyme.

- Substitute ¼ cup chopped cilantro for thyme.

ABOUT: OLIVES

These are the fruit of the olive tree, the edible part being the flesh that surrounds a hard pit. Native to the Mediterranean Basin, the olive tree is related to lilacs, jasmine and forsythia. Olives have been cultivated for millenia, primarily for their oil, which is pressed from the fruit flesh, and has significant nutritional and body balancing benefits.

Today there are thousands of olive varieties grown all over the world, and the olives vary in size, shape and color - from green to red, brown and black. Green olives are considered young and are not fully ripened. Once picked, most olives are typically cured to leach out bitter tasting compounds from the flesh. The curing process also preserves them. Traditional methods include natural fermentation, oil, salt brining, dry salt curing or lye curing. Lye curing is most often used for unripened green olives, which typically also are allowed to ferment before being placed in a brine solution.

Our favorites are salt-brined or salt-cured mature olives. When using green olives, avoid lye-cured olives.

autumn BEANS

CONTENTS

Stewed Black-eyed Peas

This combination of ingredients creates an unusual, rich flavor. Serve with sweet potatoes or a steaming bowl of Curried Millet with Squash (see recipe page 203).

SERVES 6

1 Tablespoon fresh ginger, grated
1 teaspoon cumin seeds or ground cumin
2 cups carrots, cut in thin strips, 1–2 inches long
3 Tablespoons cold-pressed extra-virgin olive oil
2 teaspoons maple syrup
2 Tablespoons fresh lime juice
¼ teaspoon cayenne pepper (optional)
4 cups black-eyed peas, drained, canned or cooked (see page 21 for instructions on cooking dried beans)
3 Tablespoons cilantro, chopped
½ teaspoon salt

1. Sauté ginger, cumin and carrots in oil 3–4 minutes or until carrots can be pierced with a fork.

2. Add remaining ingredients and cook until heated through.

autumn

beans

ABOUT: MAPLE SYRUP

This natural sweetener, originating in northeastern North America, is made from the sap of sugar or black maple trees. The trees store starch in their stems and roots before winter, which rises in the sap in the spring as sugar. Centuries ago Native Americans tapped the trees, collected the sap and concentrated it by boiling to produce the sweet syrup, having discovered the sap as a source of energy and nutrition. Further heating can reduce the syrup to produce a semi-solid spread called maple cream or maple butter. Maple syrup grades correspond to the time of sap collection, with Grade A being milder, lighter-colored early season collections, and Grade B being late season collections, with a more robust color and flavor.

Maple syrup is a source of B vitamins and is rich in trace minerals, particularly potassium, calcium, magnesium and manganese. Sucrose is the primary carbohydrate in maple syrup (about 88%), with small amounts of fructose and glucose making up the remainder. (See "A Word About...Sugars", page 12)

Curried Chickpeas with Spinach

This spicy Indian style dish takes a short time to prepare and makes a delicious whole meal.

SERVES 4

1 cup leeks, chopped
2 Tablespoons fresh ginger, grated
2 Tablespoons cold-pressed extra-virgin olive oil
2 teaspoons curry powder (add more if a stronger flavor is desired)
½ cup water
4 cups fresh spinach, chopped
¼ teaspoon cayenne pepper (add more if a hotter flavor is desired)
½ teaspoon salt
2 cups organic chickpeas, drained, canned or cooked (see page 21 for instructions on cooking dried beans)
2 cups hot cooked brown Basmati rice (see recipe page 53, brown Basmati variation)
Zest of 1 lemon (optional)

1. In large skillet, sauté leeks and ginger in oil until leeks soften. Add curry powder and sauté 1–2 seconds. Add water and cook over medium heat 5–10 minutes.

2. Stir in spinach, cayenne pepper, salt, and chickpeas. Cover, reduce heat and cook approximately 5 minutes or until spinach wilts and mixture is heated.

3. Serve over rice and garnish with lemon zest (if using).

VARIATION:

*   Substitute millet or quinoa for rice.

COOK'S TIP: MAKING A SPICE SACHET

Using a spice sachet makes it easy to include the spices you want to use to flavor a dish but don't necessarily want to bite into. Simply put your spices (for example the cinnamon stick, whole cloves and cardamom pods suggested in the header on this page) into an unbleached muslin bag or piece of cheesecloth (8 inches square), tie the packet shut with cotton twine, and place it in the cooking dish. Remove the sachet prior to serving. Muslin bags and cheesecloth are available at natural foods stores.

A sachet also is a wonderful way to flavor a soup or stew with whole fresh or dried herbs, allowing more flexibility in adjusting the depth of flavor that the herbs provide. We suggest slightly crushing the whole herbs to release their flavor before adding them to the sachet. We do not recommend using metal tea balls for sachets as the metal can impact the flavor of your herbs or spices.

Refried Beans

Refried beans are enjoyable served alone, over rice, or in a wrap.

SERVES 4

3 cups kidney or pinto beans, canned or cooked (see page 21 for instructions on cooking dried beans),
    drained and liquid reserved
½ cup liquid from beans, divided (use more if needed)
2 Tablespoons cold-pressed extra-virgin olive oil
¾ cup leeks, chopped
1 bay leaf
1 teaspoon dried oregano
1 Tablespoon ground cumin
2 teaspoons ground coriander
1 teaspoon chili powder
1 teaspoon salt
¼ teaspoon cayenne pepper

1. Using a potato masher, mash beans with ¼ cup of liquid until small pieces form. Add more
    liquid if beans are too thick.

2. Heat the oil in large skillet. Add leeks and sauté 3 minutes until soft. Mix in remaining
    ingredients. Cook on medium heat 5–10 minutes until mixture has thickened, stirring often.

VARIATION:

•   Wrap beans in a teff or rice tortilla with brown Basmati rice (see recipe page 53, brown Basmati
    variation), chopped Kalamata olives and grated almond cheese. Top with a large dollop of Vegenaise™
    dressing. (Note: Some dairy-free cheese contains casein, a milk protein. Check ingredient list on
    the package if this is a concern.)

autumn GRAINS & PASTA

CONTENTS

Mixed Wild Rice

The mixture of wild rice grains is slightly chewy and has a rich nutty flavor. Toasted sunflower seeds add a delicious crunch.

SERVES 6

1½ cups wild rice mix
3 cups water
1 Tablespoon Bragg Liquid Aminos™
½ cup toasted sunflower seeds (see "Toasting Seeds and Nuts," page 36)

1. Place rice in strainer. Run water over it and wash by rubbing the trains together lightly with hands for about a minute Rinse and drain.

2. Bring water to boil. Add Bragg Liquid Aminos™ and rice and bring back to boil. Turn heat to low and simmer 1 hour.

3. Turn off heat. Let rice stand, covered, 15 minutes. Fluff with a fork, mix in sunflower seeds and serve.

VARIATION:

• Substitute toasted pumpkin seeds or chopped almonds for sunflower seeds.

Swiss Chard and Rice Pilaf

This Moroccan style pilaf is aromatic and flavorful. It is a great accompaniment to a variety of protein dishes.

SERVES 6

1 cup brown Basmati rice
½ cup leeks, chopped in small pieces
2 green onions, chopped, including green tops
3 Tablespoons cold-pressed extra-virgin olive oil
1¾ cups water
1 vegetable broth cube (optional)
5 cups Swiss chard, cut in small pieces
⅓ cup fresh cilantro, chopped
⅛ teaspoon cayenne pepper (add more for a hotter taste)
½ teaspoon salt
½ teaspoon white pepper

1. Place rice in strainer. Run water over it and wash by rubbing the grains together lightly with hands for about 1 minute. Rinse and drain.

2. In 2½-quart sauce pan, sauté leeks and green onion in oil until soft. Add water and broth cube, if using, and bring to boil.

3. Add remaining ingredients, including rice.

4. Bring water to boil again. Cover pot and turn heat to low. Simmer 1 hour.

5. Turn off heat. Let sit covered 15 minutes. This is to allow rice to steam.

6. Fluff with a fork and serve.

ABOUT: SWISS CHARD

This green leaf vegetable with red, white or yellow stems, is related to both spinach and beets. Both the leaves and stalk can be eaten raw or prepared - the leaves provide a smooth, light texture akin to spinach or beet greens and a similarly slightly pungent, salty flavor, while the stalks are crisp and crunchy. A dark green vegetable, Swiss chard is vitamin and mineral-rich, and high in fiber, trace phytonutrients and antioxidants.

Explore the colorful varieties available at your local farmers' market or natural foods store. To store, wrap unwashed in a plastic bag and keep in the refrigerator for up to 3 days. When ready to prepare, wash thoroughly to remove all debris and dirt from the leaves and stalks. We do not recommend using aluminum pans (ever, generally, and in particular) when cooking chard as this vegetable may react with the metal, causing discoloration.

Curried Millet with Squash

The combination of curry and ginger in the millet is warming and satisfying.

SERVES 5 OR 6

1 cup millet
1 teaspoon curry powder
2 cups butternut squash or any type squash (leave skin on), diced
1 teaspoon fresh ginger, grated
½ teaspoon salt
2½ cups water

1. Place millet in bowl with water to cover. Wash by rubbing the grains together lightly with hands for about 1 minute. Pour into strainer, drain and rinse. Repeat 1–2 times (millet can have a lot of dirt sticking to it).

2. Place in 2½-quart sauce pan over medium-high heat. Toast, stirring constantly about 2–3 minutes. Remove from heat and set aside.

3. Sauté curry powder in sauce pan 1 minute or until it develops an aromatic smell. Add millet, squash, ginger, salt, and water. Bring to boil over high heat. Cover and lower heat to low. Simmer 1 hour.

4. Turn off heat and let pot stand covered 10–15 minutes before serving. Fluff with a fork and serve.

VARIATION:

• Substitute sweet potato, yam, or pumpkin for squash.

Herbed Creamy Rice Noodles

The noodles served with this creamy sauce are rich and tasty.

SERVES 4

1 teaspoon salt
1 package (16 ounces) spiral rice noodles or any type of rice noodle
⅓ cup cold-pressed extra-virgin olive oil
⅓ cup brown rice flour
½ cup almond or hemp milk
½ teaspoon white pepper
½ vegetable broth cube
½ cup fresh Italian parsley, chopped
2 teaspoons dried thyme

1. Fill 4-quart soup pot with 8 cups water and bring to boil.

2. Add salt and pasta.

3. Cook pasta according to directions on package. Drain and set aside.

4. While pasta is cooking, heat oil in 2½-quart sauce pan. Mix flour into oil, stirring 1–2 minutes or until it absorbs the olive oil and is in clumps.

5. Stir in almond or hemp milk, pepper, and vegetable broth cube. Stir constantly until mixture is thick and shiny, about 3–5 minutes. If the sauce is too thick, add more almond or hemp milk.

6. Stir in parsley and thyme and toss with noodles until well-coated.

COOK'S TIP: MAKE YOUR OWN NUT MILK

While an array of packaged organic nut and grain milks now are available generally (almond, hemp, rice, coconut, oat), it is quite easy to make your own.

We recommend investing in a nut bag, available at your local natural foods store. They are inexpensive and easy to use and clean. Cheesecloth can be a bit fussy. Alternatively, nut milker machines will do this whole process for you, and even heat the milk for lattes.

FOR ABOUT 3 CUPS MILK:

1 cup almonds or hemp seeds
3 cups water
4 Medjool dates, pitted
1/2 vanilla bean (optional)
Nut bag, cheesecloth, ultra-fine mesh screen

Soak organic seeds or nuts overnight. Rinse the nuts and add to blender with water. Note: the ratio of 1:3 is a rule of thumb. More nuts will make the milk richer, more water will make the it thinner. Add dates and vanilla, if using. Blend until thoroughly combined and nuts are finely ground. Strain mixture through nut bag, cheesecloth (folded 4-ways), or ultra-fine mesh screen. Enjoy!

Buckwheat Noodles Tossed in Sunflower Butter Sauce

This creamy, spicy sauce is a sunflower seed butter variation on a peanut sauce that complements the whole grain flavor of buckwheat.

SERVES 4

1 package (8 ounces) 100% buckwheat soba noodles

Sunflower Butter Sauce

¾ cup sunflower butter (aka "sunbutter")
¾ cup water
⅓ cup lime juice
3 Tablespoons Bragg Liquid Aminos™
1 Tablespoon agave nectar or honey
2 Tablespoons fresh ginger, grated
3 teaspoons red pepper flakes
¾ teaspoon salt
2 green onions, chopped, including green tops
⅓ cup fresh cilantro, chopped

1. Prepare buckwheat noodles as directed on package and set aside.

2. Mix all sauce ingredients, except green onions and cilantro, in a medium-size sauce pan. If sauce is too thick, add water. Cook on medium heat 5–10 minutes to blend and bring out flavor.

3. Taste for seasoning. Mix in green onions and cilantro. Cook 1 minute.

4. Mix in buckwheat noodles, heat through and serve warm or at room temperature.

VARIATION:

• Substitute rice noodles for buckwheat noodles.

autumn BREADS

CONTENTS

Corn Cakes

These crunchy corn cakes are an excellent accompaniment with soup. They are great as a snack spread with almond or sesame butter and/or jam.

MAKES ABOUT 20 CAKES

3 cups 100% organic yellow stone-ground cornmeal
1 cup gluten-free rolled oats
½ teaspoon salt
½ cup sesame seeds, toasted (see "Toasting Seeds and Nuts," page 36)
⅓ cup cold-pressed extra-virgin olive oil
3 cups boiling water

1. Preheat oven to 350°F. Oil baking sheet.
2. Toast cornmeal in dry skillet about 3 minutes, stirring frequently. The color will change from pale yellow to pale golden. Pour cornmeal into large bowl.
3. Toast oats in same skillet about 3 minutes. Let cool 1 minute and add to cornmeal. (Toasting enhances the flavor of the corn and oats.)
4. Mix in salt and sesame seeds.
5. Add oil to boiling water and mix. Add this mixture to cornmeal mixture.
6. Combine with a spoon then mix with your hands. The dough will be the consistency of play dough. Let rest 5 minutes.
7. Shape dough with your hands into flat round cakes ½-inch thick and 2-inch wide. Place on oiled baking sheet. Flatten each slightly with your palm.
8. Bake 45 minutes or until golden on bottom. Turn over and bake 10 minutes until lightly brown on both sides. The top will crack a little.
9. Take off baking sheet and cool on wire rack.
10. Cakes can be stored in an airtight container up to one week.

VARIATIONS:

• Add ½ cup agave nectar, honey or maple syrup to liquid ingredients.
• Add ½ cup raisins, dates, dried figs, or cranberries to dry ingredients before combining liquid with the dry.
• Substitute ½ cup toasted sunflower seeds, pumpkin seeds, or chopped almonds for sesame seeds.

Savory Crackers

Amaranth flour gives these crackers a delicious nutty flavor. They are excellent served with soups, with dips, or as a snack.

3 cups amaranth flour
1 cup arrowroot
3 teaspoons baking powder
1 teaspoon salt
1 Tablespoon fresh thyme, chopped or 2 teaspoons dried
½ cup sesame seeds, plus 2 Tablespoons for top of crackers
1 cup almond or rice milk
½ cup cold-pressed extra-virgin olive oil

1. Preheat oven to 350°F. Oil two baking sheets with olive oil.

2. Mix amaranth, arrowroot, baking powder, salt, thyme, and sesame seeds in medium-size bowl. Set aside.

3. Combine almond or rice milk and olive oil in small bowl and stir into flour mixture. Mix and knead lightly with your hands.

4. Divide dough into thirds. Roll one-third onto baking sheet using floured rolling pin. Make dough ⅛-inch thick.

5. Sprinkle sesame seeds over the top. Score the dough into 1½-inch pieces and bake 15–20 minutes until lightly browned. Edges will be slightly more brown than the center.

6. Allow to cool before removing scored crackers from baking sheet. When warm, dough sticks to baking sheet in the center.

7. Remove from baking sheet with spatula and place on wire rack. (If crackers stick to sheet, use a sharp knife or spatula to loosen them.) When cool, break into individual pieces.

8. Follow same procedure for remaining two-thirds of dough.

ABOUT: AMARANTH

This is a fast-growing herb plant related to spinach and native to the Andes of South America. Amaranth seeds make a nutritious and highly palatable gluten-free grain and flour. Amaranth grain, cultivated since the days of the Incas, has a rich, nutty flavor and is has one of the highest protein concentrations of any gluten-free grain. It also is rich in dietary fiber, antioxidants, calcium, iron, copper and other minerals, as well as a host of vitamins. Like quinoa, amaranth greens also are a valuable food staple and source of nutrition around the world.

VARIATIONS:

- Substitute 1 Tablespoon ground cumin for thyme.

- Add 2 teaspoons lemon zest to dry ingredients and 4 Tablespoons lemon juice to liquid ingredients.

- Substitute 1 Tablespoon sunflower seeds for sesame seeds.

- Add ½ teaspoon peppercorns to dry ingredients.

Blueberry Muffins with Corn and Quinoa

The combination of quinoa flour with the cornmeal is very flavorful and creates an attractive light golden color.

MAKES 12 MUFFINS

1½ cups quinoa flour
1½ cups 100% organic yellow or blue cornmeal
1½ teaspoons baking powder
¼ teaspoon salt
4 Tablespoons cold-pressed extra-virgin olive oil
½ cup agave nectar or honey
2 large organic eggs, lightly beaten
1¼ cups almond milk
½ teaspoon lemon zest (optional)
1 cup blueberries

1. Preheat oven to 350°F. Oil cups of muffin tin to make 12 muffins. If using non-stick muffin tins, eliminate oiling.

2. Combine quinoa flour, cornmeal, baking powder, and salt in a medium-size bowl.

3. In a separate bowl, combine oil, sweetener eggs, almond milk and lemon zest.

4. Pour wet ingredients into dry ingredients, being careful not to over-mix.

5. Gently fold in blueberries.

6. Spoon into muffin cups ¾ full and bake 25 minutes or until the muffins start to brown and a toothpick inserted into the center comes out clean.

7. Remove from muffin tin and cool on wire racks.

VARIATIONS:

• Substitute dried or fresh cranberries for the blueberries.

• Substitute 2 chopped green onions and ½ cup 100% organic corn kernels for blueberries.

Oat Bread

This bread has an excellent texture and flavor. Plus, it is easy to make. Using chick pea and fava bean flours assists the body in adjusting to the fall season. Note: We recommend using Red Star ™ active dry yeast as it is gluten-free.

2 teaspoons active dry yeast
1 teaspoon salt
¼ cup gluten-free rolled oats
1 cup oat flour
    (grind gluten-free rolled oats in blender)
½ cup chickpea and fava flour
½ cup tapioca flour
¼ cup arrowroot
¼ cup flax seed meal
2½ teaspoons xanthan gum
2 eggs
2 egg whites
2 Tablespoons cold-pressed extra-virgin olive oil
    (or coconut oil for richer taste)
3 Tablespoons agave nectar or honey
2 teaspoons lemon juice
1¼ cups almond milk heated to 110°
    (very warm to the touch)

VARIATIONS:

- Substitute millet flour for chickpea and fava flour.

- Add 1 Tablespoon each chopped fresh thyme, oregano, and parsley and 2 chopped green onions (including green tops) to batter the last minute when mixing in food processor.

- Mix 2 Tablespoons chopped fresh rosemary and ½ cup chopped Kalamata olives in batter after blending in food processor.

- Add ¼ cup seeds (sunflower, sesame, pumpkin, or combination of these).

---

1. Combine first 9 (dry) ingredients in large mixing bowl. Set aside.

2. Mix eggs, egg whites, olive oil, sweetener, and lemon juice in food processor. Add warmed almond milk and blend 1–2 seconds.

3. Add flour mixture to food processor. Mix on medium speed for 4–5 minutes. (This aerates the bread, which helps it to rise and gives it a smooth texture.)

4. Spoon batter into a well-oiled loaf pan. (Batter will fill the pan about ⅔ full and have a thick, creamy consistency.) Cover, set in warm place and let rise to top of loaf pan, approximately 30–45 minutes.

5. Preheat oven to 350°F.

6. Bake at 350°F 40–50 minutes or until a toothpick inserted in the center comes out clean and sides of bread are lightly browned.

7. Cool in the pan, on wire rack 10–15 minutes (the bread will fall about 1–2 inches after removing it from the oven.) Run a knife around inside edge of loaf pan to dislodge bread. Remove bread from loaf pan and cool on wire rack 15 minutes before slicing. This allows the bread to settle and makes it easier to cut.

8. Let bread stand 5 hours before storing. This prevents it from getting gummy.

autumn DESSERTS

CONTENTS

Apple Crisp

This recipe was given to Miriam by her mentor and dear friend, Annie Fox, about 25 years ago. It is still her favorite apple crisp recipe. The juicy apple mixture combined with the crunchy topping makes this dessert hard to resist.

SERVES 8

¾ cup apple juice
2 teaspoons cinnamon
½ teaspoon allspice
¼ teaspoon nutmeg
1 Tablespoon arrowroot dissolved in
    ¼ cup apple juice
1 teaspoon vanilla
8 MacIntosh apples, or any tart apples, sliced
½ cup raisins
½ cup dates (optional)
Pinch salt

TOPPING

2 cups rolled oats
½ cup brown rice flour
1 teaspoon cinnamon
½ teaspoon allspice
¼ cup cold-pressed extra-virgin olive oil
½ cup maple syrup
⅓ cup apple juice
1 teaspoon vanilla
½ cup almonds, chopped

1. Combine apple juice, cinnamon, allspice, and nutmeg in small sauce pan and heat to simmer. Add arrowroot mixture, stirring constantly, until thick. Remove sauce from heat. Let cool a few minutes, then mix in vanilla. Set aside.

2. Mix sliced apples, raisins, dates and salt together in large mixing bowl. Combine the mixture with the sauce.

3. Preheat oven to 400°F. Place in 9 x 13-inch baking dish. Cover with foil and bake at 400°F for 20 minutes.

4. While apple mixture is baking, combine oats, rice flour, cinnamon, and allspice in medium-size bowl. Add oil. Stir in maple syrup. Stir in apple juice, vanilla, and almonds.

5. When done, remove apple mixture from oven and spread oat topping over the top. Reduce heat to 350°F and bake 40 minutes more or until topping is browned and crisp. Serve warm or at room temperature.

VARIATIONS:

- Substitute pears for apples or use ½ pears and ½ apples.

- Substitute figs for raisins.

- Substitute sunflower seeds for almonds in topping.

Spicy Sautéed Pears

Preparing pears this way brings out their subtle flavor. It makes an excellent light dessert.

SERVES 4

4 Bartlett pears, cored and sliced thin
½ cup raisins
½ cup apple juice
1 teaspoon cinnamon
¼ teaspoon ground cardamom
¼ teaspoon nutmeg
1 teaspoon vanilla

1. Mix pears, raisins, apple juice, cinnamon, cardamom, and nutmeg in a medium-size skillet. Simmer until pears are tender. Turn off heat and slightly cool.

2. Mix in vanilla and serve warm or at room temperature.

VARIATIONS:

- Substitute apples for pears.
- Substitute chopped dried figs for raisins.

ABOUT: CARDAMOM

A member of the ginger family and native to Southeast Asia, the cardamom plant produces a seed pod that is valued as a spice and a medicinal. There are two main varieties of cardamom, one producing green pods, the other producing pods varying in shade from brown or tan to ivory. The pod, which can be used whole or ground into powder, provides a strong aroma and a slightly sweet and minty or citrus-like flavor to a variety of food dishes. Today cardamom is a key ingredient in a variety of cuisines, including Middle Eastern dishes and drinks, and Scandinavian breads.

As an herbal medicinal, cardamom is particularly favored in traditional medicine system around the world, including the Ayurvedic and Chinese Five Element systems, and the traditional systems in Japan, Korea and Vietnam. It is used to balance the digestive system, and to treat inflammations, infections, and congestion.

Almond Sandies

This is a slice-and-bake cookie that is not too sweet and has a nice crunch. The combination of oat and brown rice flour imparts a pleasing, nutty taste.

MAKES ABOUT 32 COOKIES

2 cups gluten-free oats (grind to flour in blender)
1½ cups brown rice flour
½ teaspoon salt
1 teaspoon cinnamon
1 cup toasted almonds, chopped (see "Toasting Seeds and Nuts," page 36)
¼ cup cold-pressed extra-virgin olive oil
⅔ cup maple syrup
½ teaspoon almond extract

1. Preheat oven to 350°F. Oil a baking sheet.

2. In medium-size bowl, mix oat flour, rice flour, salt and cinnamon. Stir in almonds.

3. In small bowl, mix oil, maple syrup, and almond extract. Pour into dry ingredients, stirring to form a very thick dough. Knead lightly with hands until well mixed. If dough is too sticky add more rice flour.

4. Start forming a sausage shape by rolling and pulling the dough between your hands until it is about 16 inches long and 1½ inches wide. Wrap plastic wrap around dough. Square or round the dough edges. Place in refrigerator and chill 1 hour to firm.

5. Remove plastic wrap and slice dough into ½-inch slices and place on baking sheet. Bake 15–20 minutes or until they are firm to the touch but not browned. (They will become more firm as they cool.)

6. Cool on wire rack and store in an air-tight container. (If cookies are too crisp, add a slice of apple to the container to moisten them.)

VARIATIONS:

- To use as a drop cookie, add ½ cup apple juice to the liquid ingredients. Using a tablespoon, drop batter on oiled baking sheet, flatten dough and bake as directed above.

- Add ½ cup raisins or currants to dry ingredients when stirring in almonds.

Squash Pie

This creamy pie is delicious as a dessert or snack. The filing also can be prepared as a custard without the crust. Bake pie filling in small oiled custard cups or oiled pie plate.

SERVES 8

FILLING

1 medium-size buttercup squash, or other squash
   (buttercup provides a deeper flavor)
½ cup apple juice
1½ teaspoons cinnamon
¼ teaspoon cloves
½ teaspoon nutmeg
½ teaspoon powdered ginger
¼ teaspoon salt
½ cup maple syrup, agave nectar or honey
2 Tablespoons arrowroot

1. Preheat oven to 400°F.

2. Cut squash into small pieces (peel can be left on.) Place squash in baking dish, add ¼-inch water. Cover and bake 30 minutes or until squash can be pierced with fork.

3. Prepare crust.

4. Peel skin off baked squash. Measure 3 cups squash and place in food processor. Add apple juice, cinnamon, cloves, nutmeg, ginger, salt, sweetener and arrowroot. Blend until smooth. Mixture should be thick, resembling pudding in texture.

5. Heat oven to 350°F. Pour filling into the crust, smooth the top and bake 20–25 minutes or until firm and cracked. (If crust begins to burn, cover with foil or pie crust cover.) Serve warm or at room temperature.

CRUST

1¼ cups gluten-free oats
   (ground to flour in blender)
¾ cup brown rice flour
2 teaspoons cinnamon
½ teaspoon salt
⅔ cup apple juice
⅓ cup almond, sunflower or olive oil
1 teaspoon vanilla extract
½ teaspoon almond extract

1. Mix oat flour, brown rice flour, salt, and cinnamon in a medium-size bowl.

2. In small bowl, mix apple juice, oil, vanilla and almond extracts. Pour liquid ingredients into dry ingredients.

3. Stir, then knead mixture by hand until combined. Press into oiled pie plate. Bake 5 minutes at 325°F.

VARIATION:

- Substitute sweet potato, yam, or pumpkin for squash.

winter SEASON

Shifting your food choices with winter | gluten-free & dairy-free recipes

CONTENTS

Harmony with Winter

Winter is a time of going deeper within oneself, resting, replenishing, reflecting. In the natural world, the life energy of plants and animals is gathered in their roots and body cores, during this season — resting and conserving energy in preparation for spring. Our bodies do the same: our blood vessels go deeper and our bodies contract, assisting the body in staying warm.

At each season one or more organs are considered primary in the body's intention to facilitate restoration and balance. The kidney and bladder, which process the body's water, are the organs associated with winter.

Water is an essential element of the body. It is the medium through which we transport nutrients and heat to the body through our blood, and by which we eliminate waste from the blood and lymph system. The kidneys continually filter the blood, keeping it clean and in a proper mineral and pH balance. The filtered waste is then stored as urine in the bladder for elimination. The body's ability to easily and effectively filter and remove wastes during this resting season makes balanced kidney and bladder function key during this season.

An imbalance in kidney or bladder function during this season can cause a build-up of toxins, resulting in stagnation and water retention. This may result in experiencing one or more of the following symptoms:

- Stiffness or pain in the back and/or neck
- Lethargy, low energy and vitality
- Edema, particularly in ankles, feet and hands
- Puffiness under the eyes
- Skin rashes
- Urinary tract infections
- High blood pressure
- Ear infections
- Having difficulty slowing down or relaxing

Eating in the following way supports the kidneys and bladder. It also will assist the body in maintaining warmth:

- Cut vegetables into large pieces and cook at moderate heat until tender. This gives them a longer cooking time.

- Daikon radishes assist in cleansing the kidneys. Include them with other vegetables or in soups.

- Winter is the best time to eat fried foods. Use more oil than usual in cooking and baking. Almond butter, tahini or coconut butter used as spreads or in cooking increases the amount of fat eaten which helps keep the body warm.

- Use more protein (beans, eggs, fish, seafood and poultry). Aduki beans in particular, are strengthening to the kidneys and assist in warming the body.

- Eat a higher proportion of gluten-free whole grains to vegetables. Millet and buckwheat are body heaters and are gluten-free. Other gluten-free whole grains assist in good elimination.

- Add warming spices to your cooking. They include cinnamon, allspice, nutmeg, cloves, ginger, coriander, curry and cayenne pepper.

- Use baking and roasting often as ways to cook food.

- Eat small amounts of raw foods such as salads, raw fruits and vegetables. Eat mostly cooked organic vegetables and fruits.

- Slightly increase salt intake. When using salt, we recommend using an unrefined sea or rock salt rather than regular table salt. Unrefined salts are rich in minerals and trace elements. See "A Word About...Salt," page 11.

- Include a large number of organic squashes and root vegetables such as sweet potatoes, yams, parsnips, carrots, celery root, Jerusalem artichokes, burdock root, turnips and rutabaga.

- Eat warming foods: soups, warm beverages and warm meals. Avoid iced or cold beverages.

- Put small amounts of seaweed, such as kelp, dulse, Nori and hiziki in soups, stews, vegetables or casseroles. They are rich in minerals and vitamins and assist in strengthening the body.

- Drink approximately two quarts of water each day.

- Add two cups of baking soda to baths once or twice a week to assist in removing toxins.

- Get plenty of sleep and relaxation from stress.

- Since life is more sedentary in the winter, deep breathing exercises, dancing, stretching, yoga and Tai chi chuan will help blood and lymph to circulate easily and gently in the body. This also helps to clear out possible stagnation and facilitates energy flow through the body.

- Baking breads, desserts and casseroles will warm your body as well as the kitchen.

- Roasting vegetables, potatoes, fish and poultry is another warming technique.

winter

harmony

WINTER FOODS LIST

The list below describes those we particularly recommend as in alignment with your body's desire for foods that are heavier and more concentrated. Generally, we recommend eating foods grown locally whenever possible, so that your body's rhythm matches that of your environment. While some of the foods on this list are not local to all locations, they still have valuable balancing properties at this time of the year and we recommend them during this season even if they come to you from other locations.

BEANS

Aduki
Anazaki
Black-eyed peas
Carob
Cannelini
Chickpea
Great northern
Kidney
Lentil *(all types)*
Navy
Pinto
Red
Split pea
White

GRAINS

Amaranth
Buckwheat
Millet
Oats
(gluten free)
Quinoa
(red or black)
Rice
(Basmati: brown, Brown: long and short grain, red, black and wild)
Sorghum
Teff

FRUITS

Apples
Banana
Cranberries
Dates
Dried fruits
(Apple, Apricot, Coconut, Currants, Fig, Mango, Papaya, Pear, Peach, Pineapple, Prune, Raisin)
Grapes
Kiwi
Kumquat
Oranges
Pears
Persimmon

HERBS

Chervil
Chives
Cilantro
Fennel
Oregano
Parsley
Rosemary
Sage
Savory
Tarragon
Thyme

VEGETABLES

Arugula
Beets
Red
Golden
Chyuga
Bok choy
Broccoli
Broccoli rabe
(Rapini)
Brussels sprouts
Burdock root
Cabbage
(green, Napa, red)
Cauliflower
Celery root
Daikon radish
Ginger root
Green Onions
Jerusalem artichoke
Kale *(all types)*
Leeks
Lettuce greens
(small amounts of all types except iceberg, which the body does not tolerate in any season)
Mustard greens
Okra
Parsnips
Pumpkin

Rutabaga
Spinach
Sweet potato
Swiss chard
Turnip
Watercress
Winter squash *(all types)*
Yams

We offer the following recipes as suggestions for enhancing your winter meals.

ENJOY!

winter APPETIZERS

CONTENTS

Tapenade

This tasty tapenade is great spread on toasted gluten-free bread or baked on halibut or salmon. It can be stored in the refrigerator in an airtight container for two to three weeks.

MAKES 3½ CUPS

1½ cups Kalamata olives, pitted
1½ cups green olives, salt-brined, pitted
2 green onions, coarsely chopped, including green tops
½ cup fresh parsley, finely chopped
1 teaspoon lemon zest
2 Tablespoons lemon juice
¼ cup cold-pressed extra-virgin olive oil

1. Place first six ingredients in food processor. Pulse until ingredients are chunky.

2. Pour olive oil through top of food processor and blend until mixture is in small pieces.

VARIATIONS:

•   Blend ½ cup artichoke hearts, frozen or canned (in water) with olive mixture.

•   Mix in 2 Tablespoons capers after blending.

Vegetable Pâté

This is a mild, creamy pâté that can be spread on toasted gluten-free bread or eaten as a dip with chips or rice crackers.

SERVES 6 - 8

2½ cups sweet potato or squash, grated
3 cups spinach, finely chopped
1 cup leeks, chopped in small pieces
2 Tablespoons cold-pressed extra-virgin olive oil
½ teaspoon nutmeg
½ teaspoon cayenne pepper (more for hotter taste)
1 cup ground sunflower seeds
2 Tablespoons flax meal
1 teaspoon salt
¼ cup millet, brown rice or quinoa flour
2½ cups water
3 Tablespoons Bragg Liquid Aminos™

1. Preheat oven to 375°F. Oil 8 x 8-inch baking dish.

2. Blend all ingredients in food processor until smooth.

3. Pour mixture into baking dish. Bake 50 minutes or until firm.

4. Cool before serving to allow flavors to blend. Pâté will become firmer when cool.

VARIATION:

1. Substitute 2 Tablespoons curry powder for nutmeg.

COOK'S TIP: MAKING YOUR OWN FLAX MEAL

Ground flax seed (aka flax meal) is a great source of protein, fiber, Omega 3 fatty acids, and antioxidants. It's inexpensive and has a delicious, nutty flavor. While you can buy ground flax meal at most grocery stores in the grain aisle, flax meal is best freshly ground, as exposure to air and light make it lose its flavor and some of its nutritional value.

To make your own flax meal, purchase organic whole flax seed (golden or red) from your local natural foods store and grind what you need in a blender or dedicated spice or coffee grinder. Store the seeds and any extra flax meal in the freezer, preferably in an opaque, glass container.

Quesadillas

These are fun and easy to make. Teff tortillas, either light or dark, can be found in many natural foods stores. (Note: Some dairy-free cheese contains casein, a milk protein. Check ingredient list on the package if this is a concern.)

SERVES 4

6 Tablespoons Vegenaise™ dressing, divided
4 teff tortillas
2 cups shredded jalapeño jack rice cheese, shredded and divided
4 Tablespoons canned diced chili peppers, drained (use more for hotter taste), divided
4 Tablespoons green onions, chopped and divided, including green tops
6 Tablespoons cold-pressed extra-virgin olive oil, divided

1. Spread 1½ Tablespoons Vegenaise™ on half of one tortilla. Sprinkle ⅓ cup rice cheese over Vegenaise™. Top with 1 Tablespoon chili peppers and 1 Tablespoon green onion. Fold in half.

2. Heat 1½ Tablespoons olive oil in 12-inch skillet, cook quesadillas, two at a time, over medium heat 2–3 minutes on both sides or until lightly browned and cheese is melted.

3. Remove quesadilla from skillet with a spatula. Place on baking sheet and keep warm in a 200°F oven. Repeat with remaining ingredients.

4. To serve, cut into wedges.

VARIATIONS:

• Add cooked chicken or shrimp.

• Add chopped olives.

• Add cooked vegetables.

winter SOUPS

CONTENTS

Spicy Sweet Potato Soup

This creamy, warming soup makes a fast, complete meal. It is delicious and satisfying.

SERVES 4

½ cup leeks, coarsely chopped
4 cups sweet potato or yam, cut in 2-inch pieces
3 Tablespoons cold-pressed extra-virgin olive oil
1½ Tablespoons curry powder
½ teaspoon ground cumin
1 Tablespoon fresh ginger, grated or ½ teaspoon powdered ginger
⅛ teaspoon white pepper
4 cups vegetable broth (see opposite page) or 4 cups water and 2 vegetable broth cubes
1 can light coconut milk
2 cups cooked organic chickpeas, drained, canned or cooked
    (see page 21 for instructions on cooking dried beans)
3 cups spinach, chard or kale, finely chopped

1.   Sauté leeks and sweet potatoes in olive oil in soup pot 5 minutes or until vegetables are glazed.

2.   Add curry powder, ground cumin, ginger and white pepper. Stir 30 seconds or until there is an aroma.

3.   Add vegetable broth or water with vegetable pieces. Bring to boil then reduce heat to medium-low and cook until vegetables are tender, 10–15 minutes.

4.   Add coconut milk. Blend with hand blender or food processor until partially or completely smooth.

5.   Stir in chickpeas and greens. Cook until greens are wilted, 2–4 minutes.

Vegetable Broth

In our opinion, soups are quicker, simpler and easier to make with high-quality vegetable broth cubes (see "A Word About...Broth," page 8.) That being said, home-made vegetable broth, all by itself, is the original soup. So, here's a recipe that works well. The longer cooking time gives the broth a deep, rich taste. The Kombu seaweed in this broth is high in vitamins and minerals. It also contains a natural glutamic acid, which is a tenderizer and flavor enhancer.

MAKES 6 CUPS

2 leeks, cut in large pieces
3 carrots, cut in large pieces
2 turnips, cut in large pieces
2 parsnips, cut in large pieces
3 Tablespoons cold-pressed extra-virgin olive oil
½ cup dried white beans
7 sprigs parsley
2 stalks celery or fennel, or both
2 bay leaves
2 teaspoon salt
1 teaspoon white pepper
1 strip Kombu sea weed (2–4 inches)
8 sprigs fresh thyme or 1 Tablespoon dried
Any assorted frozen vegetable trimmings and scraps, thawed
8 cups water

> COOK'S TIP:
> SAVING VEGETABLES FOR STOCK
>
> When preparing any vegetables, put trimmings in plastic bags and freeze them for later use. Vegetables that are most useful are: leeks, celery, carrots, greens beans, corn cobs, parsley, cilantro or other herb stems, broccoli stalks, and pea pods.

1. Preheat oven to 375°F.

2. Toss leeks, carrots, turnips and parsnips in olive oil. Place in a baking pan and roast 1 hour 15 minutes, tossing occasionally.

3. Place roasted vegetables in large soup pot with remaining ingredients. Bring to boil then lower heat. Simmer at least 2 hours, or up to 6 hours.

4. When ready, strain through a strainer or double layer of cheese cloth. Taste for seasoning.

5. Store tightly covered in refrigerator for 2 days or in the freezer for up to 2 months.

winter

soups

Broccoli Almond Soup

This unusual combination of ingredients creates a very tasty soup.

<u>SERVES 4 – 6</u>

1 large head broccoli
2 Tablespoons cold-pressed extra-virgin olive oil
½ cup leeks, chopped in small pieces
2 teaspoons Bragg Liquid Aminos™
1 teaspoon thyme
1 teaspoon marjoram
1 teaspoon nutmeg
1 teaspoon dill
½ teaspoon white pepper
4 cups vegetable broth (see recipe page 227) or 4 cups water with 2 vegetable broth cubes
2 Tablespoons almond butter
2 teaspoons lemon juice
2 Tablespoons toasted almonds, chopped (see "Toasting Seeds and Nuts," page 36)

1. Chop broccoli flowerets into medium-size pieces. Peel and chop broccoli stalk if tough. Set aside.

2. In soup pot, sauté leeks in olive oil 5 minutes or until soft and slightly browned. Add broccoli and sauté 2–3 minutes, until it forms a glaze. Add Bragg Liquid Aminos™, thyme, marjoram, nutmeg, dill and pepper. Sauté 30 seconds.

3. Add broth and almond butter, bring to boil. Reduce heat and simmer until broccoli can be pierced with fork. Be careful not to overcook. Blend with hand blender, food processor or blender.

4. Mix in lemon juice. Taste for seasoning and serve in bowls garnished with toasted almonds.

<u>VARIATION:</u>

•   Substitute carrots, squash or cauliflower for broccoli.

Spicy Moroccan Lentil–Chickpea Soup

This is a variation of a traditional Moroccan lentil soup called Harira. The spices create a robust flavor and keep you warm on a blustery winter day.

SERVES 6 – 8

½ cup leeks, chopped in small pieces
2 cups celery, chopped in 1-inch pieces
2 cups carrots, cut in 2-inch pieces
3 Tablespoons cold-pressed extra-virgin olive oil
2 teaspoons garam masala
½ teaspoon cinnamon
7 cups vegetable broth (see recipe page 227) or 7 cups water and 2 vegetable broth cubes
1 cup parsley, finely chopped
2 Tablespoons cilantro, finely chopped
½ cup brown or green lentils
2 cups cooked organic chickpeas
6 – 8 lemon wedges (optional)

1. In large soup pot, sauté leeks, celery and carrots in olive oil 2–3 minutes or until vegetables are glazed. Add cinnamon and garam masala and sauté 30 seconds.

2. Add vegetable broth (or water with vegetable broth cubes), parsley, cilantro, lentils and chickpeas. Bring to boil, turn heat to medium-low and cook 30–40 minutes or until lentils are tender.

3. Serve in soup bowls with lemon wedges. Squeeze lemon juice into soup before eating.

ABOUT: GARAM MASALA

An aromatic and pungent toasted dry spice mixture used for centuries throughout India and parts of Asia. Hindi for "hot mixture", garam masala is highly valued In the East Indian Ayurvedic tradition of balancing through food.

The blend is a warming spice that supports whole body balancing and reduces cravings by combining six basic tastes: sweet, sour, salty, bitter, pungent and astringent. While garam masala ingredients vary by region, typical blends comprise cumin, nutmeg, cinnamon, pepper, chili, ginger, fenugreek, and coriander. Small amounts added to soups, stews, grains or vegetables is a delicious way to support the body in colder weather. As with all spices, buy small amounts, store in glass in a cool, dark place, and use within six months.

Creamy Vegetable Soup

This delightful soup is a wonderful body-balancing soup to eat in winter. The Jerusalem artichokes, in particular, support proper kidney function, key in this season of increased carbohydrate consumption for warmth.

SERVES 6

3 Tablespoons cold-pressed extra-virgin olive oil
½ cup leeks, chopped in small pieces
1¼ cups carrots, cut in ½-inch pieces
1¼ cups celery, cut in ½-inch pieces
1½ cups Jerusalem artichokes, cut in ½-inch pieces
5 cups vegetable broth (see recipe page 227) or 5 cups water with 2 vegetable broth cubes
2 bay leaves
2 Tablespoons fresh dill, chopped or 1 Tablespoon dried
½ teaspoon nutmeg
2 Tablespoons Bragg Liquid Aminos™
2 Tablespoons parsley, finely chopped

1. In 4-quart soup pot, sauté leeks, carrots, celery and artichokes in olive oil until glazed, about 2 minutes.

2. Add vegetable broth (or water with vegetable broth cubes), bay leaves, dill, nutmeg and Bragg Liquid Aminos™. Bring water to boil. Turn heat to medium–low and cook 15 minutes or until vegetables are tender and can be pierced with a fork.

3. Remove bay leaves and blend with hand blender or food processor until vegetables are puréed, with some small pieces. Add more water if too thick.

ABOUT: JERUSALEM ARTICHOKE (AKA SUNCHOKE)

Native to North America, this perennial tuber (root vegetable) is a member of the sunflower family. It was cultivated by American Indians, who called the tubers 'sun roots' and introduced them to European explorers, one of whom declared they tasted like artichokes and carried them back to France. The tuber has a sweet, nutty, refreshing flavor, and a crispness that resembles water chestnuts. In addition to the recipes provided here for cooking them, you also can enjoy Jerusalem artichokes raw, in a salad or slaw, or as a crudité for dips.

Nutritionally, they are exceptionally rich in potassium and iron. Unlike most tubers they store the carbohydrate inulin rather than starch. Among other health benefits, inulin has a minimal impact on blood sugar levels. (See 'A Word About...Sugars," page 12) That being said, some individuals do not tolerate inulin well, so if you are new to this vegetable, start with a small dose.

Hearty Vegetable Noodle Soup

This easy-to-prepare soup will be a favorite.

SERVES 6

1 cup spiral rice noodles, uncooked
½ cup leeks, chopped in small pieces
4 cups equal amounts:
  – carrots, cut in ¼-inch pieces
  – parsnips, cut in ¼-inch pieces
  – celery, cut in ¼-inch pieces
3 Tablespoons cold-pressed extra-virgin olive oil
6 cups vegetable broth (see recipe page 227) or water with 2 vegetable broth cubes
2 bay leaves
2 teaspoons dried dill
¼ teaspoon nutmeg
2 Tablespoons Bragg Liquid Aminos™
1 cup spinach, chopped in small pieces

1. Cook noodles according to directions on package.

2. In 4-quart pot, sauté leeks, carrots, parsnips and celery in olive oil 3–4 minutes or until vegetables are glazed.

3. Add vegetable broth (or water with vegetable broth cubes), bay leaves, dill, nutmeg and Bragg Liquid Aminos™ to sautéed vegetables. Bring to boil.

4. Turn heat to medium–low and cook 12 minutes or until vegetables are slightly tender when pierced with a fork. Add spinach and cook 2–3 minutes more or until spinach is wilted.

5. Mix in rice noodles.

6. Remove bay leaves and serve hot.

VARIATIONS:

• To make chicken noodle soup: substitute organic chicken broth for vegetable broth. Add 1 cup cooked chicken pieces when adding raw noodles.

• Add 2 Tablespoons curry powder when sautéing vegetables.

winter

soups

winter VEGETABLES

CONTENTS

Sweet Potato Wedges

These are a good substitute for french fries and are an excellent accompaniment with breaded fish fillets and aduki bean burgers.

SERVES 5

3 medium sweet potatoes or yams, cut into wedges the size of french fries
4 Tablespoons cold-pressed extra-virgin olive oil
1 teaspoon salt
¼ teaspoon white pepper

1. Preheat oven to 425°F.
2. Place sweet potato wedges in large mixing bowl and toss with olive oil until all wedges are well-coated.
3. Oil a large baking sheet with olive oil. Spread wedges onto cookie sheet.
4. Bake for approximately 15 minutes. Turn wedges over and bake 15 minutes more or until lightly browned on both sides and can be pierced with a fork.
5. Sprinkle with salt and pepper, toss, and serve.

VARIATIONS:

- For spicy baked wedges: Mix 2 teaspoons dry mustard powder, 2 teaspoons paprika, 1 teaspoon dried thyme, ⅛ teaspoon cayenne pepper, 3 teaspoons Bragg Liquid Aminos™ and 4 Tablespoons olive oil in a large mixing bowl. Toss with sliced sweet potatoes and cook according to directions above.

- Toss sweet potatoes in 4 Tablespoons olive oil and bake as directed above. When done, sprinkle with a combination of 1 Tablespoon salt, 1 Tablespoon ground fennel seed and ½ teaspoon cayenne pepper.

winter

vegetables

Mashed Sweet Potato, Turnip and Parsnips

The variation in color and flavor of each vegetable in this dish creates a visually inviting and tasty combination.

SERVES 5 – 6

1¼ cups sweet potatoes, cut in ½-inch pieces
1¼ cups turnips, cut in ½-inch pieces
1¼ cups parsnips, cut in ½-inch pieces
5 cups water
1½ teaspoons salt, divided
⅓ cup Vegenaise™ dressing
½ teaspoon white pepper

> **BODY BALANCING TIP: VEGETABLE SKINS**
>
> We invite you to consider leaving the skin on the vegetables you cook. Edible vegetable skins are a rich source of vitamins, minerals and antioxidants.

1. Bring sweet potatoes, turnips, parsnips, water and ½ teaspoon salt to a boil in medium-size sauce pan. Turn heat to medium-low and cook 10–15 minutes or until vegetables can be pierced with a fork.

2. Pour out water, add Vegenaise™, pepper and remainder of salt. Purée mixture with a hand blender or in a food processor until smooth and creamy. Serve immediately.

VARIATION:

• Substitute 1¼ cups cubed celery root for sweet potato and 1¼ cups cubed rutabaga for parsnip.

Parsnip Carrot Fritters

These crispy fried treats are delicious and go well with any type of meal. They also make a great snack on their own.

MAKES 9 PATTIES

¾ cup leeks, chopped
¼ cup plus 2 Tablespoons cold-pressed extra-virgin olive oil, divided
2 cups carrots, grated
1½ cups parsnips, grated
2 teaspoons curry powder
1 teaspoon salt
¼ teaspoon white pepper
1 Tablespoon dried dill (optional)
2 beaten eggs
½ cup brown rice or chestnut flour
2 cups spinach, finely chopped

1. Sauté leeks in 2 Tablespoons olive oil in medium-size skillet until softened.

2. Mix cooked leeks together with carrots, parsnips, curry powder, salt, pepper, dill, eggs and brown rice or chestnut flour in large bowl.

3. Mix in spinach.

4. Heat rest of olive oil on medium-high heat in a large skillet. Form batter into patties about 2 inches in diameter. Place in heated oil and cook 3 minutes on both sides or until well browned. Serve warm.

winter

vegetables

ABOUT: PARSNIPS

Parsnips are an 'old-fashioned' root vegetable, more popular in medieval times than they are today. We invite you to support their comeback. Not only are they more flavorful and sweeter than their carrot cousin, they are an excellent source of soluble fiber which supports lowering cholesterol and balancing blood sugar levels. Moreover, parsnips are chock full of carotenoids, vitamin B and C, potassium, folic acid and calcium.

Parsnips are wonderful soup vegetables, and also can be baked, steamed, sauteed or boiled and served mashed with salt, pepper and olive oil.

Orange Glazed Beets

This is a simplified version of beets a l'orange and equally delicious.

SERVES 4

2 large beets (red, golden, chyugia or any combination)
1 Tablespoon orange zest
⅓ cup orange juice
2 teaspoons agave nectar
⅔ cup cold-pressed extra-virgin olive oil
1 teaspoon salt
½ teaspoon pepper

1. Preheat oven to 400°F.
2. Cut beets in slices, about ¼-inch thick. Place in a medium-size baking dish.
3. Whisk orange zest, orange juice, agave nectar, olive oil, salt and pepper in small bowl. Pour evenly over beets. Cover beets and bake for approximately 30 minutes or until beets can be pierced with a fork.

Spicy Middle Eastern Cabbage

This simple cabbage dish is both exotic and tasty.

<u>SERVES 5</u>

½ cup leeks, chopped
3 Tablespoons cold-pressed extra-virgin olive oil
½ teaspoon curry powder
½ cup ground cumin
Seeds from 3–4 cardamom pods or ¼ teaspoon ground cardamom
4–5 cups green cabbage, finely chopped
⅓ cup water
1 teaspoon salt
¼ teaspoon cayenne pepper or pepper flakes

1. In large skillet, sauté leeks in olive oil until softened.

2. Sprinkle curry powder, ground cumin and cardamom into leeks. Stir and cook 30 seconds to bring out their flavor.

3. Stir in cabbage, water, salt and cayenne pepper or pepper flakes. Cover and cook over medium-low heat 5–10 minutes or until cabbage is completely wilted. Stir occasionally.

4. Serve immediately.

winter

vegetables

Steamed Greens with Lemon

This simple way to cook greens is a fabulous addition to any winter meal.

SERVES 4

1 bunch each: Swiss chard, kale, collard greens, or 2 bunches spinach, chopped in small pieces
2 Tablespoons cold-pressed extra-virgin olive oil
¼ cup water
3 Tablespoons lemon juice
1 Tablespoon Bragg Liquid Aminos™

1. Heat olive oil in large skillet over medium heat. Stir in greens and water. Cover and steam about 5 minutes. Uncover and stir until wilted. Mix in lemon juice and Bragg Liquid Aminos™.

VARIATIONS:

*   Use any combination of dark, leafy greens.
*   Sauté ½ cup broccoli chopped in small pieces in olive oil for 2–3 minutes, add greens and stir until greens are wilted and broccoli can be pierced with a fork.

BODY BALANCING TIP: DARK LEAFY GREENS

These vegetables, among them: kale, collards, chard, cabbage, amaranth greens, turnip and beet greens, spinach, escarole, and dandelion greens, are one of the most concentrated sources of nutrition of any food. They are a rich source of minerals (including iron, calcium, potassium, and magnesium) and vitamins (including vitamins K, C, E, and many of the B vitamins.) They also provide a variety of phytonutrients including beta-carotene, lutein and zeaxanthin, which support healthy cell structure and vibrant eyesight, among many other effects. Dark green leaves even contain small amounts of omega-3 fatty acids. Greens have little carbohydrate in them, and what they do have is layered in fiber, which make them slow to digest. That is why, in general, greens have almost no impact on blood glucose.

Including dark leafy greens into your daily nutrition is one of the best ways you can support balancing and vitalizing your body at all levels.

---

winter FISH & SEAFOOD

CONTENTS

Cornmeal Crusted Orange Roughy with Tartar Sauce

This simple dish goes well with Sweet Potato Wedges (see recipe page 233.) Letting the tartar sauce chill in the refrigerator for a few hours before serving gives the flavors a chance to blend and blossom.

SERVES 4

2 pounds fish, cut in 4 pieces (orange roughy, cod, halibut or walleye pike)
1 medium lemon, sliced in half
2 teaspoons salt, divided
1 teaspoon white pepper, divided
⅓ cup millet flour
¾ cup 100% organic corn meal
½ cup Vegenaise™ dressing
2 Tablespoons water
4 Tablespoons cold-pressed extra-virgin olive oil

1. Squeeze lemon juice on both sides of fish pieces. Sprinkle 1 teaspoon salt and ½ teaspoon pepper on both sides. Set aside.

2. In a wide, medium-size bowl, mix millet flour, corn meal, remaining salt and pepper. Set aside.

3. Mix Vegenaise™ and water in another wide medium-size bowl.

4. Coat both sides of fish pieces in Vegenaise™, then dredge in cornmeal mixture, coating well.

5. On medium-high heat in 12-inch skillet, fry fish pieces in olive oil 3–4 minutes on both sides until coating is browned and fish is cooked.

6. Serve with a dollop of Tartar Sauce (see recipe below.)

Tartar Sauce

MAKES 1 CUP

¾ cup Vegenaise™ dressing
¼ cup organic dill or sweet pickle relish
2 Tablespoons green onions, finely chopped, including green tops
1 Tablespoon fresh parsley, chopped (optional)
2 teaspoons capers

1. Mix all ingredients in small bowl. Cover and chill in refrigerator 2 hours if possible.

Crab Cakes with Mustard Sauce

The combination of ingredients in these crab cakes enhances the flavor of the crab.

MAKES 9 CAKES

1 pound crab meat
2 Tablespoons Vegenaise™ dressing
⅓ cup leeks, chopped in small pieces
¼ teaspoon dried mustard powder
1 teaspoon salt
½ teaspoon white pepper
1 Tablespoon parsley, chopped
1 Tablespoon dill, chopped or 1 teaspoon dried
1 large egg, beaten
¼ cup cold-pressed extra-virgin olive oil

1. In large bowl, mix crab meat, Vegenaise™, leeks, mustard powder, salt, pepper, parsley and dill.

2. Mix in beaten egg. Mixture will be moist and thick; it will stick together. If possible, chill in refrigerator for an hour.

3. In large frying pan, heat olive oil on medium-high heat. Form crab mixture into 3-inch, medium-size patties. Cook 4 minutes on both sides, or until browned.

4. Serve with Mustard Sauce (see recipe below).

Mustard Sauce

MAKES ABOUT 1 CUP

¾ cup Vegenaise™ dressing
2 Tablespoons prepared Dijon mustard
1 teaspoon lemon juice
1 teaspoon agave nectar or honey
2 Tablespoons capers
¼ teaspoon cayenne pepper (more for hotter taste)
1 Tablespoon fresh cilantro, chopped

1. Mix all ingredients together in small bowl.

winter

fish & seafood

Curried Shrimp in Coconut Milk

This spicy dish is great served over rice.

SERVES 4

½ cup leeks, chopped in small pieces
1 Tablespoon fresh ginger, grated
1 cup carrots, cut in ¼-inch pieces
1 cup parsnips, cut in ¼-inch pieces
1 cup fennel, cut in ¼-inch pieces
1 cup celery, cut in ¼-inch pieces
3 Tablespoons cold-pressed extra-virgin olive oil
1 Tablespoon curry powder
1 vegetable broth cube in 1 cup water
½ cup light coconut milk
½ pound wild caught shrimp, peeled and deveined (see instructions page 74)
1 cup spinach, coarsely chopped

1. Sauté leeks, ginger, carrots, parsnips, fennel and celery in olive oil until glazed. Stir in curry powder for 30 seconds.

2. Pour in water with vegetable broth cube and coconut milk. Cook on medium heat 10 minutes or until vegetables are just tender and liquid is slightly thickened.

3. Mix in shrimp and spinach. Cook 3 minutes or until shrimp has curled and turned pink and spinach is wilted.

Creamy Halibut Casserole

This dish was inspired by The Barefoot Contessa. It is a variation of a dish Miriam once saw her prepare. (Note: Some dairy-free cheese contains casein, a milk protein. Check ingredient list on the package if this is a concern.)

SERVES 4

2 pounds halibut, cut into 4 pieces
1 lemon, cut in half
1 teaspoon salt
½ teaspoon white pepper, divided
½ cup leeks, cut in small pieces
3 cups carrots, cut in strips (2 inches long and ½-inch wide)
3 Tablespoons cold-pressed extra-virgin olive oil
2½ cups kale, chopped in small pieces
¼ cup water
4 Tablespoons Vegenaise™ dressing
¾ cup almond milk
½ teaspoon nutmeg
¼ teaspoon white pepper
1½ cups almond or rice, jalapeño jack or cheddar style cheese, grated (optional)

1. Preheat oven to 375°F.

2. Squeeze lemon juice on both sides of halibut pieces. Sprinkle salt and ¼ teaspoon pepper on both sides.

3. In medium-size skillet, sauté leeks and carrots in olive oil until leeks are soft and carrots are glazed. Stir in kale. Add water. Cover and cook 3 minutes or until kale is wilted. Set aside.

4. In small bowl, whisk together Vegenaise™, almond milk, nutmeg and rest of pepper.

5. Place fish in 9 x 13-inch baking dish. Spread vegetable mixture over fish. Pour Vegenaise™ mixture over vegetables. Spread grated cheese, if desired, over top of casserole.

6. Bake 30 minutes or until halibut flakes.

VARIATION:

- Substitute orange roughy for halibut.

Curried Salmon Frittata

Serve this frittata with a hot bowl of soup for a sophisticated winter brunch or luncheon.

<u>MAKES 8 PORTIONS</u>

10 organic eggs
2 teaspoons salt, divided
¼ teaspoon white pepper
⅓ cup Vegenaise™ dressing
½ cup leeks
2 Tablespoons cold-pressed extra-virgin olive oil
1 cup red cabbage, chopped in small pieces
1 cup collard greens, cut in small pieces
1 Tablespoon curry powder
2 cups cooked or smoked salmon
⅓ cup Kalamata olives, chopped in small pieces

1. Preheat oven to 350°F. Oil a 9-inch pie plate. Set aside.

2. Mix eggs, one teaspoon salt, pepper and Vegenaise™ in large bowl and set aside.

3. Sauté leeks in olive oil until soft. Stir in red cabbage, collard greens and remaining salt. Sauté until wilted and slightly soft. Mix in curry powder and cook 30 seconds.

4. Mix in salmon and olives. Evenly spread ingredients in bottom of pie plate. Pour egg mixture over salmon mixture. Bake 30 minutes or until mixture puffs and is firm. Remove from oven. Frittata will fall about one inch.

5. Cool 10 minutes. Slice and serve.

<u>VARIATIONS:</u>

• Substitute 1 cup each sweet potatoes and parsnips, chopped in small pieces, for salmon. Sauté sweet potatoes and parsnips with leeks until glazed before adding cabbage and collard greens.

• Substitute kale or Swiss chard for collard greens.

winter POULTRY

CONTENTS

Herb Roasted Chicken and Vegetables with Pan Gravy

This chicken dish is an elegant, easy-to-prepare meal. Serve with steamed greens.

1 whole organic chicken (2½ to 3 pounds)
2 Tablespoons cold-pressed extra-virgin olive oil
½ teaspoon ground sage
1 teaspoon dried thyme
1 teaspoon salt
½ teaspoon white pepper
1 large rutabaga, cut in 2 to 3-inch pieces
6 medium carrots, cut on the diagonal
3 stalks celery, cut on the diagonal
1 bay leaf

1. Preheat oven to 375°F.

2. Rinse chicken and pat dry. Place chicken, breast side up, on a rack in shallow roasting pan or Soup pot. Brush with olive oil.

3. In small bowl, stir together sage, thyme, salt and pepper. Rub outside and inside of bird.

4. Arrange rutabaga, carrots, celery and bay leaf around chicken.

5. Roast covered for 1–1¼ hours or until drumsticks move easily in their sockets and chicken is no longer pink.

6. Remove chicken from oven and let stand 10 minutes before slicing. Remove bay leaf and arrange vegetables on a serving platter with sliced chicken. Serve with Pan Gravy if desired (see recipe at right.)

Pan Gravy

MAKES 2½ CUPS

⅓ cup fat from roast chicken pan drippings
¼ cup rice flour
2 cups organic chicken broth
Salt and pepper to taste

1. After transferring chicken to serving platter, pour pan drippings into large measuring cup. Include brown bits. Skim and reserve fat (clear liquid on surface) from drippings.

2. Pour ⅓ cup fat into medium sauce pan (discard remaining fat). Stir in flour.

3. Add chicken broth and cook on medium heat, stirring frequently, until thickened and bubbly. Cook and stir one minute more. Season to taste with salt and pepper.

VARIATIONS:

1. Substitute sweet potato for rutabaga.

2. Substitute parsnips for carrots.

3. To prepare in slow cooker/crockpot: Cook all ingredients in slow cooker for 4 to 5 hours or until drumsticks move easily in their socket and the chicken is no longer pink. Cooking in a slow cooker makes the chicken very moist.

Chicken Stir Fry

This delicious and colorful stir fry can be served over any steamed grain or cooked noodles.

SERVES 4 – 6

½ cup organic chicken broth or water
1 Tablespoon arrowroot
2 Tablespoons Bragg Liquid Aminos™
½ cup leeks, cut in small pieces
1 Tablespoon fresh ginger, grated
1 cup carrots, cut in small, thin pieces
3 Tablespoons cold-pressed extra-virgin olive oil
1 teaspoon salt
½ teaspoon white pepper
2 cups fresh broccoli flowers
1½ cups red cabbage, thinly sliced
1½ cups baby bok choy, coarsely chopped
1 lb. organic cooked chicken breasts, cut in strips or pieces
3 Tablespoons fresh cilantro, chopped
½ cup toasted almonds, chopped (see "Toasting Seeds and Nuts," page 36)

1. In small bowl, mix chicken broth or water together with arrowroot and Bragg Liquid Aminos™. Set aside.

2. Sauté leeks, ginger and carrots in olive oil on medium-high heat in large fry pan or wok 3–5 minutes until leeks are soft and carrots are slightly tender. Sprinkle carrot mixture with salt and pepper.

3. Add in broccoli and cabbage. Sauté 5 minutes or until vegetables are tender.

4. Mix in baby bok choy and cook 2–3 minutes or until tender.

5. Add cooked chicken, cilantro and arrowroot mixture to vegetables. Cook 1–2 minutes or until mixture is thick and shiny.

6. Top with almonds. Serve over cooked grains or noodles.

VARIATIONS:

• Substitute organic turkey for chicken.

• Substitute cooked shrimp or scallops for chicken.

• Substitute fresh parsley for cilantro.

winter BEANS

CONTENTS

Curried Kidney Bean Stew

The nutty flavor of the kidney beans adds to the spicy richness of this stew. Serve over steamed rice or any other grain to create a whole meal.

SERVES 5 – 6

½ cup leeks, cut in small pieces
2 Tablespoons cold-pressed extra-virgin olive oil
2 cups carrots, cut in ¼-inch pieces
1½ cups fennel bulb, cut in ¼-inch pieces
3 Tablespoons fennel frawns, chopped
2 cups yams or sweet potatoes, cut in ¼-inch pieces
2 Tablespoons curry powder
3 cups water mixed with one vegetable broth cube
3 cups kidney beans, drained, canned or cooked (see page 21 for instructions on cooking dried beans)
3 cups Swiss chard, chopped in small pieces
½ cup fresh cilantro, chopped

1. Sauté leeks in large skillet in olive oil until they soften.
2. Stir in carrots, fennel and yams. Sauté until vegetables are glazed. Stir in curry powder and cook for 30 seconds. Add water and vegetable broth cube. Bring to boil, cover and lower heat to medium-low and cook 15 minutes or until vegetables can be pierced with a fork.
3. Mix in kidney beans and Swiss chard. Cover and cook 10 minutes or until chard is wilted and beans are warm.
4. Turn off heat and mix in cilantro. Serve as stew, or over any type of steamed grain.

VARIATIONS:

- Substitute cooked lentils for kidney beans.
- Substitute peeled, cubed squash for yams.
- Substitute Daikon radish for carrots.
- Substitute chopped kale, collard greens or spinach for Swiss chard.

Aduki Bean Burgers with Creamy Chipotle Sauce

Aduki beans, also known as adzuki beans, have a deep smoky flavor. They strengthen the kidneys and create warmth in the body. Baked Sweet Potato Wedges (see recipe page 233) go well with these burgers.

MAKES 8 MEDIUM-SIZE PATTIES

3 cups aduki beans, drained, canned or cooked,
    (see page 21 for instructions on cooking dried beans)
1¼ cups carrots, chopped
1¼ cups sweet potatoes or yams, chopped
½ Tablespoon ground cumin
1 Tablespoon coriander
1 teaspoon salt
1 Tablespoon Bragg Liquid Aminos™
½ teaspoon chipotle pepper or cayenne pepper
    (use more for hotter taste)
1 cup gluten-free bread crumbs
    (see "Making Your Own Breadcrumbs," page 246)
¼ cup cilantro, finely chopped
½ cup brown rice flour
5 Tablespoons cold-pressed extra-virgin olive oil

Creamy Chipotle Sauce

MAKES 1¼ CUPS

1 cup Vegenaise™ dressing
2 Tablespoons lemon or lime juice
½ teaspoon chipotle pepper powder
    (add more for hotter flavor)
½ teaspoon ground cumin

1. Mix all ingredients in a medium-size bowl and serve with aduki bean patties.

1. Steam carrots and sweet potato or yams until tender, approximately 5–10 minutes. Set aside.

2. Combine ground cumin, coriander, drained beans, salt, Bragg Liquid Aminos™, and chipotle pepper or cayenne pepper powder in food processor. Process until ingredients are reduced to a paste, scraping down sides of bowl as necessary. Mixture will be thick and a little difficult to process.

3. Place mixture in medium-size bowl. Add in bread crumbs.

4. Mix in steamed carrots and sweet potatoes or yams using potato masher. Leave small pieces of the carrots and sweet potatoes. Stir in cilantro.

5. Spread olive oil in large fry pan. Bring to medium-high heat.

6. Place brown rice flour on large plate. Form bean mixture into patties about 2 inches in diameter. Dip both sides in rice flour and fry 3–4 minutes on each side in olive oil or until browned.

7. Serve warm with a dollop of Creamy Chipotle Sauce (see recipe above.)

Aduki Beans with Squash, Carrots and Watercress

This is a delicious way to prepare aduki beans. Serve with steamed buckwheat for added warmth.

SERVES 6

1 cup dried aduki beans
3 cups water
1 vegetable broth cube
2 medium carrots, cut in 2-inch pieces
1 cup squash (butternut, buttercup, kobocha, acorn,
    carnival, or kiri), peeled and cut in 2-inch pieces
1 bunch watercress, chopped in small pieces
1 teaspoon salt
½ teaspoon pepper
2 Tablespoons Bragg Liquid Aminos™

1. Wash aduki beans and place beans, water and veg-
    etable broth cube in large sauce pan. Bring to boil,
    cover and turn heat to low. Cook about 40 minutes.

2. Add carrots and squash. Cook covered another 30
    minutes or until beans are tender. Most of the water
    will be absorbed.

3. Stir in watercress, salt, pepper and Bragg Liquid
    Aminos™. Cook 5 minutes or until watercress is
    wilted. Serve immediately.

VARIATION:

•   Substitute rutabaga for carrots.

ABOUT: WINTER SQUASH

These come in a variety of shapes and sizes. All have a hard outer rind surrounding a sweet, typically orange or yellow flesh. Because they arrive late in the growing season and have a long shelf life, winter squash have long been a valued food staple for winter and early spring, when other vegetables are harder to come by. Unlike summer squash, winter squash must be cooked - typically by baking, steaming or sautéing. The skin of all but the acorn squash is edible when cooked.

Winter squashes are a great source of complex carbohydrates and an excellent source of vitamins A, B, and C. They also are rich in carotene, trace minerals and dietary fiber. Common varieties include: acorn, buttercup, butternut, banana, delicata, pumpkin, spaghetti, turban, hubbard carnival, kobocha, or kiri. Try them all!

winter

beans

Herbed Bean Sauce Over Rice

This hearty dish has an excellent flavor. It can be prepared a day ahead and refrigerated.

SERVES 6

½ cup leeks, finely chopped
2 Tablespoons cold-pressed extra-virgin olive oil
4 cups red beans, drained, canned or cooked (see page 21 for instructions on cooking dried beans)
1¾ cups vegetable broth or 1¾ cups water with 1 vegetable broth cube
½ teaspoon cayenne pepper (add more for hotter taste)
1 Tablespoon fresh ginger, grated
1 Tablespoon ground cumin
1 Tablespoon ground coriander
1 bay leaf
1 teaspoon salt
1 Tablespoon Bragg Liquid Aminos™
¼ cup fresh cilantro, chopped
2 Tablespoons toasted almonds, chopped (see "Toasting Seeds and Nuts," page 36)
4 cups cooked red rice (see recipe, page 25)

1. Sauté leeks in olive oil in medium-size skillet until soft.

2. Place rest of ingredients, except cilantro and almonds in large sauce pan. Bring to boil, simmer about 20 minutes or until liquid has reduced and mixture is slightly thick.

3. Mix with hand blender or in food processor and blend until a chunky sauce is formed. Mix in cilantro.

4. The sauce may be prepared a day ahead and stored in refrigerator. If sauce is too thick, add a little water to return it to the original consistency.

5. Serve over rice sprinkled with toasted almonds.

VARIATIONS:

• Substitute great northern, kidney or anazaki beans for red beans.

• Substitute millet, quinoa or buckwheat for rice.

winter GRAINS & PASTA

CONTENTS

Buckwheat

Buckwheat is a wonderful, warming grain to serve in winter.

SERVES 5 – 6

1 cup buckwheat
2 cups water
pinch of salt

1. In large sauce pan, stir buckwheat for 1–2 minutes on medium heat until it turns slightly darker and there is an aroma. Turn off heat and allow to cool for 10 minutes.

2. In separate pan, bring water to boil and add salt. Remove from heat and cool 10 minutes (the buckwheat will become gummy if the water is too hot before cooking). Add buckwheat to water, bring to boil, cover and turn heat to low. Cook 45 minutes.

3. Turn off heat and let stand 15 minutes.

4. Fluff and serve.

VARIATION:

•   Mix in 5–6 Tablespoons Bragg Liquid Aminos™ and top with ½ cup toasted sunflower seeds (see "Toasting Seeds and Nuts," page 36)

Steamed Quinoa

This ancient grain comes from the high mountain regions of South America where the air is thin. It is a highly nutritious, warming grain with a delightful, nutty flavor. Wonderful in winter, serve it with vegetables or as a side dish with soup.

MAKES 5 SERVINGS

1 cup quinoa (white, red or black)
2 cups water
¼ teaspoon salt

1. Place quinoa in strainer. Run water over it and wash by rubbing the grains lightly with hands for about one minute. Drain and rinse.

2. Bring water and salt to a boil in sauce pan. Add quinoa and resume boiling. Reduce heat to low, cover and cook 30–40 minutes or until water is absorbed and white rings are visible.

3. Turn off burner and allow to stand 15 minutes.

4. Fluff and serve.

VARIATIONS:

• Add one vegetable broth cube to water before cooking.

• Sauté until tender finely chopped ½ cup leeks, 3 cups combination of carrots, celery and fennel. Mix into cooked quinoa along with 1 Tablespoon curry powder, 3 Tablespoons chopped cilantro, ½ cup raisins and ½ cup toasted pine nuts.

• Mix in 1 cup dried cranberries and 1 cup chopped or slivered almonds when quinoa is done.

• Mix in 1 Tablespoon lemon zest and 2 finely chopped green onions when quinoa is done cooking.

ABOUT: QUINOA

This ancient grain originated in the Andean region of South America, where it has been an important food for 6,000 years. It is not a grass and is valued both as a green leaf vegetable and for its seed (it is closely related to beets and spinach.) Incans held quinoa as sacred, referring to it as the "mother of all grains". The seed has an exceptionally high protein content (12-18%), is chock full of minerals and, unlike wheat or rice, has a balanced set of essential amino acids for humans, making this gluten-free, easily digestible grain an unusually complete protein source among plant foods. In fact, NASA is considering quinoa as a crop for long-duration manned spaceflights.

Red Rice

Here is a pretty and colorful variation on a traditional grain dish.

SERVES 6

1 cup red rice
2 cups water
1 vegetable broth cube

1. Place rice in strainer. Run water over it and wash by rubbing the grains lightly with your hands for about 1 minute. Drain and rinse.

2. Bring water and vegetable broth cube to a boil in 2½-quart sauce pan. Add rice. Resume boiling, reduce heat to low, cover and cook 1 hour. Turn off heat. Allow to sit (covered) for 15 minutes. Fluff and serve.

> ABOUT: RED RICE
>
> Also known as Bhutanese or Himalayan rice (short-grain) or cargo rice (long grain), red rice refers to an unhulled rice variety with a red hull or bran. The grain has a nutty flavor and high nutrient value, thanks to the presence of the hull. Red rice is rich in dietary fiber, B vitamins, minerals and antioxidants. When cooked, the natural red color in the rice hull, leaches out and dyes the rest of the dish red to pink, making the dish a colorful accompaniment to winter meals.

Wild Rice

Wild rice has a delicious nutty flavor. Cooking it in combination with brown rice makes for a visually-attractive and highly-nutritious grain dish.

SERVES 5 - 6

2 cups water
½ cup wild rice
½ cup brown Basmati rice or any type brown rice
1 Tablespoon Bragg Liquid Aminos™

1. Place wild rice and Basmati rice in strainer. Run water over it and wash by rubbing the grains together lightly with hands for about one minute. Rinse and drain. Bring water to boil in medium-size sauce pan.

2. Mix in wild and Basmati rice and Bragg Liquid Aminos™. Resume boiling, cover and turn heat to low. Cook 1 hour. Turn off heat and allow to stand 15 minutes or more. Fluff and serve.

VARIATIONS:

• Add 1 cup toasted, chopped almonds (see "Toasting Seeds and Nuts," page 36) before serving.

• Add 1 cup raisins before serving.

ABOUT: WILD RICE

Contrary to its name, wild rice is not a member of the true rice family, although it is related, and is another grain-producing grass. Native to North America, both short-grain and long-grain varieties exist. Because wild rice resists cultivation and is difficult to harvest, this grain is more expensive than true rices. Nonetheless, its nutty flavor, chewy texture and nutrient-rich composition makes it a highly attractive grain.

Wild rice is higher in protein, vitamins and minerals than true rice, including brown or red rice, and is low in fat. It also is an excellent source of dietary fiber. Like true rices, it is gluten-free. Your local natural foods store carries this grain, as do larger supermarkets.

winter

grains & pasta

Kasha Varishkas or Buckwheat and Noodles

This dish is a classic winter-warming "comfort food," served with love by generations of Jewish mothers in Eastern Europe. While we've tweaked the recipe a bit, we kept in all the comfort and love.

SERVES 6

1 cup rice spiral pasta or quinoa corn noodles
3 cups cooked buckwheat (see recipe page 256)
½ cup leeks, chopped in small pieces
1 Tablespoon fresh ginger, grated
1 Tablespoon cold-pressed extra-virgin olive oil
1 Tablespoon coconut oil
1 vegetable broth cube dissolved in 1 cup hot water
½ teaspoon white pepper

1. Cook noodles following directions on package. Set aside.

2. Sauté leeks and ginger in olive and coconut oils on medium-high heat in large skillet until softened and lightly browned.

3. Add water with dissolved vegetable cube and pepper. Cover and cook 1–2 minutes. Mix in buckwheat and cook 10 minutes more or until water is absorbed. Mix in cooked noodles and serve.

Creamy Lasagna with Squash

This lasagna is rich, creamy and satisfying. The raw lasagna noodles will cook to the right consistency as they bake in the sauce. The recipe is in three parts: squash blend, creamy sauce, filling. (Note: Some dairy-free cheese contains casein, a milk protein. Check ingredient list on the package if this is a concern.)

SERVES 8

SQUASH BLEND

3 Tablespoons cold-pressed extra-virgin olive oil
½ cup leeks, chopped
4 cups acorn, buttercup or butternut squash, baked and mashed
½ teaspoon salt
1½ teaspoons dried thyme

1. Sauté leeks in olive oil until tender. Mix in mashed squash, salt and thyme. (If squash is too thick, mix with water for thinner consistency.) Set aside.

CREAMY SAUCE

⅓ cup cold-pressed extra-virgin olive oil
½ cup brown rice flour
4 cups almond milk, divided
2 vegetable broth cubes
¼ teaspoon ground nutmeg
2 Tablespoons parsley, finely chopped (optional)

1. Heat olive oil in medium-size sauce pan. Mix in rice flour and stir 30 seconds. Pour in 1 cup almond milk and vegetable broth cubes. Stir until very thick and shiny. Continue to stir in remaining almond milk, one cup at a time until sauce is slightly thick. Mix in nutmeg and parsley and set aside.

FILLING

1½ cup grated almond cheese, divided
½ cup Kalamata olives, chopped in small pieces, divided
2 cups frozen or canned (in water) artichoke hearts, drained, chopped roughly, divided
2 cups spinach, chopped and divided
12 rice lasagna noodles (1 box), uncooked

TO ASSEMBLE LASAGNA:

1. Preheat over to 375°F.
2. Place four raw lasagna rice noodles next to each other slightly overlapping in bottom of 9 x 13-inch baking dish. If needed, add another noodle in extra space at end of baking dish.
3. Spread half of squash mixture over noodles.
4. Sprinkle half olives, then half artichoke hearts, then half spinach over squash.
5. Pour one third of sauce over entire mixture.
6. Sprinkle one third of grated cheese over sauce.
7. Repeat steps 2–6 one more time.
8. Lay remaining four noodles over mixture, cover with remaining sauce, and sprinkle with remaining cheese.
9. Bake at 375°F for 45–50 minutes or until noodles are tender. Let lasagna cool for about 10–15 minutes before serving.

(recipe continues on next page)

winter

grains & pasta

COOKS TIP: ROASTING SQUASH

Roasting squash can intensify this root vegetable's flavor, and is an ideal means for carmelizing the flesh.

1. Pre-heat oven to 400°F

2. Wash outer surface of squash, and cut in half length-wise if small, in multiple pieces if large. Cutting larger squashes can be a challenge. Use a cutting board and a sharp knife, and slice enough off the side of the squash resting on the cutting board so it does not roll while you cut. Using a rocking motion with the knife blade helps. Cover the back of the blade with a clean dish towel and rest your hand on that as you rock the knife.

3. Remove seeds and threads using the edge of a soup spoon.

4. Season inner surface with salt and pepper and, if desired, olive oil.

5. Place pieces in baking pan and roast 40-45 minutes or until flesh is easily pierced all the way through with a fork. For a more carmelized flesh, place squash flesh side down in pan. For a moister squash, place in pan flesh side up and add an inch or two of water to bottom of pan.

6. Remove from oven, allow to cool, and scoop out flesh.

VARIATIONS:

*   Substitute the following vegetable mixture for the squash mixture:

    2 Tablespoons cold-pressed extra-virgin olive oil
    ½ cup leeks, finely chopped
    1½ cups carrots, cut in ¼-inch pieces
    1 teaspoon salt
    4 cups kale, finely chopped
    1 teaspoon ground cumin
    1 teaspoon ground coriander

*   Add 2 teaspoons curry powder to creamy sauce when adding vegetable broth cubes.

winter BREADS

CONTENTS

Pizza

This pizza is fun and easy to prepare. While we can make our own gluten-free pizza crust from scratch, the prepared Namaste™ pizza flour mix is fabulous. Using it ensures that we actually will make pizza, which makes everyone happy. (Note: Some dairy-free cheese contains casein, a milk protein. Check ingredient list on the package if this is a concern.)

MAKES 6 - 8 SERVINGS

CRUST

Use a package of Namaste™ gluten-free pizza crust mix.

1. Follow the instructions on the package for one pizza crust and include in the flour mix:

   1 teaspoon salt
   1 teaspoon Italian herb blend (see "Italian Herb Blend," page 265)
   2 teaspoons cold-pressed extra-virgin olive oil in place of 1 teaspoon olive oil as package directs

2. Cook pizza crust (with added ingredients) according to package directions.

3. Remove crust from oven.

PESTO

1½ cups fresh basil
¼ cup sun-dried tomatoes (canned in olive oil, or dried, soaked in water until moist)
1 Tablespoon pine nuts
¼ teaspoon salt
½ cup cold-pressed extra-virgin olive oil

1. Blend all ingredients in food processor until smooth.

TOPPINGS

½ cup frozen or canned artichoke hearts (in water), drained, quartered
¾ cup spinach, chopped
8–10 Kalamata olives, pitted and chopped
1½ cups Jalapeño Jack almond cheese, grated

TO ASSEMBLE PIZZA:

1. Spread the ingredients over the top of crust in the following order: pesto, artichoke hearts, spinach, Kalamata olives, almond cheese.

2. Brush outside edges of crust with olive oil.

3. Bake 10–15 minutes on lowest rack in oven or until almond cheese melts completely.

4. Remove from oven, slice and serve warm.

Focaccia

We think this gluten-free variation on the traditional recipe outshines the original!

MAKES 1 LOAF

2 cups brown rice flour
½ cup tapioca flour
½ cup arrowroot
3 teaspoons xanthan gum
2 teaspoons agar powder
2 Tablespoons fresh rosemary, finely chopped
1½ teaspoons salt
3 teaspoons dry active yeast
2 teaspoons agave nectar or honey
1½ cups warm water (105°F)
4 large eggs
4 Tablespoons cold-pressed extra-virgin olive oil
1 teaspoon lemon juice

TOPPING

2 Tablespoons cold-pressed extra-virgin olive oil
½ teaspoon salt
1 teaspoon Italian herb blend (see "Italian Herb Blend," see above)

> **COOK'S TIP: ITALIAN HERB BLEND**
>
> Don't have a jar of this blend handy? Make your own... in minutes! Oregano leads the way in this blend of dried herbs. Mix together equal parts oregano, marjoram, thyme and rosemary. Some blends also include dried basil and/or sage. Enhances soups, stews, poultry, pizza and focaccia.

1. Preheat oven to 350°F.

2. Place brown rice flour, tapioca flour, arrowroot, xanthan gum, agar powder, rosemary and salt in food processor.

3. In small bowl, mix sweetener in warm water. Sprinkle yeast over water and stir until dissolved. Set aside to foam, about 4 minutes.

4. Add eggs, olive oil, lemon juice and dissolved yeast to food processor. Blend 3 minutes. Dough will be soft and sticky.

5. Transfer dough to oiled baking sheet. Flatten and spread olive oil on with pastry brush. Sprinkle salt and Italian herbs over top of dough. Cover and let rise in a warm place 30 minutes or until doubled in size.

6. Bake 20 minutes or until lightly browned. Remove from oven and let cool on wire rack 5 minutes. Remove from baking sheet with spatulas at both ends and cool on wire rack. Serve warm or at room temperature.

Buckwheat Pancakes

These are easy and fun to make. They are delicious topped with maple syrup, jam or applesauce.

MAKES 6–8 PANCAKES

1 cup buckwheat flour
1 teaspoon aluminum-free baking powder
1 teaspoon cinnamon
1 teaspoon nutmeg
½ teaspoon salt
¼ cup plus 3 Tablespoons cold-pressed extra-virgin olive oil, divided
1 cup almond milk
1 Tablespoon agave nectar or maple syrup
1 egg

1. Mix buckwheat flour, baking powder, cinnamon, nutmeg and salt in medium-size bowl.

2. Mix ¼ cup olive oil, almond milk, agave nectar and egg in medium-size bowl.

3. Combine wet and dry ingredients.

4. Heat remaining olive oil in large skillet on medium-high heat. The skillet is the right temperature to cook pancakes when water splashed onto skillet sputters. Drop pancakes onto skillet to desired size. When bubbles form and pancakes get puffy, approximately 2–3 minutes, flip pancakes and cook another 2–3 minutes.

5. Serve warm.

VARIATIONS:

- Add ½ cup sliced bananas, blueberries, raspberries or blackberries to dry ingredients.
- Add ¼ cup chopped almonds to dry ingredients.
- Prepare in waffle maker.
- Substitute 1 cup sorghum flour and ¼ cup tapioca flour for buckwheat flour.
- Substitute ½ cup brown rice flour for ½ cup buckwheat flour.

Buckwheat Sweet Potato Muffins

This muffin is spicy, moist and satisfying.

MAKES 12 MUFFINS

2 cups sweet potato, pumpkin or winter squash, coarsely grated
2 eggs
¾ cup vanilla almond milk
½ cup maple syrup
3 Tablespoons cold-pressed extra-virgin olive oil
2 teaspoons orange zest (optional)
½ cup buckwheat flour
1 cup sorghum flour
¼ cup tapioca flour
2 teaspoons aluminum-free baking powder
½ teaspoon baking soda
1½ teaspoons cinnamon
1 teaspoon powdered ginger
½ teaspoon nutmeg
½ teaspoon salt

1. Preheat oven to 400°F degrees. Grease a non-stick 12-cup muffin tin.

2. Combine grated sweet potato, eggs, almond milk, maple syrup, olive oil, and orange zest in medium-size bowl. Set aside.

3. Combine buckwheat, sorghum flour, tapioca flour, baking powder, baking soda, cinnamon, ginger, nutmeg and salt in medium-size bowl.

4. Mix dry ingredients into wet ingredients, a little at a time, stirring to blend after each addition.

5. Fill muffin cups ¾ full with batter.

6. Bake 20–25 minutes or until lightly browned on top and a toothpick inserted into the center comes out clean.

7. Remove from oven and cool on a rack 5–10 minutes. Remove muffins from tin and serve warm or cool thoroughly on rack.

VARIATIONS:

- Add ½ cup chopped almonds to dry ingredients.
- Add ½ cup raisins, currants, dates or dried cranberries to dry ingredients.

Orange Almond Scones

Hot scones on a cold winter's day... Enjoy them with a friend, with a hot cup of green or herbal tea. They are fabulous fresh from the oven!

MAKES 8 – 10 SCONES

1¼ cups sorghum flour
½ cup tapioca flour
1 teaspoon baking soda
½ teaspoon salt
4 Tablespoons cold-pressed extra-virgin olive oil
½ cup currants or raisins
4 Tablespoons agave nectar or honey
⅔ cup almond milk
1 large egg, lightly beaten
2 Tablespoons orange zest
1 teaspoon almond extract
2 Tablespoons almond milk, to brush top (optional)

> **ABOUT: TAPIOCA**
>
> A starch extracted from the root, or tuber, of the cassava plant, native to the Amazon. The starch, which is white and has a slightly sweet flavor, makes an excellent gluten-free flour that is light, soft and fine. The starch also is a valued thickening agent and, in pearl form is the basis of tapioca pudding.

1. Preheat oven to 400°F. Oil baking sheet with olive oil.

2. Mix sorghum and tapioca flour, baking soda and salt in medium-size mixing bowl.

3. Pour olive oil into flour mixture until lumps form. Stir in raisins or currants.

4. Combine sweetener, almond milk, egg, orange zest and almond extract in another bowl. Mix liquid ingredients into the dry ingredients.

5. Drop the dough, about 2–3 inches in diameter and ¾-inch thick, onto baking sheet using a tablespoon. Place about an inch apart. Brush the tops with almond milk, if desired.

6. Bake 10–13 minutes or until the tops are browned and a toothpick inserted in the center comes out clean.

VARIATIONS:

- Substitute chopped dates for currants.

- Add ½ cup chopped or slivered almonds into dry ingredients or spread on top of scones before baking.

winter DESSERTS

CONTENTS

Creamy Rice Pudding

This flavorful, creamy pudding is the perfect winter comfort food.

SERVES 6 – 8

2 cups cooked Basmati rice
1½ cups light coconut milk
1½ cups almond milk
⅓ cup agave nectar or honey
½ teaspoon salt
1 teaspoon cinnamon
½ teaspoon ground cardamom
¼ cup raisins
1 teaspoon vanilla

1. Place rice, coconut milk, almond milk, sweetener and salt in medium-size sauce pan. Bring to boil and let cook on medium-low heat for about 25 minutes, stirring occasionally.

2. Mix in cinnamon, cardamom and raisins and cook 30 minutes more or until most of the liquid has been absorbed and the pudding is thick and creamy. Remove from heat. Let cool for about 5 minutes and mix in vanilla. Pudding will continue to thicken as it cools.

3. Serve warm or at room temperature.

VARIATIONS:

• Substitute chopped dates for raisins.
• Mix in ½ cup chopped almonds along with vanilla.

Carrot Cake with Coconut Almond Frosting

This is a delicious variation on carrot cake. The creamy, moist frosting is an excellent substitute for cream cheese frosting.

MAKES ONE 9X13-INCH CAKE

2¼ cups brown rice flour
½ cup tapioca flour
2 teaspoons aluminum-free baking powder
1 teaspoon baking soda
½ teaspoon sea salt
1 teaspoon cinnamon
¼ teaspoon cloves
½ teaspoon nutmeg
1 cup almonds, chopped
1 cup raisins
¾ cup cold-pressed extra-virgin olive oil
¾ cup agave nectar or honey
3 eggs
¾ cup almond milk
1½ teaspoons vanilla
2 cups carrots, grated

1. Preheat oven to 350°F. Grease 9 x 13-inch baking dish.

2. Combine brown rice flour, tapioca flour, baking powder, baking soda, salt, cinnamon, cloves and nutmeg in a large bowl. Mix in almonds and raisins.

3. Mix olive oil, sweetener, eggs, almond milk and vanilla in a medium-size bowl.
   Mix in grated carrots.

4. Add carrot mixture to flour mixture. Pour into baking dish and bake 45 minutes or until a toothpick inserted into cake comes out almost clean (this will create a moister cake).

5. Place on cooling rack and frost cake when partially cooled with Coconut Almond Frosing (see recipe above.)

Coconut Almond Frosting

MAKES 6 CUPS (enough for a 9x13-inch sheet cake or 9-inch round cake)

½ cup cold-pressed extra-virgin olive oil
1 cup agave nectar or honey
1 cup almond milk
3 Tablespoons arrowroot dissolved in ½ cup almond milk
2 cups almonds, chopped in small pieces
2 cups unsweetened coconut
½ teaspoon almond extract

1. Combine oil, sweetener, almond milk and arrowroot mixture in medium-size sauce pan. Bring to a boil over medium heat. Boil 3 minutes, stirring frequently.

2. Remove from heat and mix in almonds, coconut and almond extract.

VARIATIONS:

• Substitute mashed sweet potato or pumpkin for carrots.

• Bake in two 8-inch round cake pans. Cut parchment paper or paper bag to fit inside of each pan. Oil the paper and pour batter into both pans. Bake for 30 minutes or until a toothpick inserted into center of cake comes out almost clean.

Cinnamon Raisin Almond Cookies

The combination of spices gives these cookies an excellent flavor.

1¾ cups sorghum flour
¼ cup arrowroot
¼ cup tapioca flour
½ teaspoon salt
2 teaspoons aluminum-free baking powder
½ teaspoon baking soda
1½ teaspoons cinnamon
½ teaspoon allspice
¼ teaspoon nutmeg
½ cup raisins
½ cup almonds
¼ cup cold-pressed extra-virgin olive oil
¾ cup maple syrup
⅓ cup applesauce
2 teaspoons orange zest (optional)
1 teaspoon vanilla
⅓ cup almond milk

1. Preheat oven to 350°F. Oil baking sheet.
2. Mix sorghum flour, arrowroot, tapioca flour, salt, baking powder, baking soda, cinnamon, allspice and nutmeg in large mixing bowl. Stir in raisins and almonds.
3. Mix olive oil, maple syrup, applesauce, orange zest, vanilla and almond milk in medium-size bowl.
4. Add wet ingredients to dry ingredients.
5. Using two tablespoons, drop cookie dough onto baking sheet, two inches apart (use one spoon to scoop batter, the other to scrape off batter.) Bake 15 minutes or until browned around the edges and firm to the touch.
6. Place on cooling rack.

VARIATIONS:

• Substitute ½ cup gluten-free oatmeal for ½ cup sorghum flour.
• Substitute dates or dried cranberries for raisins.

Valentine Cookies

This is one of Miriam's favorite cookie recipes. She discovered this recipe during her Alaska days years and years ago. They make an excellent valentine gift.

NUMBER OF COOKIES DEPENDS ON SIZE OF COOKIE CUTTER

1¼ cups gluten-free rolled oats, ground to flour in blender
1¼ cups brown rice flour
1 cup almond meal or whole almonds, ground in food processor or blender
1 teaspoon cinnamon
¼ teaspoon salt
⅓ cup almond or sunflower oil
¼ cup water
½ cup maple syrup
½ teaspoon almond extract
1½ cups raspberry jam (optional)
1 cup coconut (optional)

1. Preheat oven to 350°F. Oil 2 baking sheets.

2. Combine oat flour, brown rice flour, ground almonds, cinnamon and salt in large bowl.

3. In another bowl, combine almond or sunflower oil, water, maple syrup and almond extract.

4. Combine liquid ingredients and dry ingredients. When dough gets too thick to stir, mix with your hands. Let dough rest about 5 minutes until all liquid is absorbed. If dough is too thin to roll out, mix in more brown rice flour.

5. Form dough into two balls. Spread brown rice flour on cutting board and rolling pin and roll out one dough ball ¼- to ⅓-inch thick. Cut with heart-shaped cookie cutter. Place on non-stick baking sheets and bake 15–20 minutes or until cookies are lightly browned on the edge.

6. Remove from oven and place cookies on cooling rack. They will harden as they cool.

7. When cookies have cooled about 5 minutes, spread raspberry jam (if using) over the top of each cookie. Press the tops into coconut, if desired.

winter

desserts

holiday COOKING

Shifting your food choices with the holidays | gluten-free & dairy-free recipes

CONTENTS

Holiday Harmony

We love holidays. What a wonderful way to celebrate living and gratitude for family and friends. Meal preparation and sharing takes on a special meaning during holidays.

November and December are chock-full of celebratory occasions, and almost constitute a season by themselves, one with its own traditional "seasonal" dishes. So, we added a section just for this time of year.

In this section, we put together delicious gluten-free and dairy-free variations on traditional holiday dishes that will allow you to enjoy this season of celebration without compromising your nutrition or your palate.

Still, the nature of this "season" is larger meals with rich food, high in starchy ingredients. You can assist your body with digestion and balance by:

- Staying hydrated. Drinking up to two quarts of water a day is helpful. Some ways to drink water easily in a colder season include:

  – warm water
  – lemon water (room temperature or warm)

- Drinking ginger tea, mint tea or lemon water after a meal to assist the digestive process

- Moving your body in some way daily — e.g., stretching, yoga, walking, to assist with blood and lymph flow

- Refrain from consuming refined sugar, gluten products, alcohol, dairy, or excessive caffeine

holiday BEVERAGES

CONTENTS

Hot Mulled Apple Cider

Spiced apple cider is a favorite drink at holiday time.

SERVES 8 – 12

8 cups unfiltered apple cider or apple juice
3 cinnamon sticks
½ teaspoon whole allspice
½ teaspoon whole cloves
2 oranges, thinly sliced

1. Pour apple cider into large pot.
2. Add cinnamon sticks, allspice, and cloves.
3. Gently heat to simmering.
4. Keep at very low heat in pot or transfer to crock pot to keep warm.
5. Garnish with orange slices and ladle into cups.

VARIATION:

• Substitute 3 Tablespoons cider mulling mix for cinnamon sticks, allspice, and cloves.

ABOUT: APPLE CIDER

"Cider" refers to the juiced pressed from fresh apples, which is not subsequently filtered, sweetened or pasteurized. As a result, the juice tends to be darker and more opaque than pasteurized apple juice, due to the fine apple particles that remain in suspension. Fresh ciders vary in taste depending on the apples chosen for pressing. Like whole apples, apple cider is rich in vitamin C, and antioxidants, including flavonoids.

You'll find this seasonally produced beverage at your local farmers' market or natural foods store in the fall, following the apple harvest. Keep your cider in the refrigerator and drink it often as it does not have a long shelf life. Serve your hot mulled cider in a glass or ceramic container as cider can react with metals, giving the beverage a bitter, metallic taste.

Holiday Nog

This dairy-free nog is surprisingly similar in taste to traditional eggnog.

SERVES 6 - 8

1 cup butternut squash or sweet potato, cubed
2 cups vanilla-flavored almond, or rice milk
3 Tablespoons agave nectar or honey
¼ teaspoon nutmeg
¼ teaspoon vanilla extract

1. Steam or bake squash until tender. Let cool.
2. Combine all ingredients in blender or food processor and blend until smooth.
3. Refrigerate 30 minutes or more before serving to allow flavors to blend.

holiday APPETIZERS

CONTENTS

Pumpkin Hummus

The pumpkin in this recipe makes the hummus both flavorful and festive in color. Serve with rice cakes or gluten-free crackers or chips.

<u>MAKES 2½ CUPS</u>

2 Tablespoons tahini
2 Tablespoons lemon or lime juice
1 teaspoon ground cumin
1 teaspoon cold-pressed extra-virgin olive oil
⅛ teaspoon cayenne pepper
¾ teaspoon salt
2 cups pumpkin or squash purée, canned or cooked (see "Roasting Squash," page 262)
2 Tablespoons fresh parsley, chopped
1 Tablespoon toasted pumpkin seeds (see "Toasting Seeds and Nuts," page 36)

1. Place all ingredients in food processor, except pumpkin seeds. Blend until smooth. Taste for seasoning.

2. Spoon hummus into small serving bowl and sprinkle pumpkin seeds on top.

BODY BALANCING TIP: SALT BRINED FOODS

We recommend salt-brined foods over foods preserved in vinegar. Salt brine curing, which has been used by cultures around the world for thousands of years, occurs via lactic acid bacteria, which carry out their reactions without the need for oxygen. Because of this, the changes that they effect do not cause drastic changes in the composition of the food. In addition, lactic acid bacteria may improve the nutrient value of food by introducing B vitamins in the pickling process. Moreover, these bacteria contribute to the healthy microflora of human mucosal surfaces.

By contrast, vinegar begins with an alcohol fermentation initiated by yeast. Yeast is a fungus and, for a variety of reasons we endeavor to stay away from all forms of fungi, or fungi-processed foods (see "A Word About… Allergens", page 7.) Also, while the raw material used to make vinegar historically has been a fruit juice (typically grape or apple), today many commercial vinegars used for pickling are made synthetically from natural gas and petroleum derivatives, or from corn sugar.

Olive and Almond Pâté

This tasty pâté goes great with corn chips, rice crackers or gluten-free bread.

MAKES 3 CUPS

½ cup leeks or green onions, chopped, including green tops
2 Tablespoons cold-pressed extra-virgin olive oil
1 can (6 ounces) green olives preserved in salt brine
1 cup water
¼ cup raw almonds
¼ cup sunflower seeds
1 Tablespoon Bragg Liquid Aminos™
¼ cup rice flour
2 teaspoons fresh thyme, chopped or ½ teaspoon dried
2 teaspoons fresh sage, chopped or ½ teaspoon dried

1. Preheat oven to 350°F. Oil 8 x 8-inch baking dish.

2. In medium-size skillet, sauté leeks in olive oil on medium heat until wilted and slightly browned.

3. Combine all ingredients in food processor and purée.

4. Spread mixture into baking dish.

5. Bake 45 minutes, until top is firm.

6. Place in refrigerator about 1 hour to allow flavors to blend.

7. Serve garnished with a sprig of fresh parsley.

holiday

appetizers

Sweet Potato Latkes with Homemade Applesauce

These sweet potato latkes are a delicious variation on the traditional ones.

1 cup sweet potatoes, grated
½ cup celery root or celery, grated
½ cup parsnip, grated
½ cup spinach, chopped and steamed
½ cup leeks, grated
1 teaspoon salt
2 Tablespoons brown rice flour
1 teaspoon curry powder
1 teaspoon ground cumin
⅓ cup almond milk, if needed
2 eggs, slightly beaten or ¼ cup sweet potato pureé
⅓ cup cold-pressed extra-virgin olive oil

1. Mix all ingredients except olive oil together in a large mixing bowl. Add almond milk if batter is too thick.

2. Heat olive oil in large skillet on medium-high heat until oil sputters.

3. Form into 2-inch patties and cook 3–4 minutes on each side until browned.

4. Place on paper towel to drain.

5. Serve hot with dollop of Vegenaise™ dressing and/or Homemade Applesauce (see recipe at right).

Homemade Applesauce

MAKES ABOUT 3 - 4 CUPS

9 medium tart apples, quartered, cored, and peeled.
1 cup apple juice
½ cup agave nectar or honey (optional)
¼ teaspoon cinnamon

1. Combine apples, apple juice, sweetener (if using) and cinnamon in large pot. Bring to boil, reduce heat to low, cover and simmer 8–10 minutes or until apples are tender. Remove from heat.

2. Purée with hand blendor or food processor to desired texture.

3. Serve warm or chilled.

VARIATION:

• For a sweeter version, combine the following ingredients using previous directions.

   3 cups sweet potatoes, grated
   2 Tablespoons dates, chopped
   2 Tablespoons raisins
   ¼ cup almond, chopped (optional)
   ½ teaspoon salt
   2 Tablespoons brown rice flour
   2 eggs, lightly beaten

holiday SOUPS

CONTENTS

Curried Squash Apple Soup

This simple soup is elegant and satisfying.

SERVES 6

½ cup leeks, chopped
3 Tablespoons cold-pressed extra-virgin olive oil
5 cups squash (butternut, buttercup, kiri, acorn), cut in 2-inch pieces, peeled and seeds removed
2 apples, cored and cubed in 2-inch pieces
1½ Tablespoons curry powder
6 cups vegetable broth or 6 cups water with 2 vegetable broth cubes

1. Sauté leeks in olive oil on medium-high heat until soft. Add squash and apples, and sauté until they glaze.

2. Add curry powder and sauté 1–2 seconds or until fragrant.

3. Add vegetable broth or water with vegetable broth cube. Bring to a boil, reduce heat to medium-low and cook until squash and apples are tender.

4. Purée squash mixture with a hand blender or in a food processor until smooth.

5. Serve in individual bowls.

VARIATIONS:

•   Substitute pumpkin or sweet potato for squash.

•   Substitute pears for apples.

•   Eliminate apples.

Leftover Turkey Soup

This is a good way to use leftover turkey and also tastes great.

<u>SERVES 6 – 8</u>

½ cup leeks, chopped
1 Tablespoon fresh ginger, grated
2 cups carrots, chopped in ½-inch pieces
1 cup celery, cut in ½-inch pieces
3 Tablespoons cold-pressed extra-virgin olive oil
6 cups organic turkey or organic chicken broth
2 bay leaves
3 Tablespoons Bragg Liquid Aminos™
1 Tablespoon dried thyme
1 Tablespoon dried dill
½ teaspoon nutmeg
2 cups Swiss chard, coarsely chopped
1½ cups cooked turkey, cubed

1. Sauté leeks, ginger, carrots, and celery in olive oil in soup pot until glazed.

2. Add chicken or turkey broth, bay leaves, Bragg Liquid Aminos™, thyme, dill, and nutmeg. Bring to boil and reduce heat to medium-low. Cook 15 minutes or until vegetables are cooked through.

3. Add Swiss chard and turkey pieces. Cook 5 minutes or until chard is wilted.

4. Serve in individual bowls.

<u>VARIATIONS:</u>

•   Add 2 cups cooked rice noodles with turkey and greens.

•   Substitute chicken for turkey.

holiday SALADS

CONTENTS

Mixed Greens and Pomegranate Salad with Creamy Chive Dressing

Pomegranate adds a festive touch to this salad.

SERVES 6

3 cups mixed salad greens
1 cup arugula, torn in small pieces
½ cup pomegranate seeds

1. Mix salad greens and arugula in salad bowl.
2. Toss with Creamy Chive Dressing (see recipe below) and sprinkle with pomegranate seeds.

Creamy Chive Dressing

MAKES ¾ CUP

½ cup Vegenaise™ dressing
3 Tablespoons lemon juice
¼ cup water
2 Tablespoons fresh chives, chopped

1. Mix all ingredients in small bowl.

ABOUT: POMEGRANATE

Native to Persia and the Himalayan ranges, this ancient and colorful fruit has a scarlet red leathery skin enclosing a white membrane and ruby red, jewel-like edible seeds, also known as 'arils'. These arils can be eaten whole or pressed to produce pomegranate juice. With a flavor comparable to cranberries and a pleasant crunchy texture, pomegranate arils provide a tangy accent to dishes, as well as a bright splash of color. To remove the arils from the fruit, cut the pomegranate in half, and push the membrane inside out, allowing the seeds to remain together.

Pomegranate arils are rich in vitamin C, dietary fiber, and a host of antioxidants. In the East Indian Ayurvedic tradition of body balancing through food, pomegranate has been used extensively as a medicinal remedy for thousands of years. Among other uses, it is valued as a blood tonic and a digestive system balancer.

holiday

salads

Crunchy Romaine Salad with Honey Lemon Dressing

This is an elegant salad that will dress up any meal.

SERVES 6

4 cups romaine lettuce, torn in small pieces
1 carrot, grated
3 Tablespoons raisins
2 Tablespoons toasted almonds, chopped (optional)

1. Place all ingredients in large salad bowl and toss with Honey Lemon Dressing (see recipe below).

Honey Lemon Dressing

MAKES ¾ CUP

½ cup fresh lemon juice
¼ cup cold-pressed extra-virgin olive oil
3 Tablespoons agave nectar or honey

1. Mix all ingredients in a small bowl.

VARIATION:

•   Substitute lime or orange juice for lemon juice.

Festive Cranberry Salad Dressing

This dressing is festive and has a great flavor.

MAKES 2 CUPS

¾ cup cranberries
1 cup orange juice
⅓ cup cold-pressed extra-virgin olive oil
½ teaspoon fresh rosemary, coarsely chopped

1. In a small bowl marinate cranberries in orange juice for 2–3 hours.
2. Add olive oil and rosemary and blend in blender or with a hand blender.

ABOUT: CRANBERRIES

This round, dark red, tart berry, a close relative of the blueberry, grows on evergreen shrubs in acidic bogs. Native to North America, the cranberry long has been valued as a food source, dye, and medicinal by Native Americans. Cranberries are rich in vitamin C, dietary fiber, manganese and an array of antioxidants.

holiday

salads

holiday FESTIVE DINNERS

CONTENTS

Roasted Turkey

Cooking turkey with a combination of lemon, herbs, and chicken broth enhances the flavor and makes it moist.

SERVES 10 – 12 WITH SOME LEFTOVERS

1 (12-14 pound) organic turkey
1 lemon, cut into wedges
½ cup cold-pressed extra-virgin olive oil
Salt and pepper to taste
3 sprigs fresh rosemary
3 sprigs fresh thyme
3-5 cups organic turkey or organic chicken broth (enough to cover the bottom of the pan ½-inch)
2 bay leaves

1. Preheat oven to 325°F. Squeeze lemon juice over turkey. Place squeezed lemon wedges inside the cavity. Rub olive oil, salt, and pepper over the entire turkey.

2. Tuck rosemary and thyme under breast skin. Place stuffing (if using) into cavity and tie legs together.

3. Pour broth into roasting pan. Mix bay leaves into broth. Put roasting rack into pan and place turkey, breast side up, onto rack. Cover with foil, creating a tent. Roast until meat thermometer reaches 180°F when inserted into thickest part of the breast and thigh (without touching bone), approximately 2–3 hours.

4. About 30 minutes before turkey is done, remove foil and turn oven to 450°F. Roast until turkey is golden brown.

5. Remove from oven and allow turkey to stand about ½ hour before slicing.

holiday

festive dinners

Apple Cranberry Stuffing

The fruit and herb combination in this stuffing make it particularly flavorful. The stuffing can be baked separately, also. Breads made with a millet-rice blend make great stuffing.

SERVES 6 - 8

2 cups leeks, finely chopped
2 cups celery, chopped in ¼-inch pieces
4 cups apple, chopped in ½-inch pieces
¼ cup cold-pressed extra-virgin olive oil
¼ cup coconut oil, melted
8 cups gluten-free bread, lightly toasted and cut into
    ½-inch pieces
2 teaspoons poultry seasoning
¼ teaspoon nutmeg
1 cup dried fruit-sweetened cranberries,
1 cup toasted almonds, chopped in small pieces
    (see "Toasting Seed and Nuts," page 36)
2 vegetable broth cubes dissolved in 3 cups boiling water,
    or 3 cups vegetable, organic turkey, or organic
    chicken broth (for use if baking stuffing separately)

1. Preheat oven to 350°F.

2. Sauté leeks, celery, and apple in olive oil 2–3 minutes or until a glaze forms.

3. In large bowl, mix together cubed bread, poultry seasoning, nutmeg, cranberries and almonds. Add leek/celery/apple mixture. Add broth, if baking separately, and combine.

4. Stuff mixture into turkey or place in a 9 x 13-inch baking dish, if baking separately.

5. If baking separately: Cover dish with foil and cook for 30 minutes or until stuffing is soft. Stir every 10 minutes to assist in liquid absorption.

6. Remove foil in the last 10 minutes of baking to let stuffing slightly crisp.

7. Remove from oven and serve.

COOK'S TIP: POULTRY SEASONING

This is a blend of dried herbs and spices that can add a deeper flavor to poultry, which is naturally mild-tasting. Thyme and sage form the base of the seasoning blend. The blend typically is applied as a dry rub patted onto the poultry flesh, or is combined with stuffing before the stuffing is put into the bird. Use only small amounts of poultry seasoning, as its strongly flavored herbs and spices can be overpowering if over-applied.

Here's a simple recipe for making your own poultry seasoning. Feel free to embellish it with pinches of nutmeg, oregano, savory, parsley or cloves. Custom-blended poultry seasoning, made with high-quality herbs and packaged in a pretty glass jar, makes a wonderful holiday gift.

RECIPE:

Combine the following:

3 parts thyme
2 parts sage
2 parts marjoram
1 part rosemary
1 part white pepper

Wild Rice Stuffing

This stuffing has a nutty flavor and is an excellent variation to bread stuffing. It can be prepared three to four days before serving.

SERVES 6 - 8

3 cups water
1 vegetable broth cube
1½ cups wild rice blend
1 cup carrots, cut in ¼-inch pieces
1 cup celery, cut in ¼-inch pieces
1 cup leeks, chopped in small pieces
1 Tablespoon fresh ginger, grated
3 Tablespoons cold-pressed extra-virgin olive oil
1 Tablespoon fresh thyme, chopped or 2 teaspoons dried
1 Tablespoon fresh sage, chopped or 2 teaspoons dried
1 Tablespoon Bragg Liquid Aminos™
Zest of 1 orange (optional)
½ cup toasted almonds, chopped (see "Toasting Seeds and Nuts," page 36)

1. In sauce pan, bring water and vegetable broth cube to boil.

2. Place rice in strainer and rinse by rubbing grains together with your palms, running water over it at the same time. Add to boiling water. Resume boiling. Turn heat to low and cook 1 hour. Turn off heat and allow cooked rice to stand covered 15 minutes. Fluff with a fork.

3. Sauté carrots, celery, leeks and ginger in olive oil 5 minutes or until glazed. Mix in thyme, sage, Bragg Liquid Aminos™, orange zest and almonds.

4. Mix cooked rice into vegetable mixture. Taste for seasoning and stuff into turkey, or serve separately.

VARIATION:

• Substitute 3 Tablespoons coconut oil for olive oil for richer taste.

holiday

festive dinners

Turkey Gravy

Teff flour gives this a hearty, rich taste and a dark rich color. For a lighter flavor, use the brown rice flour.

MAKES 2 CUPS

¼ cup cold-pressed extra-virgin olive oil
½ cup teff or brown rice flour
1½ - 2 cups chicken or turkey broth, turkey drippings, or vegetable broth (½ vegetable broth cube dissolved in 1½ cups boiling water)
1 Tablespoon fresh parsley, chopped (optional)

1. Heat olive oil in 2-quart sauce pan.

2. Mix flour with olive oil until a paste is formed.

3. Stir in the broth, stirring constantly until gravy is thickened and shiny. Add more liquid if a thinner consistency is desired. Mix in parsley.

VARIATION:

• Substitute chestnut flour for teff flour. Chestnut flour creates a rich, nut-like flavor.

BODY BALANCING TIP: PARSLEY

Native to southeastern Europe, and related to celery, dill, cumin and fennel, parsley has been cultivated for at least 2,000 years and was valued as a medicinal first. Traditionally, it has been used around the world to balance a host of disorders, including as a tonic to strengthen the bladder, to balance high blood pressure, and as a kidney stimulant. Besides being rich in vitamins, minerals and antioxidants, parsley has a volatile essential oil with substantial aromatherapeutic properties, including as a diuretic, antiseptic, detoxifier and digestive aid.

Parsley is delicious raw, as a salad green or chopped fine as an accent green. It also goes well with soups, stews, or tossed with pasta and grains. Italian, or flat-leaf parsley has a stronger flavor that stands out in soups, stews and other cooked foods. Curly parsley shines in salads and other contexts where texture is important.

To store, trim stems and place in a glass of water in the refrigerator. Including parsley in your diet from time to time is a wonderfully supportive way to assist your body in balancing naturally.

Stuffed Squash with Wild Rice Stuffing and Hearty Gravy

This is a colorful and festive vegetarian main dish. People love it! Some of it can be made in advance for ease of preparation.

SERVES 6 - 8

1 large Hubbard squash
4 cups water
1 vegetable broth cube (optional)
2 cups wild rice blend or long grain Basmati rice
1 cup carrots, cut in ¼-inch pieces
1 cup celery, cut in ¼-inch pieces
3 Tablespoons cold-pressed extra-virgin olive oil
  or coconut oil
1 cup leeks, chopped
1 Tablespoon fresh ginger, grated
1 Tablespoon fresh thyme or 2 teaspoons dried
1 Tablespoon fresh sage or 2 teaspoons dried
1 Tablespoon Bragg Liquid Aminos™
Zest of one orange (optional)
½ cup toasted almonds, chopped
  (see "Toasting Seeds and Nuts," page 36)

SQUASH

Squash may be cooked a day ahead and refrigerated.

1. Preheat oven to 400°F.

2. Place whole squash in roasting pan. Add water to measure 1 inch deep.

3. Bake uncovered in oven 30 minutes or until squash can be pierced with a knife. It should be slightly firm.

4. Remove from oven and when slightly cooled, slice off stem end. The opening should be large enough to put in stuffing. Scrape out seeds and set aside.

RICE

This can be cooked up to 3–4 days ahead and refrigerated.

1. Bring water and vegetable cube to boil.

2. Place rice in strainer and rinse by rubbing grains together with your palms and running water over it at the same time. Add to boiling water. Resume boiling. Turn heat to low and cook 1 hour.

3. Turn off heat and allow cooked rice to stand 15 minutes. Fluff with a fork.

4. In a skillet, sauté carrots, celery, leeks, and ginger in olive or coconut oil 5–10 minutes or until glazed. Mix in thyme, sage, Bragg Liquid Aminos™, zest and almonds.

5. Mix cooked rice into vegetable mixture. Taste for seasoning.

GLAZE

1 cup orange juice
1 Tablespoon agave nectar or honey
½ teaspoon cinnamon

1. Mix all ingredients in small bowl.

(Recipe continues on next page.)

1. Brush glaze in cavity of cooked whole squash. Spoon rice, prepared as above, into squash cavity.

2. Brush top of whole squash with more glaze if desired.

3. Place in baking pan with water 1 inch deep. Bake in 400°F oven 15–20 minutes to warm through.

4. Slice through squash lengthwise and stuffing mixture and serve topped with Hearty Gravy
(see recipe at right.)

VARIATION:

• Substitute 3 acorn or carnival squashes for the Hubbard squash and cook as follows:

   1. Slice squash in half or in quarters lengthwise. Remove seeds.

   2. Bake at 400°F face side down in water measuring 1 inch deep for 30 minutes until slightly tender when pierced with a knife. Remove from oven.

   3. Brush glaze in cavity of each piece cooked squash and mound prepared rice on squash pieces.

   4. Brush rice mounds with more glaze if desired and bake as above.

Hearty Gravy

Using teff flour gives this gravy a hearty, rich taste and a darker color. If a lighter flavor and color is desired, use brown rice or chestnut flour.

This can be made two to three days in advance. Heat through the day it is served, it may be necessary to add more liquid.

MAKES 2 CUPS

¼ cup cold-pressed extra-virgin olive oil
½ cup teff, brown rice or chestnut flour
1-1½ cups water mixed with 2 vegetable broth cubes
¼ teaspoon white pepper
1 Tablespoon fresh parsley, chopped (optional)

1. Heat olive oil on medium heat in 2-quart pot.

2. Mix flour with olive oil until a paste is formed.

3. Stir in vegetable broth or water with vegetable cube, stirring constantly until gravy is shiny and thick. Add more liquid if a thinner consistency is desired. Mix in parsley if using.

holiday FISH & SEAFOOD

CONTENTS

Creamy Curried Halibut

The ingredient combination in this quick and simple recipe produces an elegant and flavorful result.

SERVES 4 – 6

4 halibut fillets, 6 ounces each
4 Tablespoons lemon juice
Salt and white pepper to taste
¾ cup Vegenaise™ dressing
1 Tablespoon cilantro, finely chopped
1 Tablespoon curry powder

1. Preheat oven to 350°F.

2. Wash halibut fillets, pat dry and place in 9 x 13-inch baking dish. Rub lemon juice over top of fillets and sprinkle with salt and pepper to taste.

3. In small bowl, mix Vegenaise™, cilantro and curry powder.

4. Spread Vegenaise™ dressing mixture over the top of the fillets approximately ¼-inch thick. Add water to baking dish, ¼-inch high.

5. Place in oven and bake 15–20 minutes uncovered, or until halibut can be flaked with a fork. Remove from oven and serve.

ABOUT: HALIBUT

This cold water fish, related to flounder, is one of the largest saltwater fish, averaging about 300 pounds. It has a mildly sweet flavor and requires little seasoning. Halibut also is noted for its dense, firm texture, akin to chicken.

An excellent source of high quality protein with a low fat content, halibut also is rich in essential minerals, vitamins B12 and B6, and omega-3 essential fatty acids, which support a balanced and vitalized cardiovascular system. If you eat fish, we invite you to include halibut in your diet periodically. It is a delicious way to be of assistance.

Orange Ginger Salmon

This marinade adds a gourmet touch to the salmon.

<u>SERVES 6</u>

4 salmon fillets, 6 ounces each, wild sockeye or coho
Salt and white pepper to taste
¼ cup plus 2 Tablespoons Bragg Liquid Aminos™
¼ cup plus 2 Tablespoons agave nectar or honey
¼ cup plus 2 Tablespoons cold-pressed extra-virgin olive oil
2 Tablespoons fresh ginger, grated
½ cup orange juice

1. Preheat oven to 400°F.

2. Place fillets, skin side up, in 9 x 13-inch baking dish.

3. In small bowl, mix all marinade ingredients together and pour over fish in baking dish.

4. Bake salmon about 15 minutes uncovered or until salmon flakes.

5. Place cooked salmon fillets on serving platter and cover with foil. Place in 200°F to keep warm.

6. Pour cooking liquid from salmon into a sauce pan. Bring to boil and cook until sauce becomes thick and is reduced to half. Add salt and pepper to taste. Pour over cooked salmon and serve.

holiday

fish & seafood

holiday VEGETABLES

CONTENTS

Orange Maple Mashed Yams

Not overly sweet, this harmonious combination of flavors complements a holiday meal.

SERVES 4 – 6

4 large sweet potatoes or yams
6 Tablespoons pure maple syrup
¼ cup freshly squeezed orange juice or 4 Tablespoons frozen orange juice concentrate
½ teaspoon salt
2-4 Tablespoons extra virgin olive oil, divided

1. Preheat oven to 350°F.

2. Scrub the sweet potatoes or yams well. Pierce all over with a fork and rub olive oil over the skin.

3. Place in oven and bake until fork pierces through easily, 30–60 minutes (depending on size). If desired, they can be baked hours ahead or even the day before serving.

4. Allow to cool enough to handle. Remove skins and place the pulp in large bowl.

5. Mash with pulp potato masher or hand blender. Mix in maple syrup, orange juice and salt. Taste for seasoning. (Add more maple syrup and/or orange juice to suit your taste.) Place mixture in sauce pan and heat until warm, or bake as follows:

6. Oil a 9 x 13-inch baking dish with 1 Tablespoon olive oil. If desired, spread the remaining olive oil on the mixture. Cover and bake at 350°F until heated through.

holiday

vegetables

Baked Sweet Potatoes and Apples

The combination of the sweet potatoes, tart apple and lemon zest creates a deliciously sweet and tangy taste.

4 medium-size yams, sliced in ¼-inch rounds
3 medium-size tart apple, quartered, cored and sliced in ¼-inch wedges (leave skin on)
½ cup apple juice
½ cup pure maple syrup
2 teaspoons cinnamon
Zest of 1 lemon

1. Preheat oven to 400°F.

2. In a 9 x 13-inch baking dish, place yams and apples in alternate layers.

3. Combine apple juice, maple syrup, cinnamon and lemon zest in a 2-cup measuring cup. Pour evenly over top of potato/apple mixture.

4. Cover with foil and bake 30 minutes or until potatoes and apples can be pierced with a fork. Baste mixture with liquid from pan 2–3 times while baking. Remove foil and serve warm.

VARIATION:

•   Before baking, combine potatoes and apples together instead of alternate layering.

Golden Mashed Root Vegetables

This recipe is a great substitute for mashed potatoes. The sweet potatoes and carrots give this a lovely golden color. Mash the vegetables the same way you like mashed potatoes, smooth or lumpy. Either way they are delicious.

SERVES 4

2 medium-size celery roots, peeled and cut in 1-inch pieces
1 large sweet potato, peeled and cut in 1-inch pieces
3 medium-size carrots, cut in 1-inch pieces
2 medium turnips, cut in 1-inch pieces
1 vegetable broth cube
2 Tablespoons almond milk
2 Tablespoons Vegenaise™ dressing
1 teaspoon salt
½ teaspoon white pepper
½ teaspoon nutmeg

1. Combine celery root, sweet potato, carrots, and turnips in large sauce pan. Add cold water to cover by 1 inch. Add vegetable cube, cover and bring to boil over high heat. Reduce heat to medium–low, and cook until vegetables are tender when pierced with fork, 15–20 minutes. Drain in colander, and return to pan. (Save leftover liquid to use in soups or other dishes for vegetable broth.)

2. Mash vegetables with almond milk and Vegenaise™ to desired consistency. If mixture is too thick add more milk or cooking liquid. Mix in salt and pepper and nutmeg.

ABOUT: TURNIPS

A member of the mustard family, this small, round fleshy root vegetable has a smooth skin that can range from white to yellow, green, or scarlet. Inside, the flesh is creamy white and crisp textured. Raw turnips are sharp flavored with a somewhat sweet peppery taste that mellows when cooked.

While a starch vegetable, turnips have about one-third the calories of night shade potatoes, and are an excellent source of dietary fiber, folic acid, trace minerals, and vitamins B6, C, and E. Turnip greens, which have a spicy pepper flavor, are abundant in antioxidants, vitamin A, C and K, and lutein, a compound found to support eyesight vitality.

Enjoy turnips raw as a snack or julienned in a salad, or add them to stews, soups or served on their own as a side dish. Turnip greens are a wonderful soup green, and make a spicy side dish sautéed with olive oil.

holiday

vegetables

Brussels Sprouts with Almonds and Orange

These Brussels sprouts are tasty and festive. They provide a wonderful complement to any holiday meal. When selecting Brussels sprouts, choose only those that are firm and fully green for the best flavor.

SERVES 4 – 6

4 cups Brussels sprouts
2 Tablespoons orange juice
2 Tablespoons lemon juice
1 teaspoon agave nectar or honey
½ teaspoon salt
¼ teaspoon white pepper
¼ cup cold-pressed extra-virgin olive oil
½ cup toasted almonds, chopped (see "Toasting Seeds and Nuts," page 36)
1 Tablespoon orange zest

1. Discard and trim off yellow leaves and bases from Brussels sprouts. Cut into quarters.

2. Place in a large sauce pan. Add water to cover. Bring mixture to boil in salted water. Lower heat to medium and cook 5–8 minutes or until they can be pierced with a fork. Remove from heat and drain.

3. In serving bowl, whisk together orange and lemon juices, sweetener, salt, white pepper and olive oil.

4. Toss sprouts with orange juice mixture, almonds, and zest.

5. Serve immediately, or reserve in warm oven.

ABOUT: BRUSSELS SPROUTS

Related to wild cabbage, forerunners to the modern Brussels sprouts were cultivated in ancient Rome. The leafy green buds look like miniature cabbages and are at their best from autumn through early spring.

Like their cousin the cabbage, Brussels sprouts are a nutrient-dense food. They are rich sources of vitamins C, K, A, folic acid, trace minerals, and an excellent source of dietary fiber. They also are believed to have cancer rebalancing properties, particularly with respect to colon cancer.

Brussels sprouts typically are steamed, roasted or sauteed. However prepared, avoid overcooking. Overcooking releases a compound with a sulfurous odor, which can be unpleasant to smell, and gives this delightful vegetable an undeserved reputation.

Green Beans Almandine

The almonds and water chestnuts add a nice crunch to this classic recipe.

SERVES 4

3 cups green beans, ends removed
3 cups boiling water
1 teaspoon salt, divided
⅓ cup leeks, finely chopped
3 Tablespoons cold-pressed extra-virgin olive oil
½ cup slivered almonds
¼ cup water chestnuts (optional)
¼ teaspoon white pepper

1. Boil green beans in water with ½ teaspoon salt for 10 minutes or until beans can be pierced with a fork. They should be slightly firm. Drain and set aside.

2. In large skillet, sauté leeks in olive oil over medium heat 5–8 minutes or until soft. Add almonds and water chestnuts, if using, and sauté 5 minutes or until almonds are slightly browned.

3. Mix in green beans and remaining salt and pepper. Cook until beans are heated through, about 5 minutes. Serve warm.

holiday

vegetables

❄

Spinach with Raisins and Pine Nuts

A simple and sophisticated dish that goes well with any holiday meal.

SERVES 4

4 Tablespoons raisins
4¼ cups fresh spinach, chopped, or 1 package frozen, drained
2 Tablespoons cold-pressed extra-virgin olive oil
4–5 green onions, thinly sliced, including green tops
4 Tablespoons pine nuts, toasted (see "Toasting Seeds and Nuts," page 36)
½ teaspoon salt
¼ teaspoon white pepper

1. Place raisins in small bowl and pour enough boiling water over them to cover. Soak 10 minutes until they have plumped. Drain water.

2. In a skillet, cook spinach on medium-high heat with only the water that clings to the leaves after washing. Cook 1–2 minutes until leaves are bright green and wilted.

3. Remove spinach from skillet, cool and chop roughly with sharp knife.

4. Sauté green onions with olive oil in skillet on medium heat 2–3 minutes or until soft. Add spinach, raisins, pine nuts, salt and pepper. Cook 2–3 minutes to warm through and serve.

ABOUT: PINE NUTS

Also known as pinoli or pignoli, these are the edible seeds of pine trees and have been eaten in Europe and Asia since the Paleolithic period. They are rich in protein (up to 34%), minerals, vitamins A, D, and C; and are a good source of dietary fiber. The oil is highly valued for its antioxidant and anti-inflammatory properties. Pine nuts are typically sold unshelled and these need to be refrigerated as the oil in the nut deteriorates quickly (within days) at room temperature.

Red Cabbage and Caramelized Fennel

Eating fennel with a heavy meal is beneficial because it aids in digestion. This fragrant, tasty, and colorful dish makes a great addition to your holiday meals. Serve warm or at room temperature.

SERVES 8

1½ Tablespoons fennel seeds or 1 Tablespoon ground fennel
2 medium fennel bulbs
2 Tablespoons cold-pressed extra-virgin olive oil
1 teaspoon salt
6 cups red cabbage, sliced into ¼-inch strips
1 cup apple cider

1. In heavy sauce pan over medium heat, toast fennel seeds until fragrant, about 2 minutes. Transfer seeds to clean coffee mill or grinder, or mortar and pestle. Grind to powder. Set aside. If using fennel powder, toast in sauce pan until it smells fragrant, about 1–2 seconds. Set aside.

2. Trim top and bottom of fennel; reserve fronds for later use. Cut out fennel core and slice bulbs into ¼-inch slices.

3. In large skillet, over medium heat, warm olive oil and add sliced fennel and salt. Sauté 10–15 minutes until fennel gets soft and is slightly browned and glazed.

4. Mix in cabbage and apple cider. Turn heat to high and bring to quick boil. Cover, reduce heat to low and cook about 20 minutes until cabbage is tender and glazed-looking.

5. Uncover and stir in ground fennel seeds or toasted fennel powder. Cook over high heat, stirring occasionally until liquid evaporates, about 5 minutes. Remove from heat.

6. Roughly chop reserved fennel fronds and stir into cabbage mixture.

VARIATION:

•   For a sweeter taste, add 1 apple chopped in ½-inch pieces with the cabbage.

holiday

vegetables

holiday CONDIMENTS

CONTENTS

Cranberry Sauce

This cranberry sauce has an excellent flavor.

2 cups fresh cranberries
Zest of 1 small orange
Juice of 1 small orange plus enough water to equal 1 cup
1 cup water
6 cloves
1 medium-size apple, peeled, cored, and chopped (leave skin on)
½ cup agave nectar or honey
½ cup maple syrup
¼ teaspoon cinnamon
1 Tablespoon vanilla

1. Place all ingredients except cinnamon and vanilla in a medium-size sauce pan. Cook on medium heat until cranberries have popped and texture is mushy, 10–20 minutes. Blend with hand mixer or blender until mixture has very small pieces.

2. Remove from heat and mix in cinnamon and vanilla. Let cool; then refrigerate for several hours. It is best made a day ahead of serving. Sauce will be thick.

Cranberry Orange Sauce

This sauce is simple to make and quite tasty. The orange adds a special and festive touch.

MAKES ABOUT 3½ CUPS

2 cups fresh cranberries
1¼ cups apple, diced in ¼-inch pieces
Juice and grated zest from 2 small tangerines or oranges
⅔ cup pure maple syrup

1. Combine all ingredients and cook in small sauce pan over moderate heat until cranberries pop and become mushy, about 10–20 minutes.

2. Let cool and serve. It can be made a day before serving.

holiday

condiments

holiday BREADS

CONTENTS

Date Cranberry Quick Bread

Applesauce is added to provide moisture. Tapioca flour holds the bread together in place of gluten flours, and the xanthan gum allows the bread to fluff.

MAKES 8 – 10 SLICES

1½ cups sorghum flour
½ cups tapioca flour
1 teaspoon xanthan gum
½ teaspoon salt
1 teaspoon cinnamon
2 teaspoons baking powder
½ teaspoon baking soda
½ cup dates, chopped
2 Tablespoons orange juice
⅓ cup cold-pressed extra-virgin olive oil
½ cup maple syrup
2 eggs
⅓ cup applesauce
¼ cup almond milk
1 teaspoon vanilla
2 Tablespoons orange zest
¾ cup fresh or frozen cranberries, coarsely chopped

> **COOKS TIP: QUICK BREAD GIFTS**
>
> These quick breads and biscuits are fun to make. For gift giving, you can bake the quick breads in mini-loaf pans and wrap them decoratively. These recipes fill about 3 small (5½ x 3⅜-inch size) loaf pans.

1. Oil loaf pan and preheat oven to 350°F.

2. Combine sorghum, tapioca flour, xanthan gum, salt, cinnamon, baking powder and baking soda in large bowl. Mix in dates and orange juice. Set aside.

3. Combine olive oil, maple syrup, eggs, applesauce, almond milk and orange zest in a medium-size bowl.

4. Pour liquid ingredients into dry ingredients. Stir. If batter is too thick, add more almond milk. Mix in cranberries.

5. Pour into loaf pan and bake 50–55 minutes or until a toothpick inserted in the center comes out clean.

6. Remove from oven and cool on wire rack 15 minutes. Remove from loaf pan, place on wire wrack to cool. Slice when cool.

Rosemary and Sage Biscuits

These are a Thanksgiving tradition at the Jwalan Muktikā School of Illumination. We love the rich, nutty flavor of the buckwheat, which creates a dark brown color. If you prefer a lighter biscuit, use sorghum flour.

MAKES ABOUT 12 BISCUITS

⅓ cup cold-pressed extra-virgin olive oil
1¼ cups almond milk
2 Tablespoons agave nectar or honey
1½ Tablespoons dried sage, or 4 Tablespoons chopped fresh
¼ teaspoon dried rosemary, crumbled or 1 Tablespoon chopped fresh
2 cups buckwheat or sorghum flour
2 teaspoons baking powder
½ teaspoon salt

1. Combine oil, almond milk, sweetener sage and rosemary in large bowl. Allow mixture to stand 15–20 minutes to enhance the flavor of the herbs.

2. Meanwhile, preheat oven to 400°F. Lightly oil baking sheet.

3. Mix flour, baking powder, and salt in medium-size bowl.

4. Mix liquid ingredients into dry ingredients until just moistened.

5. Use large spoon, or ¼ cup measure, to drop ¼ cup portions of batter onto oiled baking sheet.

6. Bake 15–20 minutes, or until edges begin to brown.

7. Remove from baking sheet and serve.

ABOUT: SORGHUM

This ancient, drought-resistant cereal grain is grown around the world. It originated in Africa, having been cultivated in Egypt in antiquity. Sorghum seed is rich in protein and minerals and has a high tannin content, making it rich in antioxidants, higher even than blueberries in certain strains. Its bland flavor makes it a fabulous gluten-free flour for baking. Sweet sorghum, a variety with a high sugar content, is used to make a molasses-like syrup sweetener.

Herbed Dinner Rolls

These rolls are easy to make and will be enjoyed at your holiday meals. They are best eaten within two days. However, they can be kept in the freezer up to two months. Wrap them tightly in plastic wrap and then again in foil.

MAKES 12 ROLLS

3 cups gluten-free high-protein flour blend (see below)
2 teaspoons xanthan gum
1 teaspoon salt
1 Tablespoon gluten-free active dry yeast
1 Tablespoon rosemary, chopped
1 Tablespoon chives, chopped
3 Tablespoons agave nectar or honey
1 Tablespoon cold-pressed extra-virgin olive oil
1½ cups warm water (110°F)

GLUTEN-FREE, HIGH PROTEIN FLOUR BLEND

1¼ cups chickpea flour
1 cup arrowroot
1 cup tapioca flour
1 cup brown rice flour

1. Mix the flour blend ingredients together in a bowl.

2. Lightly oil large baking sheet.

3. Combine gluten-free flour blend, xanthan gum, salt, yeast, rosemary and chives in bowl.

4. Transfer mixture to food processor. Add sweetener, olive oil, and water. Mix on high speed 4 minutes. (This aerates the dough, assisting it to rise.)

5. Using large ice cream scoop (approximately ¼ cup capacity) or large soup spoon, scoop out 12 balls of dough. Place on baking sheet with ample space between balls.

6. Cover with light cloth or paper napkin and let dough rise in warm place 30 minutes or until doubled in size. Preheat oven to 350°F.

7. Bake 25 minutes, until rolls are slightly brown. Remove from oven, brush each roll with olive oil and bake 10 more minutes or until rolls are golden brown. They are done when they sound hollow when tapped.

VARIATION:

• Spread sesame or poppy seeds on rolls before letting them rise.

Pumpkin Bread

The spice combination and the pumpkin make this bread moist and fragrant.

MAKES 1 LOAF

1¾ cups sorghum flour
½ cup tapioca flour
¼ cup arrowroot
1 teaspoon xanthan gum
1 teaspoon cinnamon
1 teaspoon powdered ginger
¼ teaspoon cloves
½ teaspoon nutmeg
2 teaspoons baking powder
½ teaspoon baking soda
½ teaspoon salt
½ cup raisins
⅓ cup extra-virign olive oil or melted coconut oil
½ cup maple syrup
2 eggs
1 cup pumpkin purée
¾ cup almond milk
1 teaspoon vanilla

ABOUT: XANTHAN GUM

This thickening agent is produced by the Xanthomonas campestris bacterium, in its process of breaking down simple sugars, typically glucose or sucrose. The gum's ability to vastly increase the viscosity of a liquid makes it highly attractive for a wide variety of uses.

Note: Many commercial sources of xanthan gum use wheat, corn or soy for the sugar substrate. Check the ingredient list on the package or call the company if this is a concern. We recommend Bob's Red Mill™, as a certified gluten-free source.

1. Preheat oven to 350°F. Oil loaf pan.

2. Blend sorghum, tapioca flour, arrowroot, xanthan gum, cinnamon, ginger, cloves, nutmeg, baking powder, baking soda and salt in a large mixing bowl. Blend in raisins.

3. In another bowl, mix olive oil, maple syrup, eggs, pumpkin purée, almond milk and vanilla.

4. Pour liquid ingredients into dry ingredients and mix well.

5. Pour batter into loaf pan and bake 1 hour or when a toothpick inserted in the center comes out clean.

6. Place on cooling rack 10–15 minutes. Remove bread from loaf pan and let cool on cooling rack before cutting.

holiday SWEETS

CONTENTS

Carob Fudge

This fudge recipe is worth the effort! Quite simply, it is divine.

MAKES ABOUT 14, 1-INCH SQUARES

½ cup carob powder
1 teaspoon cinnamon
½ cup tahini
¼ cup pure maple syrup
1 Tablespoon arrowroot
¼ cup water
1 teaspoon vanilla extract
⅛ teaspoon mint extract (optional)
½ cup toasted almonds, chopped in small pieces (optional, see "Toasting Seeds and Nuts," page 36)

1. Toast carob powder in dry sauce pan, stirring over low heat until it darkens slightly and starts to clump. Sift carob through strainer, mix in cinnamon, and set aside.

2. Combine tahini and maple syrup in sauce pan and cook, stirring over low heat until smooth and thick. Mix arrowroot in water until dissolved. Add arrowroot mixture to tahini mixture and stir constantly until mixture becomes thick and shiny. Remove from heat.

3. Stir carob, vanilla and mint extract (if using) into mixture. Mix in almonds if desired. Press fudge mixture into an oiled 8 x 8-inch baking dish.

4. Keep in refrigerator overnight before cutting into 1-inch squares.

ABOUT: FONDANTS & HOLIDAY SWEETS

The four Holiday Sweets recipes (Carob Fudge, Almond Spice Balls, Sugar Plums and Cranberry Treats) taste terrific, make great gifts, and can be served throughout the holidays. They can be safely stored in an airtight container in the refrigerator for about 30 days.

Almond Spice Balls

We recommend making these spice balls a day in advance. Giving the flavors time to blend together and expand enhances the delectability of these treats. Note: This recipe requires soaking almonds for five hours.

MAKES 12 BALLS

¾ cup almonds, whole, soaked 4–5 hours in 1½ cups water
¾ cup raisins, soaked 1 hour in ½ cup water
½ cup dates, soaked 1 hour in ¼ cup water
¼ teaspoon cinnamon
⅛ teaspoon cardamom
½ teaspoon grated lemon peel
⅓ cup shredded coconut

1. Drain soaked almonds and dried fruit. Discard water.

2. Blend almonds, raisins and dates in food processor until smooth. Mix in cinnamon, cardamom and lemon peel.

3. Form into ½-inch balls and roll in coconut. Store in airtight container in refrigerator.

Sugar Plums

A wonderful, easy-to-make variation on this traditional holiday treat.

MAKES 10 BALLS

⅔ cup dried black mission figs
⅓ cup almonds, whole, toasted (see "Toasting Seeds and Nuts," page 36)
⅓ cup, plus 2 Tablespoons, carob powder, divided
½ teaspoon cinnamon
¼ cup pure maple syrup
1 Tablespoon orange zest
1 teaspoon almond extract

1. Blend figs, almonds, 2 Tablespoons carob powder and cinnamon in food processor. Pulse until mixture is the size of peppercorns.

2. Add maple syrup, orange zest and almond extract. Pulse until blended.

3. Form into ½-inch balls and roll in ⅓ cup carob powder. Store in airtight container in refrigerator.

holiday

sweets

Cranberry Treats

These festive treats are quick and easy to make.

MAKES 20 BALLS

1 cup pine nuts
1 cup sunflower seeds
1 cup almonds, chopped
2 cups dried cranberries sweetened with fruit juice
3 Tablespoons maple syrup
1 teaspoon vanilla
2 teaspoons nutmeg
½ cup coconut flakes

1. Combine pine nuts, sunflower seeds, and almonds in food processor and pulse until coarsely ground. Add dried cranberries and pulse 4 times.

2. Add maple syrup, vanilla and nutmeg. Pulse until mixture sticks together. Add water if mixture is too dry. Add more maple syrup if a sweeter taste is desired.

3. Roll mixture into 1-inch balls.

4. Place coconut flakes on a flat dish. Roll balls in coconut flakes to coat.

5. Store in airtight container in refrigerator.

ABOUT: NUTMEG

This spice is derived from the fruit of the nutmeg tree, native to Australia, Southeast Asia, and the Pacific Islands. Nutmeg itself is from the seed, while the spice mace comes from the red membrane covering the seed. A valued ingredient in both Indian and Indonesian cooking, ground nutmeg also has a long history as a medicinal. Its antimicrobial properties make nutmeg a valuable pickling spice and its essential oil, diluted, soothes sore muscles, toothaches and arthritic pain. In the East Indian Ayruvedic tradition of body balancing through food, ground nutmeg is used to balance the body humours and soothe the digestive system.

Do include nutmeg in your cooking, and use it sparingly, as excessive consumption can cause unpleasant side effects in some people.

holiday DESSERTS

CONTENTS

Pumpkin Pie

This crust, originally called Mim's crust, was developed for Miriam by her mentor, Annie Fox about 30 years ago. The wonderful crunch and rich flavor of this crust make it a favorite recipe. For a crowning touch top with a dollop of Almond Cream when serving (see recipe page 324.).

SERVES 6 – 8

CRUST

1¼ cups gluten-free oats, ground to flour in blender
¾ cup brown rice flour
2 teaspoons cinnamon
½ teaspoon sea salt
⅔ cup apple juice
¼ cup almond or olive oil
½ teaspoon almond extract
1 teaspoon vanilla

1. Combine oat and rice flours, cinnamon and salt in a medium-size bowl. Set aside.

2. Combine apple juice, oil, almond and vanilla extracts in a small bowl.

3. Pour liquid ingredients into dry ingredients. Mix with spoon, then knead with your hands until well mixed. The consistency of the dough will be like a regular pie crust.

4. Oil a 9-inch pie plate and press dough into plate.

5. Pre-bake at 350°F for 5 minutes and remove from oven. Set aside. Makes one 9-inch crust.

FILLING

2 cups pumpkin purée
2 Tablespons arrowroot dissolved in ¼ cup almond milk
½ cup agave nectar, honey or pure maple syrup
3 teaspoons pumpkin pie spice
½ cup vanilla almond or coconut milk
2 Tablespoons arrowroot mixed in ¼ cup almond milk
½ teaspoon salt
1 teaspoon vanilla extract

1. Place all ingredients in a medium-size bowl and blend with hand blender or food processor until smooth.

2. Pour into pre-baked pie crust. Place foil or pie crust protector around crust to prevent burning.

3. Bake at 425°F for 15 minutes, then reduce heat to 350°F and bake for 35–40 minutes or until pie is firm. Remove from oven and cool on wire wrack.

VARIATION

• Substitute 2 eggs for arrowroot in almond milk.

COOK'S TIP:
CUSTOM-BLENDED PUMPKIN PIE SPICE

Combine:

2 teaspoons cinnamon
1½ teaspoons powdered ginger
¼ teaspoon ground cloves
¼ teaspoon nutmeg.

Mock Mincemeat Pie

The large pieces of ginger add a pungent taste to this pie and are a wonderful surprise when you bite into one. Bragg Liquid Aminos™ gives the pie a deep flavor similar to a true mincemeat pie.

SERVES 6 – 8

CRUST

1½ cups gluten-free oats, ground to flour
    in blender
1¼ cups brown rice flour
3 teaspoons cinnamon
1 teaspoon salt
1 cup apple juice
⅓ cup almond or cold-pressed extra-virgin
    olive oil
1 teaspoon vanilla extract
½ teaspoon almond extract

1. Combine oat and rice flours, cinnamon and salt in a medium-size bowl. Set aside.

2. Combine apple juice, oil, vanilla and almond extracts in small bowl.

3. Pour liquid ingredients into dry ingredients. Mix with spoon, then knead with your hands until well mixed.

4. Place in refrigerator about 15 minutes. Break off ⅓ piece of dough and set aside. It will be used later.

5. Oil a 9-inch pie plate. Press remaining dough in pie plate.

FILLING

4 apples, peeled, cored and cut into
    1-inch pieces
1 cup raisins
½ cup currants
Juice and rind of ½ medium-size orange
½ cup apple juice
3½-inch slices of fresh ginger
1 teaspoon cinnamon
½ teaspoon cloves
2 Tablespoons arrowroot
¼ cup apple juice
2 Tablespoons Bragg Liquid Aminos™

1. Mix the first eight ingredients in a large pot and simmer 15–20 minutes until apples are mushy.

2. Dissolve arrowroot in apple juice and pour into apple mixture. Stir constantly until mixture becomes thick and shiny. Stir in Bragg Liquid Aminos™.

3. Pour mixture into pie crust.

4. Roll out the saved ⅓ of dough with floured rolling pin to ⅛-inch thick. Cut out shapes (i.e., trees, ornaments, candles) of your choice. Arrange cutouts around top of pie.

5. Bake 30 minutes or until crust is lightly browned.

holiday

desserts

Stuffed Baked Apples with Almond Cream

This simple dessert adds lightness to finish a heavy holiday meal. The Almond Cream topping provides a delightful, elegant touch.

SERVES 6

6 apples
1½ teaspoons cinnamon, divided
6 drops pure vanilla extract, divided
3 cups dried fruit: raisins, currants, figs, dates, or any combination
1 cup apple juice

1. Preheat oven to 350°F.
2. Core apples. Pierce through skin once or twice with a knife.
3. Sprinkle ¼ teaspoon cinnamon and 1 drop vanilla into center of each apple. Spread with your finger. Stuff cavity with raisins, currants, figs, or dates.
4. Stand the apples in baking dish and pour apple juice over top of apples until it is ½ inch from bottom of baking dish.
5. Cover and bake until the fruit is tender, approximately 40 minutes.
6. Serve warm or at room temperature with a dollop of Almond Cream (recipe at right.)

VARIATIONS:

- Substitute pears for apples.
- Mix grated orange or lemon rind with dried fruit.

Almond Cream

This is an excellent substitute for whipped cream. It goes especially well with pumpkin pie or cranberry pudding.

2 cups blanched almonds or almond meal
1 cup water
4 Tablespoons agave nectar or honey

1. Combine almonds or almond meal in blender with water. Blend until almonds are smooth and creamy. If mixture is too thick, add more water. Add honey or agave nectar. Continue blending until smooth. Serve over dessert.

VARIATION:

- Add 1 Tablespoon orange zest when adding honey or agave nectar.

COOK'S TIP: BLANCHING ALMONDS

Blanched almonds are simply almonds with the skin removed. Slivered almonds typically are blanched first. Here's a quick and simple method for blanching almonds.

1. Place almonds in bowl and pour boiling water over them, just to cover.

2. Let sit for about 1 minute or less. (Any longer and the nuts lose their crispness.)

3. Drain and rinse twice under cold water, pat dry, and slip skins off.

Cranberry Pudding

This recipe is unique because it makes its own sauce as it bakes. Served warm with a dollop of Almond Cream (see recipe opposite) or vanilla dairy-free frozen dessert, or, it makes an a sophisticated holiday dessert that is not too sweet. This pudding also is delicious at room temperature without any topping.

MAKES 6 SERVINGS

1½ cups gluten-free rolled oats, blended to consistency of cake flour in blender
2 teaspoons baking powder
¼ teaspoon baking soda
1½ cups fresh cranberries, coarsely chopped
1 cup Medjool dates, chopped in small pieces
1½ teaspoons cinnamon
Zest of 1 orange
⅔ cup vanilla flavored almond milk
½ cup maple syrup
¼ cup organic molasses
1 teaspoon vanilla extract
1½ cups water
1 Tablespoon cold-pressed extra-virgin olive oil

1. Preheat oven to 350°F. Lightly oil 1½ to 2-quart casserole or 9 x 13-inch baking dish.

2. Combine oat flour, baking powder, baking soda, cranberries, dates, cinnamon and orange zest in large mixing bowl. In another bowl, combine almond milk, maple syrup, molasses, and vanilla.

3. Pour liquid ingredients into dry ingredients. Pour mixture into prepared baking dish.

4. Whisk water and oil in small bowl. Pour over batter in baking dish. (This may seem like too much water. It is no mistake. It will cook into a moist consistency.)

5. Bake about 50 minutes, until pudding is cake-like and sauce bubbles around edges.

holiday

desserts

❄

Pumpkin Cake

This cake is spicy and moist. It was developed by our chef friend, Adrienne Swiatek. We frost this cake with whipped maple syrup, aka maple cream, which can be purchased at natural foods stores and larger supermarkets. Note: Some varieties of prepared maple cream contain dairy. Check the ingredient list on the jar if this is a concern. If maple cream is unavailable, whipped honey can be substituted.

MAKES 12 SERVINGS

1½ cups sorghum flour
¼ cup tapioca flour
¼ cup arrowroot
1 teaspoon xanthan gum
2–3 teaspoons pumpkin pie spice (see "Custom-Blended Pumpkin Pie Spice," page 322)
½ teaspoon salt
1 teaspoon baking powder
1 teaspoon baking soda
2 eggs
1 cup pumpkin puree
1 cup maple syrup
½ cup olive oil
Whipped maple syrup, also known as maple cream, to cover cake

1. Preheat oven to 350°F.

2. Combine sorghum and tapioca flours, arrowroot, xanthan gum, pumpkin pie spice, salt, baking powder and baking soda in large bowl. Set aside.

3. In another bowl, combine eggs, pumpkin pureé, maple syrup, and olive oil.

4. Pour liquid ingredients into dry ingredients. Pour into oiled 9 x 13-inch baking dish or bunt pan. Bake 35–40 minutes or until a toothpick inserted in the middle comes out clean.

5. Remove from oven and place on cooling rack. If using bunt pan, cool for 15 minutes, then remove from pan.

6. When cake has cooled, spread whipped maple syrup over top. If using a bunt pan, mix a little water with whipped maple syrup to thin slightly. Drizzle over top of cake.

VARIATION:

Substitute Coconut Almond Frosting (see recipe page 271) for the whipped maple syrup.

Carob Date Brownies

The combination of apples and dates makes a moist brownie.

MAKES ABOUT 12, 2-INCH SQUARES

½ cup rice flour
½ cup sorghum flour
¼ cup tapioca flour
1 teaspoon baking powder
½ teaspoon salt
1 teaspoon cinnamon
¼ teaspoon nutmeg
½ teaspoon ground cardamom (optional)
½ cup carob powder
⅓ cup cold-pressed extra-virgin olive oil
⅓ cup pure maple syrup
1 egg
6 Tablespoons water
1 cup pitted Medjool dates, chopped in small pieces
1 medium apple, grated
½ cup almonds, chopped (optional)

1. Preheat oven to 350°F, and oil an 8 x 8-inch baking dish.

2. Combine flour, arrowroot, baking power, salt, cinnamon, nutmeg, cardamom and carob powder in large bowl.

3. In another bowl, mix oil, maple syrup, egg and water.

4. Mix liquid ingredients into dry ingredients. Add dates and grated apple. Mix well.

5. Spread mixture into baking dish. Sprinkle with almonds then press almonds into batter. Bake 30 minutes or until a toothpick comes out clean when inserted in center. Brownies will be moist like chocolate brownies.

6. Let brownies cool slightly and cut into 2-inch squares before serving.

VARIATION:

• Frost with Carob Fudge Frosting (see recipe page 330)

Date Bars

These bars are easy to prepare and use dates as the sweetener. If date sugar is not available, you can substitute pure maple syrup.

MAKES ABOUT 12, 2-INCH SQUARES.

¾ cup Medjool dates, chopped
8 Tablespoons cold-pressed extra-virgin olive oil
¼ cup date sugar
⅓ cup applesauce
¼ cup vanilla-flavored almond milk
⅛ cup water
½ teaspoon vanilla
1 cup gluten-free rolled oats
¼ cup sorghum flour
2 Tablespoons tapioca flour
¼ cup almonds, chopped
1 teaspoon cinnamon
¼ teaspoon baking soda
¼ teaspoon salt

1. Preheat oven to 350°F. Oil an 8 x 8-inch baking dish.

2. Combine dates, olive oil, and date sugar in large bowl. Stir in applesauce, almond milk, water, and vanilla.

3. Stir oats, sorghum flour, tapioca flour, almonds, cinnamon, baking soda, and salt into date mixture until ingredients are moistened.

4. Let stand for 10–15 minutes to allow flour and oats to absorb the liquid.

5. Press evenly into baking dish. Bake 25 minutes or until lightly browned and slightly firm.

6. Remove from oven and place on cooling rack. Cut into 2-inch squares.

7. Store in an airtight container.

ABOUT: DATE SUGAR

Made from dehydrated dates that are ground into small bits, this granulated unprocessed sweetener adds a rich sweetness to recipes. It can be used as an alternative to brown sugar. However, because it does not blend or dissolve easily when added to other ingredients, and it does not melt as easily as other granulated sugars, its application can be somewhat limited.

Date sugar is composed of roughly equal amounts fructose and glucose, with some sucrose. In addition, the dehydrated fruit flesh contains proteins, minerals, vitamins and antioxidants in trace amounts. Date sugar is a part of Mediterranean and Middle Eastern cooking, and can be found in Middle Eastern specialty food stores, as well as natural foods stores.

Apricot Thumbprint Cookies

These cookies are one of Miriam's favorites. The combination of oat and brown rice gives these cookies an "old-fashioned" taste. Miriam makes then every season.

MAKES ABOUT 2 DOZEN COOKIES

1¼ cups gluten-free rolled oats ground to flour in blender
1¼ cups brown rice flour
1 cup almond meal or whole almonds, ground in blender
1 teaspoon cinnamon
¼ teaspoon salt
⅓ cup almond or sunflower oil
¼ cup water
½ cup maple syrup
½ teaspoon almond extract
1 cup apricot jam, fruit juice sweetened, divided
1 cup coconut

1. Preheat oven to 350°F. Oil 1 baking sheet.

2. Combine oat flour, brown rice flour, ground almonds, cinnamon, and salt in large bowl.

3. In another bowl, combine almond or sunflower oil, water, maple syrup, and almond extract.

4. Pour liquid ingredients into dry ingredients. Mix with spoon, then mix with your hands. Dough will be the consistency of pie dough. Let dough rest 10–15 minutes until liquid is absorbed.

5. Form dough into ½-inch balls. Place on baking sheet. Make an indentation with your finger or thumb on top of each ball.

6. Bake 15–20 minutes or until cookies are lightly browned on top and bottom. Remove from oven and place cookies on cooling rack. Cookies will harden as they cool.

7. When cookies are almost cold, fill indentation with 1 teaspoon apricot jam. Place coconut in flat dish and press jam section of cookie in coconut.

VARIATION:

- Substitute any flavor of fruit sweetened jam for apricot jam.

holiday

desserts

Carob Cookies with Carob Frosting

These cookies are rich, chewy and "chocolate-y".

MAKES ABOUT 15 COOKIES

1 cup sorghum flour
¾ cup brown rice flour
¼ cup carob powder
1½ teaspoons baking powder
½ teaspoon baking soda
1 teaspoon cinnamon
¼ teaspoon salt
½ cup dates, cut in small pieces
½ cup chopped almonds (optional)
⅔ cups organic vegetable shortening, softened
   (e.g. Spectrum unrefined palm oil)
¾ cup maple-flavored agave nectar or maple syrup
⅓ cup applesauce
2 teaspoons vanilla extract
¼ teaspoon mint oil (optional)

1. Preheat oven to 350°F. Oil 2 baking sheets.

2. Mix sorghum and rice flours, carob powder, baking powder, baking soda, cinnamon and salt in large mixing bowl.

3. Stir in dates and almonds (if using).

4. In a medium-size bowl, mix shortening with hand blender or electric mixer until smooth. Mix in sweetener, applesauce, vanilla and mint oil (if using).

5. Mix wet ingredients into dry ingredients.

6. Using two tablespoons, drop cookie dough onto baking sheet (one to scoop batter, the other to scrape off batter) 1½ inches apart. Bake 15–20 minutes or until cookies are slightly firm on top.

7. Remove from baking sheet and cool on wire racks. Cookies will become firmer as they cool.

8. Frost with Carob Fudge Frosting (see recipe at right.)

Carob Frosting

MAKES ABOUT 1½ CUPS

½ cup carob powder
1 teaspoon cinnamon
½ cup tahini
¼ cup maple syrup
1 Tablespoon arrowroot
   mixed with ½ cup water
2 teaspoons vanilla
⅛ teaspoon mint oil (optional)

1. Toast carob powder in dry sauce pan, stirring over low heat until powder darkens slightly and starts to clump. Sift in strainer, add cinnamon and set aside.

2. Mix tahini and maple syrup in small sauce pan over medium heat until smooth. Stir in arrowroot mixed in water and stir until thick and shiny.

3. Remove from heat and mix in vanilla and mint oil. Add carob-cinnamon mixture and blend.

4. Spread over cookies. Frosting will become firmer as it cools.

Gingerbread Cookies

Molasses, fresh ginger and orange juice give these cookies an old fashioned flavor.

1½ cups sorghum flour
1¾ cups gluten-free oats, ground into flour
¼ cup tapioca flour
1 teaspoon xanthan gum
1 teaspoon cinnamon
1 Tablespoon powdered ginger
¼ teaspoon ground cloves
½ teaspoon salt
1 teaspoon baking soda
½ cup cold-pressed extra-virgin olive oil
¼ cup agave nectar or honey
¼ cup molasses
⅓ cup applesauce
1 Tablespoon grated orange zest (optional)
2 Tablespoons orange juice
Whipped maple syrup (also known as maple cream), or whipped honey
Raisins, dried cranberries, almonds for decoration (optional)

1. Preheat oven to 350°F.

2. In medium-size bowl, combine sorghum, oat and tapioca flours, xanthan gum, cinnamon, ginger, cloves, salt and baking soda. Set aside.

3. In another bowl, mix olive oil, sweetener, molasses, applesauce, orange zest and orange juice.

4. Pour liquid ingredients into dry ingredients. Dough should be thick, resembling pie crust dough. If too thin, mix in more sorghum flour. Let dough rest 5–10 minutes until it becomes more firm.

5. Cut dough into 4 pieces. Roll each piece on floured cutting board with floured rolling pin. Roll to ⅛-inch thick. Cut into desired shapes with cookie cutters. Carefully place on baking sheet with spatula (dough can fall apart easily).

6. Bake 10 minutes or until cookies are slightly firm to the touch. (They will become firmer when cooled.) Remove from cookie sheet, cool on cooling rack.

7. Frost each cookie with whipped maple syrup and decorate with dried fruit as desired. The maple syrup spread will become firm as cookies cool.

8. If eliminating frosting, press decorations on cookies before baking.

holiday

desserts

Index by Key Ingredient

Notes

Notes

Notes

Notes